"So often people are enthused by the vision and possibilities ⸺
only to be stymied by the details of how to get started to acti⸺
vision. The Sharing Solution *offers a practical, step-by-step approach for a whole
range of collaborative ventures. Its easy-to-read and accessible information provides
a great resource for the more community-oriented future we must move toward.*"

— Kathryn McCamant, Architect and Developer, CoHousing
Partners, McCamant & Durrett Architects; co-author of
CoHousing: A Contemporary Approach To Housing Ourselves

"*From the neighborhood level to the global, sharing may be the single most important
strategy to reduce our environmental impact, gain financial health, promote equity
and have fun.* The Sharing Solution *provides valuable advice and how-to tips for
seasoned sharers and new converts. [It's] a tremendously valuable resource for us all,
and a must-read for those who want to chart a new path: a more sustainable, more
compassionate and more fun one.*"

— Annie Leonard, Author and Host of *The Story of Stuff*; *Time Magazine*
2008 Hero of the Environment

"*In good times, sharing lessens our impact on the environment and builds bonds
among people; in tough times, it's how we can get by together. Whatever you might
want to share—from cars to housing to power tools to bulk food purchases—this
canny, thorough book offers detailed advice on how to make clear sharing
agreements and minimize potential confusion and conflict.*"

— Ernest Callenbach, Author of *Ecotopia* and *Ecotopia Emerging*

"*Amidst the sweeping trend toward privatization that has dominated recent decades,
this book is a welcome reminder of that other, almost forgotten, defining element in
American culture: the pursuit of the common good.* ...The Sharing Solution *offers
great practical advice on how to act on our best instincts toward sustaining our
society as well as ourselves in the twenty-first century.*"

— Bruce Sievers, Senior Fellow, Rockefeller Philanthropy Advisers; Visiting
Scholar, Stanford University

26 in 26
Neighborhood Resource Centers
26 Neighborhood Strategies in a 26 month time frame
A Grant Funded by the LSTA
(Library Services & Technology Act)

CITY OF
RIVERSIDE

Riverside Public Library

NOLO Products & Services

Books & Software

Nolo publishes hundreds of great books and software programs on the topics consumers and business owners want to know about. And every one of them is available in print or as a download at Nolo.com.

Plain-English Legal Dictionary

Free at Nolo.com. Stumped by jargon? Look it up in America's most up-to-date source for definitions of cutting edge legal terminology. Emphatically not your grandmother's law dictionary!

Legal Encyclopedia

Free at Nolo.com. Here are more than 1,200 free articles and answers to frequently asked questions about everyday consumer legal issues including wills, bankruptcy, small business formation, divorce, patents, employment and much more. As *The Washington Post* says, "Nobody does a better job than Nolo."

Online Legal Forms

Make a will, or living trust, form an LLC or corporation or obtain a trademark or provisional patent at Nolo.com, all for a remarkably affordable price. In addition, our site provides hundreds of high-quality, low-cost downloadable legal forms including bills of sale, promissory notes, nondisclosure agreements and many more.

Lawyer Directory

Find an attorney at Nolo.com. Nolo's unique lawyer directory provides in-depth profiles of lawyers all over America. From fees and experience to legal philosophy, education and special expertise, you'll find all the information you need to pick a lawyer who's a good fit.

Nolo's Aim:
to make the law...

- easy-to-understand
- affordable
- hassle free

Keep Up to Date!

*Old law is often bad law. That's why Nolo.com has free updates for this and every Nolo book. And if you want to be notified when a revised edition of any Nolo title comes out, sign up for this free service at **nolo.com/ legalupdater.***

"Nolo is always there in a jam."
—NEWSWEEK

Please note

We believe accurate, plain-English legal information should help you solve many of your own legal problems. But this text is not a substitute for personalized advice from a knowledgeable lawyer. If you want the help of a trained professional—and we'll always point out situations in which we think that's a good idea— consult an attorney licensed to practice in your state.

1st edition

The
Sharing Solution

How to Save Money,
Simplify Your Life &
Build Community

By Attorneys Janelle Orsi & Emily Doskow

FIRST EDITION   MAY 2009

Editor   LISA GUERIN

Cover Design   SUSAN PUTNEY

Proofreading   ANI DIMUSHEVA

Index   VICTORIA BAKER

Printing   DELTA PRINTING SOLUTIONS, INC.

Orsi, Janelle, 1979-
    The sharing solution: how to save money, simplify your life & build community /
by Janelle Orsi and Emily Doskow. -- 1st ed.
        p. cm.
    Includes bibliographical references and index.
    ISBN-13: 978-1-4133-1021-4 (pbk. : alk. paper)
    ISBN-10: 1-4133-1021-4 (pbk. : alk. paper)
    1. Sharing. 2. Sharing--Economic aspects. 3. Cooperation. I. Doskow, Emily.
II. Title.
    BJ1533.G4O77 2009
    179--dc22
                        2009009111

Quantity sales: For information on bulk purchases or corporate premium sales, please
contact the Special Sales Department. For academic sales or textbook adoptions, ask
for Academic Sales. Call 800-955-4775 or write to Nolo, 950 Parker Street, Berkeley,
California 94710.

Dedication

To our partners, Catherine and Luan, with whom we have the incredible good fortune to share each day.

And to President Barack Obama, with whom we all share the task of creating a better world.

Acknowledgments

First and greatest thanks go to our editor, Lisa Guerin, who truly shared the work of creating this book through her valuable contributions to both structure and substance, and whose intelligence and sharp wit we appreciate so much.

We are grateful to Marcia Stewart for her early and enthusiastic support and for shepherding us through the acquisitions process so smoothly and so quickly, and to Nolo's production department for the wonderful look of the book.

We heartily thank all the sharers who were and are our inspiration. We would like to specially honor the community of sharers who provided many sparks of inspiration and ideas that led to this book—Diane Dodge, Cecilie Surasky, Carolyn Hunt, Teo Surasky, and Jill, Pauline, and Carmel H. Guillermo-Togawa.

We also extend much gratitude to others whose real-life sharing practices informed and illuminated for us the practical ins and outs of sharing, including Terry Lim, Jane Cavanaugh, Karen Hester, Diana Shapiro, Laurence Schectman, Matt Nichols, Karen Mitchell, John Abrams, the Barn-Raisin' Babes and the Maxwell Park Neighborhood Home Improvement Group, and the countless others whose examples have paved the way for a more sharing world. We also greatly appreciate the carsharing expertise and input from Chris Ganson, Matt Nichols, Rick Hutchinson, and Lorraine Wilde.

Many thanks to Elena Condes—without her devotion to the sharing of birthday cake, *The Sharing Solution* might not exist.

Luan Stauss is due much appreciation for the title, as well as for the home improvement group forms and ideas—and, as ever, for her unflagging support and engagement in the process.

A huge thank you goes to Catherine Shaffer whose enthusiasm, insights, and delightful presence were a constant throughout the writing of this book. And many thanks to Tom and Jackie Orsi, whose support helped make this book possible, among countless other things.

Table of Contents

Part I: Sharing Basics

4 Thank You For Sharing: Communicating, Making Decisions, and Resolving Conflict

5 Putting Your Arrangement in Writing

Part II: Sharing Solutions

6 Sharing Housing

7 Sharing Household Goods, Purchases, Tasks, and Space

Appendixes

Index

Your Sharing Companion

We first learn about sharing as children, when we are taught to share our toys with others. Over time, most of us share less—even though most of us also have more "toys" now than we did when we were young. They are just different kinds of toys: bigger and more expensive. Especially in recent decades, our culture has encouraged each of us, or at least each family unit, to have our own things and to handle our own responsibilities.

Recently, however, people are finding this lifestyle less attractive. Maybe it's the high cost of living. Maybe it's the fact that we work longer hours than ever. Maybe it's the resulting disconnect we feel from our communities and families. Or maybe it's something in the air—such as smog, carbon emissions, or global warming.

For a variety of reasons, people are looking for ways of living that are more sustainable—not only environmentally sustainable, but also economically and personally sustainable. One of the most sustainable choices we can make is *sharing*.

Sharing contributes to the greater good in lots of ways. First, it's nice. It can help people feel connected to their neighbors, coworkers, and even strangers. It builds community and meets our needs in creative ways. It sets a good example for our children.

Second, it's economical. Almost every type of sharing we discuss in this book will save you some money—sometimes more, sometimes less, but always some.

Third, it's green. Most kinds of sharing result in fewer resources being used, and that's good for the planet. Sharing also makes it possible to afford more environmentally friendly choices, such as solar panels, grey water systems, and community supported agriculture.

In many ways, sharing is already an integral part of our society. We share the sidewalks, streets, and highways—and the cost of building and maintaining them. We share public schools, public utilities, and public services, all of which we pay for through our taxes.

Most of us share in ways that are closer to home, too. Do you leave your child with your neighbor once in a while so you can run to the store, returning the favor when your neighbor has a quick errand to do? Do you pick up riders when you drive to work in the morning? Are you part of a vacation timeshare? Do you have roommates or live in a condominium? All of these things involve sharing.

Increasingly, people are taking sharing to new levels. Most things can be shared, from lawnmowers to motor homes, from an hour of babysitting to a full-time nanny. This book provides all the information you need to start sharing in any—or every—area of your life.

Part I explains sharing basics, including what you might want to share; who you can share with; what issues you should consider and discuss at the outset; how to communicate, make decisions, and resolve disputes in your sharing group; and how to make a written sharing agreement. In this section, we cover:

- how to set up practical and logistical details
- how to plan for foreseeable and unforeseeable changes
- how to deal with legal issues that might arise in connection with your sharing arrangement
- how to manage the people aspects of sharing, like differing needs and communication styles, and
- how to deal with conflict in productive ways.

Part II provides detailed solutions, information, ideas, tips, and tools for particular types of sharing, including:

- how to share simple things, like tools and food from your garden
- how to share bigger things, like a car, a job, or office space
- how to share help, like a nanny or a caregiver for an elder, and
- how to share the most important things, like your home.

Each chapter in Part II contains a number of sharing solutions, practical strategies you can use to create sharing arrangements for the topic that chapter covers, such as transportation, food, or work. Each chapter highlights the ways sharing benefits you, through demonstrating your "triple bottom line": the personal, environmental, and financial benefits of sharing.

The ultimate beauty of sharing is that it's a solution we create for ourselves. It's not a government program, nor is it the "latest and greatest" product marketed to us on billboards. It's a solution based on our own needs and lifestyles, in our own communities. It's a way for each of us to shape our own lives in positive ways and simultaneously benefit the world as a whole. In that respect, sharing is more than a simple trend: Some might even say our society is moving toward a sharing revolution. We hope you'll use *The Sharing Solution* to become part of it.

Part I:
Sharing Basics

Getting Started

Would you like to save time and money? Learn new skills and teach others what you know? Use fewer resources and reduce your carbon footprint? Get to know your neighbors and build community? You can get all of these valuable benefits—and many more—through sharing.

"Share" is a word of many meanings. As children, we "share" our crayons by letting others *borrow* them. We "share" our cookies by *giving* some to a friend or by *exchanging them for* some cheesy crackers. During "sharing time," we *tell* our stories. We "share" a bike with our little sister and *take turns* using it. We "share" a task by *cooperating* to build a fort or put away our toys. At night, we "share" a bedroom, where we sleep *together with* our siblings. As adults, we "share" homes by *dividing the space* with someone else, we share in the ownership of a company by *buying* "shares" of corporate stock, we "share" information by *making it available* on the Internet, and we flock to see *"Cher"* on her final concert tour.

We won't be covering all these ways to share in this book. For example, while we're all in favor of donating money or time to charitable causes, giving away things you no longer need, and helping out people who've fallen on hard times, that's not what this book is about. As we use the term, "sharing" refers to two or more people coming together to pool property, resources, or obligations or to do or create something together. In other words, the sharing arrangements we talk about in this book are mutual and reciprocal. Everyone involved is giving something *and* getting something, through endeavors like:

- **co-owning** property or pooling resources
- **sharing use** of property, either by taking turns or through simultaneous use
- **cooperating** to perform a task, make decisions, share responsibilities, or collectively purchase goods or services, and
- **exchanging** goods or services in a barter process.

This chapter will help you get started. Here, you'll find information, ideas, and tools you can use to figure out your sharing goals and what you might like to share. To decide whether and what you'd like to share, start by considering your needs, wants, and personal preferences. For example, if you love to be surrounded by others, you might want to consider shared housing. If you want to build community with your neighbors but need lots of time and space to yourself, a neighborhood home improvement group or shared garden might better suit your needs. Using the worksheets in this chapter, you'll be able to put together some sharing ideas that will really work for you.

SKIP AHEAD

For those who are already sharing or have a sharing plan. You may have picked up this book because you are planning to share something—for example, you want to share a car with your neighbor or a nanny with a friend—or are already sharing, and want to make sure you've considered all the important details. You may still benefit from considering your sharing goals and using some of the worksheets in this chapter, but it you're anxious to get started, you can skip ahead to Chapter 2 (if you don't yet have your sharing partners) or Chapter 3 (if you already know whom you plan to share with or are already sharing).

What Are Your Sharing Goals?

People make sharing arrangements for different reasons. Your sharing goals will often determine what you decide to share, and in what ways. In our experience, most people share for one or more of these reasons:

- to save money or acquire property (or the right to use it)
- to save time and reduce work and effort
- to live in a more "green" way
- to build community, and
- to get help with a project or learn a skill.

Financial and Property Goals

If you're looking to save money, sharing is a very effective strategy. Sharing cuts the costs of buying, maintaining, and using property or hiring someone to provide services. Rather than paying the full cost of a care provider, truck, magazine subscription, or lawnmower, for example, you and each person you share with can shoulder a fraction of the cost. Sometimes, you can save almost all of what it would cost you to buy property by sharing with people who already own it. If, for example, you join a neighborhood tool sharing group, you might get to use a variety of expensive tools that others have contributed, without having to buy anything.

You can use the worksheet below to brainstorm about your sharing goals relating to money and property. We've provided a few examples to help you get started; ideas for all of these categories—and more—are covered in Part II. You'll find a blank copy of this form in Appendix B.

Money and Property Worksheet

How I Spend Money	How Much I Spend Per Month	Ways to Share and Possible Savings
Food		Buy bulk food and share with neighbors or coworkers; may save $100 per month.
Car/ Transportation		Carpool to work; give up my car and use a carshare service. Could save up to $300 per month.
Housing		
Entertainment/ Vacations/ Recreation		Find enough people who also want to share a vacation home; explore fractional ownership; buy into an existing sharing group.
Household goods		
Child care		
Pets		
Utilities/Phone/ Internet		
Clothes		
Healthcare		
Other		

Time and Efficiency Goals

Sharing can also save you time—for most of us, something that is at a premium. It's amazing how spending time sharing actually gives you more free time. For example, if you share meals with four coworkers, you'll have to spend the time to make lunch for five once a week, but you'll save the time it would take you to make your own lunch on the other four days. Below is a worksheet for you to consider how you might open up some of your time by sharing, with some sample entries; a blank copy is in Appendix B.

Where Does the Time Go?

Many of us feel that we have less leisure time than ever before, but Americans actually have more "free" time than we did 40 years ago, to the tune of at least 45 minutes per day. (We spend a lot of it watching television, though, so it often feels like less.) We spend an average of three quarters of an hour per day shopping, and approximately the same amount of time caring for others. And we spend nearly two hours each day on "household work," which includes cooking, household chores inside and out, and caring for pets. By sharing even part of that work with someone else, we can free up hours of time per week.

Time and Efficiency Worksheet

How I Spend Time	Ways to Save Time by Sharing
Commuting	Arrange a jobsharing situation that allows each of us to telecommute.
Home repair/ Housework/Yard work	Start a neighborhood home improvement group. Start a skills-sharing group so I learn more about how to do things and become faster.
Caring for others (children, adults, pets)	Hire a shared caregiver with the family down the street.
Working	
Running errands	
Preparing meals	
Other	
I would like more time for:	Make time for taking Spanish class after work: Start a dog-walking share so I can come home later once or twice a week.

Environmental/Green Goals

Sharing is one of the easiest ways there is to start living a greener life. Adopting even one of the examples below can make a real difference in the resources you consume and, therefore, a real difference in the health of your community and the planet. Appendix B includes a blank copy of the chart below.

Calculate Your Footprint

One way to find out how you're doing in the green department is to use an online "footprint" or carbon emissions calculator. For example, the U.S. Environmental Protection Agency provides a personal emissions calculator, which tells you how many pounds of carbon dioxide are released into the atmosphere from your activities each year. It also shows you how much you can reduce your emissions by making some changes in your daily patterns and consumption. You can find the calculator at: www.epa.gov/climatechange/emissions/ind_calculator.html

Other footprint calculators express your impact based on the number of acres of biologically productive land that are required to support your lifestyle. The results can be arresting. For example, the average person in the United States has a footprint of about 24 acres, but the Earth only has about 27 billion biologically productive acres available. When we divide that by 6.7 billion people, we find that the Earth can sustainably provide us with only four acres apiece. This mean we are currently extracting the Earth's resources much faster than they can be replenished. At this rate, we're going to need a new Earth soon. To calculate your footprint in acres, try these calculators: www.myfootprint.org or www.thefootprintnetwork.org.

Environmental Worksheet

Green Goals	Ways to Live More Sustainably By Sharing
Drive less	
Buy fewer consumer goods	Share items like a vacuum cleaner, tools, or BBQ.
Obtain food from more sustainable sources	Start a community food garden or join a community supported agriculture (CSA) program.
Reduce home energy use and use renewable energy sources	Find others who are interested in solar energy and reduce costs through collective bargaining. Start a home energy savings group.
Reduce waste	
Be greener at work	
Buy environmentally friendly products	
Other	

Community Building Goals

Getting to know your neighbors, coworkers, and friends you might not have met yet is another way that sharing can improve your quality of life.

If participating more in the life of your community, or being part of building community yourself, is one of your reasons for sharing, here is a worksheet with examples that will help you start thinking about what might work in your own life. A blank copy is in Appendix B.

Community Building Worksheet

Community Building Goals	Ways to Build Community by Sharing
Get to know neighbors	Plan a neighborhood potluck block party. Start a goods-sharing group or a disaster-preparedness group.
Help neighbors and get help in return	Offer to share child care or pet care with a neighbor.
Get to know coworkers better	Start a mealsharing group.
Other	

Returning to Community

In his 2000 book, *Bowling Alone*, Robert Putnam found that Americans'
engagement in civic life—measured by things like membership in local
groups, churches, and social and work-related organizations, participation
in local and national politics, and time spent with family, friends, and
neighbors—had fallen by 25% – 50% since the late 1960s. His follow-up
book, *Better Together*, (www.bettertogether.org), explores ways that some
communities are working together to increase civic engagement in the 21st
century. One way to start is by the simplest of mealsharing programs—the
dinner party. Only 38% of Americans entertain friends or family at home at
least once a year; surely we can do better than that.

Goals Related to Getting Help

You may have noticed that many of the suggestions in the worksheets
above are overlapping—for example, starting a neighborhood home
improvement group is a way to save time and get to know your
neighbors. Arranging a carpool saves time and reduces your carbon
footprint. Many of the ideas listed above also fall into the category of
getting help—with projects (home improvement), with caring for others
(sharing a caregiver or nanny), or with learning a skill (starting a group
to share skills at your workplace). Use the chart below to consider the
things you might need help with. Our version includes some examples;
you'll find a blank copy in Appendix B.

What Can Be Shared?

Now that you've thought out why you want to share, it's a short step
to considering what you could share to meet those goals. There are
unlimited ways of sharing, and nearly unlimited things to share, too.
Here are some ideas.

Getting Help Worksheet

What I Could Use Help With	Ways to Get Help by Sharing
House care	Start a neighborhood home improvement group.
Yard care	Let neighbors know they can have some of my berries if they help pick them when they ripen. Talk to neighbors in apartment building about starting a shared garden in my back yard.
Taking care of other possessions	Offer to let neighbor use my driveway to work on his car if he'll teach me how to change the oil.
Meal preparation	
Chores and errands	
Child care	
Elder care or care for other adults	
Other	

Things That Can Be Shared

You can share ownership or use of *tangible objects*, like:

- a vehicle, including a car, truck, motorcycle, motor scooter, or RV
- a bicycle or scooter
- a canoe, kayak, paddleboat, or surfboard
- a boat or airplane
- household appliances, like a vacuum cleaner, washer and dryer, sewing machine, or extra refrigerator or freezer
- gardening and yard work equipment, such as a wheelbarrow, weed whacker, shovels, rakes, lawnmower, tree trimmer, or snow blower
- tools for carpentry and home repair, like a circular saw, painting equipment (tarps, rollers, brushes, and so on), a lathe, or a tile saw
- tools for working on a car or other vehicle
- an emergency preparedness kit
- recreational gear, like a tent, skis, camping stove, beach chairs and umbrella, bike rack, scuba gear, or sports equipment (bats, balls, tennis rackets, and so on)
- a work of art
- a piece of expensive jewelry, or
- clothing, such as formal wear, business attire, and specialized sports clothing (like a wetsuit or ski jacket).

You can share ownership or use of *spaces*, like:

- a house, apartment, condominium, or other living space
- a work space, garage, or studio
- a retail building, office space, commercial kitchen, or selling space
- a laundry or storage room, or
- outdoor space, such as a yard, garden, swimming pool, tennis or other sport court, or play equipment (like a swing set, tree house, or jungle gym).

You can share *services, privileges, or subscriptions,* like:

- season tickets to a sports team, music or dance series, or theater group

- newspaper or magazine subscriptions, or
- services, like a nanny, elder care worker, house cleaner, or gardener.

You can pool resources and purchasing power to *bargain collectively for goods and services*. For example, you could:

- form a buying club for food, dry goods, or other household staples
- cooperate to purchase things that are cheaper to buy in large quantities, such as a cord of firewood, a tank of propane fuel, or a ton of gravel, mulch, or potting soil
- form a purchasing group to bargain collectively for expensive services, such as solar power, or
- take part in community-supported agriculture, by joining with others to "adopt" a farm.

You can share your time, skills, or expertise to *cooperate with others* to:

- create a child care cooperative or a simple babysitting trade with one or two neighbors or friends
- establish a dog walking tradeoff
- set up a mealsharing group or trade cooking skills for something else
- carpool to work, to school, or for a long-distance trip
- start a neighborhood home improvement group, or
- offer to swap skills—for example, teach your neighbor to build a bookcase if she'll show you how to make pasta.

Ways to Share Things

You may choose to share in many different ways, including:

- **Shared ownership.** Each sharer owns a part interest in something, such as a house or car.
- **Shared responsibility.** The sharers agree to do something together, like trade child care or hire a gardener.
- **Shared use.** The sharers all use something, even though everyone might not have an ownership share.

In most cases, you can set up your sharing situation in whatever way best suits your group's needs. For example, if you're sharing a car with

Form a Sharing Group or Network

Some people first decide what they want to share, and then seek out other sharers. Another way to get some sharing started is to get together a group of people who are interested in exploring ways to share. These might be neighbors, coworkers, or anyone else you see on a regular basis. (For more ideas about who to share with and how to connect with them, see Chapter 2.) Once your "Sharing Circle" or "Sharing Group" comes together, you can brainstorm all kinds of ways to share, and will probably come up with many ideas you may not have thought of on your own.

Forming a sharing group has the added benefit of creating a network of reciprocity. For example, Baracka shares his washer and dryer with Daniel, who provides occasional childcare for Carmel, who shares her storage shed with Mayumi, who shares her sailboat with Baracka. Everyone gives and receives through the group, even though the sharing relationships aren't directly reciprocal.

If you form a group of people to brainstorm sharing ideas, you might each want to complete the worksheet, "What Could I Share?" below. You can compile the answers on a spreadsheet or just pass around the filled-out sheets. Once everyone's ideas are in the mix, sharing arrangements will begin to develop naturally. Individual group members can approach each other with sharing proposals and sort out the details on their own.

another person, you could split use equally by trading off days or weeks, or you could agree that one of you gets the car more often. You could share costs equally or one of you could do the minor repairs yourself while the other foots more than half of the bill for major repairs. You could agree that other people may—or may not—borrow the car, that you'll both chip in to buy a car seat that your kids will share or a bike rack for the roof, or that one of you will pay a bit more to buy a new hybrid in exchange for getting to claim the tax deduction. This is one of the best things about sharing: For the most part, you get to decide how to structure the arrangement.

The exception is when you are sharing something that has some kind of legal or regulatory rules attached to it. For example, many shared housing situations must be designed to comply with local laws, such as zoning restrictions that may limit how many families can share a home or how you may use property. But regardless of whether you have to consider legal issues or not, there are certain common practical and logistical issues that you should consider in any sharing situation to help you create a solid sharing plan, ensure that you meet everyone's needs, plan for changes and unforeseeable events, and so on. These issues are covered in Chapter 3, which lists the 20 questions that every sharing group should consider.

In the chapters that follow, you'll learn much more about these ways of sharing and the different considerations involved in each.

Your Sharing Ideas

The following worksheet is a tool for you to fill out on your own or use together with a group of people who are exploring sharing ideas together. It will help you:

- think of ways you might share and how sharing might benefit you
- think of things you already own that you might be able to share, and
- think of things that you can't afford to own, but that you could borrow from, or purchase with, someone else. (Vacation home, anyone?)

The worksheet will also help you brainstorm ways that you can partner with others to make purchases, or cooperate with them for things like pet care and home repair. We provided examples throughout to help get you started; you'll find a blank copy in Appendix B.

What Could I Share?

Categories of Things to Share	What I Have to Share	What I Hope to Get Through Sharing
Tangible Items		
Household appliances	A bread machine	Perhaps others will share bread that they make.
Household goods		
Electronics		Video camera: I don't own one, but it would be great to have occasional access to one.
Tools		A circular saw: Dave across the street does some repairs and construction; we could buy it together and share its use.
Vehicles	Pickup truck	Help with expenses of keeping the truck through allowing others to use it regularly.
Work equipment	Massage table: I hardly ever use it. I could advertise for someone who wants to use it sometimes.	Copy machine: Too expensive for my home office, unless my neighbor who also works at home regularly would share the cost.
Recreation/ Hobbies	Season tickets to the Durham Bulls games	Want to share some games and defray the cost of the tickets.

What Could I Share? (continued)

Categories of Things to Share	What I Have to Share	What I Hope to Get Through Sharing
Fitness/ Outdoors		Elliptical trainer: Ron and Sue down the street have said that they want one too. We could keep it in my basement and they could have a key to the outside basement door. We could use an online calendar to schedule use.
Clothing/ Accessories		Wetsuit
Other	Typewriter	
Space		
Housing		
Yard		
Laundry room		It would be GREAT to have access to someone's laundry room.
Storage space	I have plenty of room in the crawl space of my house to share.	

What Could I Share? (continued)

Categories of Things to Share	What I Have to Share	What I Hope to Get Through Sharing
Vacation home		
Work space		
Other		
Services, privileges, and subscriptions		
Services		Housecleaning: Maybe my house mate will share the cost with me.
Privileges	I have 10 guest passes for the YMCA and am happy to take anyone with me.	
Subscriptions		
Other		

What Could I Share? (continued)

Categories of Things to Share	What I Have to Share	What I Hope to Get Through Sharing
Purchasing		
Food		I would like to take part in Community-Supported Agriculture.
Goods/ Supplies	Firewood: I will be getting a delivery and could share the cost.	
Utilities		
Other		

What Could I Share? (continued)

Cooperation	Ways to Cooperate with Others
Carpools and rides	I drive from Raleigh to Atlanta frequently for business. I could advertise online to look for a rider to share the cost.
Child care	
Adult care	
Pet care	I could do a pet sitting exchange, to try to get occasional cat sitting when I'm in Atlanta.
Meals	
Gardening/ Yard work	
Home repair/ Improvement	
Chores/ Errands	
Skills	I can teach bicycle repair; I would like to learn how to cook.
Other	

Now that you've brainstormed and crunched some numbers and even dreamed a little, you can look over your list and decide where you want to start sharing. As is true of many things, it's often easiest to start small, with an arrangement to share something relatively simple, like tools or appliances. If that is a success, you could move on to thinking about sharing larger or more involved things, such as a vehicle, childcare, or physical space, like a yard.

Sharing: The Bigger Picture

This book is full of sharing ideas that almost anyone could implement. More and more, people are consciously choosing to integrate sharing into their daily lives, and society will feel the effects in countless beneficial ways.

But as we bring about a more sharing world, change will come not just from individuals, but also from businesses, nonprofits, community leaders, developers, and lawmakers. All of these entities play a role in creating the tools and resources that help us share, such as city-wide carsharing programs and public tool lending libraries.

In Part II of this book, each chapter includes a box entitled "The Bigger Picture." For those interested in helping to spread sharing beyond their own homes, these boxes provide a short list of ideas about how businesses, leaders, lawmakers, and others can help society share in bigger ways.

The Triple Bottom Line: The Benefits of Sharing

In the second part of this book, each chapter covers a particular type of sharing. These chapters include a section that describes your "triple bottom line." The triple bottom line is the essence of why we share—because it's good for our pocketbooks, it's good for the planet, and it's good for the social world we live in. Later chapters provide information about specific sharing scenarios, such as shared housing or a shared car. Here's the triple bottom line as it applies to sharing in the most general sense.

Social and Personal Benefits

These are some of the ways that your life and society as a whole will be better because of sharing. For example, sharing can help everyone:

- get to know our neighbors and make neighborhoods safer
- make friends
- find resources and referrals more easily
- find new ways to relate to friends, relatives, coworkers, and neighbors
- lighten our load of responsibilities
- create more free time
- meet the needs of seniors and people with disabilities
- increase resources and opportunities for low-income households
- support small businesses and buy local
- access better nutrition, and
- access higher quality goods.

Environmental Benefits

Sharing is as green as it can be, because it:

- uses space, energy, and resources more efficiently
- reduces consumption
- reduces waste
- reduces energy use
- helps us invest in green products, alternative energy, and durable goods
- shrinks your carbon footprint
- sets a green example for others, and
- helps take cars off the road.

Financial Benefits

The financial bottom line is undoubtedly important to you. The benefits of sharing are evident here. Through sharing, you can:

- spread the cost of owning high quality and durable goods
- reduce the cost of caring for a child or other family member

- reduce the cost of food, fuel, and supplies
- accomplish home repairs without paying for labor
- spread the risk of loss, damage, and depreciation
- share homeownership and build equity
- save money through collective buying, and
- get access to luxury items you couldn't afford alone.

We hope that this chapter has given you lots of ideas about things you can share and the many benefits of having more sharing in your life.

Finding Sharing Partners

Some sharing arrangements spring up naturally among people who already know one another. In many situations, the makeup of a sharing group is determined by the type of share its members have in mind. For example, if you want to share a nanny, you may be looking to go in with a friend whose children are the same age as yours. Appliances, tools, or a vehicle are usually easiest to share with neighbors. And often, the idea to share housing comes up among a group of close friends.

If you have an idea for sharing, you'll naturally first consider whether you could do it with people you already know. But the world is full of potential sharers, and one of the benefits of sharing is getting to know people you might otherwise not have crossed paths with. This chapter explains how to find people to share with among your neighbors, your coworkers, and friends (both those you know and those you haven't met yet).

Who Can I Share With?

Depending on what you're sharing, your sharing partners might be:

- friends
- family members
- neighbors
- coworkers
- members of your church, temple, mosque, or other spiritual community
- parents of your children's friends
- people with similar interests to yours, or
- people you meet only for the purpose of sharing.

As you can see, you already know some of these people well, and others not so much, so you'll have to do your best to figure out whether some of them will be good sharers. There are lots of different people who can share well, and the qualities that will be most important in a sharing partner depend on what you're sharing and how. Most likely, you'll have a different set of criteria for someone who occasionally takes care of your children than for someone who occasionally uses your ladder, for example. But responsibility and reliability will be important for both.

There are some qualities that good sharers generally, well, share. A *good sharer*:

- pays attention to detail, is thoughtful, and plans ahead
- can be flexible and adaptable
- has a generous spirit and doesn't hold grudges
- doesn't worry constantly about being taken advantage of (for example, someone who will suspiciously track every nickel and dime your group spends might become a problem)
- communicates honestly and clearly
- cares about your needs and wishes
- meets commitments, and
- is pleasant to be around.

Sharing Is for Introverts, Too

In interviewing people for this book, we learned that sharing isn't just for outgoing extroverts who love to be around other people; we found plenty of introverts sharing, too. This surprised us at first, but on further reflection, it makes sense. In modern society, where many of us live away from our families and in neighborhoods where people don't know each other, our "community" often consists of the circles of friends we develop through social activities. This can make it difficult for introverts, who tend to be less outgoing and social, to build community for themselves. Sharing provides opportunities for introverts to meet people with common interests.

Cohousing is a good example of the type of sharing that might appeal to a more reserved personality (cohousing is covered in Chapter 6). Cohousing offers private living areas, which meets people's need for personal space and solitary time. At the same time, there are extensive shared facilities and activities in cohousing, including shared laundry, shared yard space, some shared meals, and shared group activities such as gardening and home improvement projects. The large group gatherings often revolve around a structured activity, in contrast to unstructured parties where people are expected to mingle and chat. These structured activities are welcoming to introverts, who can take part in the activities and feel a sense of belonging, without feeling pressured to be the life of the party.

If you don't already know who you'd like to share with, go back to the worksheets you completed in Chapter 1. For your one or two top sharing ideas, think about who might make sense as a sharing partner, using these questions to get you started:

- Do you want to share something that's stationary, such as a large appliance? If so, it makes sense to share with neighbors. You also might consider sharing with someone who spends a lot of time at your home or vice versa, such as a parent, sibling, or close friend.
- Is your sharing idea motivated by green goals? If so, sharing with someone nearby—again, a neighbor or someone who spends time at your home or vice versa—will probably do the most to reduce your carbon footprint.
- Do you plan to share something that requires a lot of responsibility, such as child care or cohousing? In that case, you'll want people whom you trust and who are compatible with you. Looking for sharing partners among your friends makes sense.
- Are you going to be sharing something expensive, like a house or a boat? If so, your fellow sharers should be people whose financial sense you trust and whose resources you know a little bit about—again, either people you already know or people who are willing to share financial information with you. They should also be trustworthy and responsible.
- Will your sharing arrangement involve a fair amount of contact, like a weekly mealsharing group or a regular child care share? If you'll be seeing your fellow sharers regularly, make sure you really like them! This seems obvious, but don't ignore it. If you have a neighbor whom you find slightly annoying, you might want to think twice before agreeing to a weekly food exchange with him. Instead, choose neighbors you like and want to know better.

Sharing With Your Neighbors

Sharing with your neighbors often makes sense, for the obvious reason that it is inconvenient to share a lawnmower that is kept across town (it won't do much to save you time or reduce your carbon footprint, either). If you are lucky enough to live in one of those neighborhoods where everyone knows each other or where there's an existing neighborhood association, then you've got a head start on creating a more sharing community. If not, there are a lot of things you can do to build community right where you are.

Often, breaking the ice with your neighbors is the hardest part. You might feel kind of silly if you've lived across the street or down the hall for years and have never said so much as a hello. Don't worry; this happens all the time. You can reverse this pattern by starting with a smile, nod, or wave. Your neighbors probably feel just as silly as you do about never saying hi, and will be happy that you made the first move.

As you get bolder, you might comment on their lovely bougainvillea or mention how adorable their pug is. You could even go out on a limb and offer them some plums from your tree, ask whether you can pick some of their lemons, or ask how they'd feel if you practiced drums once or twice a week. They will probably be pleased that you thought of them. Sometimes, all people need is to be acknowledged or considered.

Once you have begun to melt the social ice cap in your neighborhood, you can take some more active steps to pull people together. We suggest three ways to start: a neighborhood questionnaire or survey, a block party, and a neighborhood bulletin board or email list.

Survey Your Neighbors

We're starting with the survey, but you also could start with a party. We know one woman who printed flyers inviting her neighbors to her house on a Sunday afternoon and delivered the flyers in person. The party was a lot of fun, and neighbors exchanged contact information so they could build on the social connections they made.

But you can start with information gathering, too. Create a questionnaire and take it door to door. Invite your neighbors to fill it out, and explain that you want to help neighbors learn more about each other and build a closer community. You could then either tally up the results yourself or copy the surveys and distribute a full packet to each neighbor. That should get people thinking and give them lots to talk about at the block party.

Here's a sample letter with a questionnaire:

Dear Neighbor,

I just read a really interesting book called "The Sharing Solution," where I found a lot of tips and ideas for saving money, simplifying my life, and living more sustainably by sharing resources with others. It gave ideas for forming child care, dog-walking, gardening, and home repair co-ops, sharing cars, rides, tools, and household appliances, and sharing meals, among many other things. It got me thinking that it would be nice for all of us to know each other better, and we might even find more ways to share resources and cooperate.

Please take some time to fill out this questionnaire and return it to me at 2424 Heinz Street. I'll make copies of everyone's answers and distribute them to the group. This includes everyone living on Heinz Street between 9th and 11th.

I would also like to invite you to a neighborhood block party to be held on May 1. By then, we will all have read each other's neighbor questionnaires, which will give us lots to think and talk about. It should also be a lot of fun!

Thanks so much for taking the time to complete this questionnaire! If you have any questions, please feel free to email me at Janelle@ sbcglobal.net or call me at 510-555-1212.

Sincerely,

Janelle

Janelle (2424 Heinz Street)

Neighbor Questionnaire

Name: _____

Address: _____

Phone number: _____

Email address: _____

Would you like to join a neighborhood email listserv? ☐ Yes ☐ No

Emergency contact (someone we can call if we think you need emergency help): _____

Home phone: _____ Work phone: _____
Cell phone: _____

How long have you lived in this neighborhood? _____

Where are you from originally? _____

What do you like to do for fun? _____

What kind of work do you do? _____

What city do you work in? _____

Do you drive to work? ☐ Yes ☐ No

Would you be interested in carpooling if a neighbor works near you?
☐ Yes ☐ No

Do you own a car?   ☐ Yes ☐ No

Would you ever be interested in sharing a car with a neighbor?
☐ Yes ☐ No

If you work from home, are you interested in sharing office equipment?
☐ Yes ☐ No

Do you have children?   ☐ Yes ☐ No
If so, how many and how old? _____

_____

Would you ever like to trade child care with other neighbors, whether through casual babysitting, sharing a child care provider, or otherwise?
☐ Yes ☐ No

Do you have pets? ☐ Yes ☐ No
If so, who are they?_____

Would you ever like to coordinate with neighbors to take turns walking dogs or caring for other animals? ☐ Yes ☐ No

Would you be interested in joining a neighborhood gardening group? ☐ Yes ☐ No

Would you be interested in joining a neighborhood home improvement group, which will meet to work on home repair and building projects at each member's house? ☐ Yes ☐ No

Would you like to be invited to neighborhood games nights?
☐ Yes ☐ No

Would you be interested in doing mealsharing with neighbors?
☐ Yes ☐ No

Do you have a fruit tree that you'd like help harvesting or fruit you'd like help eating? ☐ Yes ☐ No

Do you or does anyone in your household have any disabilities or health problems you would like your neighbors to know about, or you might need help with? ☐ Yes ☐ No
If so, what are they? _____

_____

Would you be interested in sharing any of the following:
    ☐ Tools, ladders, etc.
    ☐ Washer and dryer
    ☐ Household appliances, like vacuum cleaners
    ☐ Household goods and electronics
    ☐ Toys and sports equipment

Have a Block Party

Now that you've collected all the information, here are some ideas for planning your neighborhood block party, step by step.

Step 1: Talk to the neighbors you know best, especially the ones you think will be most helpful and enthusiastic, and ask whether they want to share in planning the party.

Step 2: Pick a date when the weather will likely be nice and people will probably be available. If you plan the party for Memorial or Labor Day, for example, you run the risk that your neighbors will be out of town for the three-day weekend.

Step 3: Get any required permits. If you're planning to actually block off the street, rather than holding your party on the sidewalk, a cul-de-sac, someone's front yard, or a public spot, you may need to deal with a bit of red tape. Most of the time, this is a simple process; you just need permission from your city to block off the street for a few hours. Some cities may require you to get signatures from your neighbors (usually from about 75% of households on your block). You might have to pay a fee for the permit.

Once you have the permit, the city may supply road barricades for you a day or two before the party, or you can block off the street with clever use of trash cans and yellow tape. The city might want you to get insurance for the event; if so, it should tell you how to get it. There might also be limits on the times of day when you can have the party and the amount of noise you can make. Also find out the city's policy about alcohol; there may be a law requiring that alcohol be consumed on private property only. (If that's the case, you can set up a bar in someone's yard.)

Most of this information should be available on your city's website. If you can't find it, call the department of public works or the main city phone number and ask how to get the information you need.

Step 4: Print invitations and go door to door inviting neighbors. While you are talking to people, ask whether they'd like to help plan an activity or coordinate part of the event (such as overseeing the barbecues, setting up, cleaning up, organizing a game, and so on). Keep an eye out for a charismatic neighbor who can rally folks for a relay race or be an announcer for the talent show. On the invitation, ask that people bring something to grill, a side dish, or drinks. Also ask that they bring their own dishes, so that no paper or plastic is wasted.

Step 5: Plan activities. Here are some ideas:
- chalk art on the side walks
- one of those big inflatable bouncing cages (it's an expense, but will be a major draw for neighborhood kids)
- badminton, croquet, or some other sport in someone's front yard
- limbo
- talent show or performances by the neighborhood band
- relay races
- bean-bag toss
- piñatas
- neighborhood history walk, and
- icebreaker games that help people to meet and learn about each other.

Step 6: Gather supplies. Depending on your planned activities, you might need to collect:
- a bucket of thick sidewalk chalk
- a bunch of tables and chairs
- large umbrellas to block the sun
- a couple of grills
- sports and games equipment
- a stereo or sound system
- trash cans
- street barricades, or
- coolers and ice.

Step 7: On the day of the party, try to meet and greet everyone who comes, and introduce them to someone else.

When people arrive, have everyone put on a name tag. Use a big one with room for them to also answer a question that you put on it or to mention something about themselves that they'd like to share. For example, "my name is _____, and my favorite [sport/animal/thing to do in my free time, etc.] is _____."

And have a great time!

Set Up a Neighborhood Bulletin Board or Email List

A neighborhood email list or discussion group can work wonders for bringing people together. There are a lot of hosting sites for a listserv, but the most commonly used—probably because it's one of the simplest—is www.yahoo.com. You'll need a moderator who takes responsibility for adding members (at their request), and you'll need to agree on what types of posts are acceptable. Many neighborhood email groups agree that they'll post only announcements of interest to the neighborhood, and refrain from sharing jokes, political commentary, or personal information. This means it's fine to post the time and location of the neighborhood garden meeting or that you want to borrow a lawnmower, is fine, but not all the reasons why you hate the mayor.

If some folks on your block don't use email, it's a nice idea to print out the messages and post them on a bulletin board in front of someone's house, unless you feel the information is too private.

If you are successful, your neighborhood email postings will start to look like this:

- *"I will be getting a load of soil [firewood/mulch/bricks] delivered to my house. It's cheaper if I buy more than _____. Would anyone like to go in on it with me?"*
- *"Help! I just harvested 8,000 zucchinis from my garden. I'm putting them on my front porch. Please come take some! If you have a good zucchini recipe, please let me know!"*
- *"I'm making a trip to the dump [thrift store/electronics recycling center/propane refill station]. Do you have anything you'd like me to take? "*
- *"I broke my foot, and I need help bringing in the lawn furniture before the storm hits. Can anyone come over and help me?"*
- *"Don't forget! Tomorrow is street cleaning day! Move your car to the south side of the street."*

- *"Neighbors are going to get together at my house on Thursday at 7 to talk about what we can do about the recent rash of car thefts."*
- *"Has anyone seen little Susie's Pooh-Bear? She left it somewhere again."*

Many of the ideas described in other chapters of this book are neighbor-related. Once you bring your neighborhood together, the door is open to suggesting all kinds of sharing with your neighbors.

Sharing With Your Coworkers

Coworkers are another good group of candidates for sharing arrangements. You see them practically every day, so you can easily hand things off to each other if you are taking turns using them. Magazine subscriptions, portable tools (like a cordless drill or socket set), or camping equipment are all easily shared among people who work together.

Do you work near a wholesale club or outlet that sells things in bulk? If so, you can take a trip during your lunch hour with coworkers, then divide up that giant bag of apples, wheel of cheese, or wall of toilet paper into portions you can actually eat or find room for in your home.

There are also things that you can share while you are at work. For example, sharing lunch has become increasingly popular in workplaces, in part because it's hard to find a good lunch for under $10 these days. And let's face it, at some point most of us get tired of the lunch options near our workplaces. Take turns providing lunch for a small group. If there are ten of you, you'll probably have to cook only twice a month. Not bad, considering it's in exchange for 18 free lunches a month.

Some coworkers share bikes or cars while at work. For example, maybe you need a car while you are at work, but would like to avoid morning and evening rush hour. So you take a train to work, meet your coworker, get in the car parked at the train station, and then the two of you have the car at work all day if you need it. (An alternative is to lobby for a company car.)

You and your coworkers could also pool resources—and perhaps ask your employer to chip in—to improve the office environment. There are lots more ideas about sharing with your coworkers in Chapter 8 (about sharing food) and Chapter 11 (about work-related sharing).

As is true with your neighbors, getting to know your coworkers is the first step. Many companies sponsor email bulletin boards where employees can post non-work-related items like things for sale or where someone's band is playing that night. You can use this resource as a way to find others who want to share—or just to propose a potluck lunch so people can get to know each other. Most workplaces also have an actual bulletin board where you can pin up a notice.

Finding Sharers Online

Depending on what you are hoping to share, you might need to look beyond the people you already know to find a suitable sharer. Perhaps you don't know anyone who's looking to share a house or something else you want to share. Sharing a horse, a boat, an RV, or another big ticket item requires finding someone else who is interested in the same thing and ready to make the investment when you are.

The Internet is an incredibly useful tool for finding people with similar interests. Most people are probably familiar with online classified ad sites, like craigslist (www.craigslist.com) and social networking sites, such as Facebook (www.facebook.com). But there are also more specific sites that can help you find the precise kind of share you're looking for. There are websites that connect people who want to carpool, share housing or garden space, and much more. Some websites even contain interactive maps to help you find nearby sharers. We list many of these sites in the chapters that follow and in Appendix A.

Seeking Sharers

Just for fun, here are some of the sharing posts that showed up during one week on a San Francisco Bay Area craigslist:

- Sourdough starter to share or trade
- Share a ride to Portland?
- Looking for family to share a nanny
- Daily carpool from Fremont to Palo Alto
- Looking for a tenancy-in-common partner for a duplex
- Looking to share a pickup truck
- Monthly vegan potluck
- Women's makeup club
- Studio share available now
- Do you need vegetable gardening space? Share my yard
- Looking to share street vendor space
- Discussion group for seniors starting worker-owned business.

Join Established Sharing Programs

There are many existing sharing groups and programs out there, including established cooperative grocery stores, tool lending libraries, cooperative nursery schools, city-wide carsharing programs, community-supported agriculture programs, group housing, and much more. We describe many of these in the chapters that follow, and provide resources to help you find out whether there are established groups in your area.

20 Questions to Ask When You Share

Alva and Bobbie just started college. They could each use a car for occasional errands, visiting friends and family, and, of course, road trips. But neither can afford a decent car, even a used model of less than recent vintage.

After reading a newspaper article about vehicle sharing, Alva realizes this could be the answer to their car-related dreams. Alva and Bobbie have this conversation about it:

Alva: "Hey Bobbie, I heard about this cool idea called "carsharing!" Do you want to share a car with me?"

Bobbie: "Sure! Great idea!"

Alva: "Wonderful, we can go buy a used car tomorrow! You can use the car on odd days of the month and I'll take the car on the even days."

Bobbie: "Deal!"

Alva: "Deal!"

Whoa! Wait a minute! Alva and Bobbie just sped into a sharing agreement full throttle. Before they get too far down the road, they may want to slow down and consider some basic questions like these:

- Who will own the car and whose name(s) will be on the title? Will one own a larger share than the other?
- How long will they be sharing this car? Who gets the car if someone moves away or decides to stop sharing?
- How do they share expenses for the car? What if one of them uses the car a lot more than the other?
- Whose name is on the insurance? Are both liable for damages if one person gets in a wreck?
- Will other people get to use the car or share it with them? How many? How will they decide who can join the group?
- Who will take the car in for tune-ups and repairs?
- What happens if the car needs major repairs that one of them can't afford?
- What if Alva really needs to use the car on an odd-numbered day? Will they stick to the schedule no matter what or try to be more flexible?
- Are there any rules about the use of the car? Can they eat in the car? Are dogs allowed to ride in the car? Who gets to program the radio station buttons?

As you can see, even relatively straightforward sharing arrangements may involve more than meets the eye. Questions about ownership, responsibilities, privileges, and rules are bound to come up as you put your sharing plan into practice. Groups that can anticipate these issues and agree on how to handle them have the best chance of success—and will spend the least amount of time later dealing with disagreements and misunderstandings.

Chapters 1 and 2 covered *what* you might want to share and *who* you might want to share with. This chapter will help your group decide *how* it wants to share. Here we provide 20 basic questions you may want to consider and discuss when forming a sharing arrangement. You can use these questions to help guide your planning conversations and make sure everyone in your group agrees about how your sharing arrangement will work.

At the end of this chapter, you'll find a worksheet listing each of these questions and providing space for you to jot down your thoughts. You can do this individually or as a group. It may not be quite as amusing as a good old fashioned game of "20 Questions," but it can be interesting and revealing. Without realizing it, sharers sometimes have different expectations about what they'll be sharing, how often, for what reasons, or with whom. By working through these issues early on, you'll build the foundation for a smooth sharing operation. (Chapter 4 offers communication tips for sharers, including ways to raise and discuss tough issues.)

Don't be daunted by the number of issues to consider: If you're setting up a relatively simple sharing arrangement (for example, sharing a yard with your neighbor), you may be able to skip some questions and answer others in only a minute or two. If you're setting up a more complicated arrangement (for example, sharing childcare with several other families), you'll need to consider each question more thoroughly— and it will be time well spent.

In Part II, we provide more detail, tips, and considerations specific to different types of sharing arrangements. These should also be part of your discussion.

When you're done, you can use this chapter's worksheet and the other sample agreements in this book as a template for your written sharing agreement, if you decide to make one. For the reasons discussed in Chapter 1, we think you should.

1. Why Are We Sharing?

As discussed in Chapter 1, people decide to share for many different reasons: to save money, time, or the environment; to build community; to lighten their load and responsibilities; to simplify their lives; and so on. Your sharing group can work well even if members are motivated by different goals. In fact, that's the beauty of sharing: It allows you to meet the needs of a diverse group with one activity or arrangement.

Talking about why each member wants to share is a great way to start your discussion about how your group will work. Many of the decisions you'll need to make—about cost, obligations, use of the shared item, and more—will largely depend on each member's motivation for sharing. Talking about these goals will help prevent potential misunderstandings later and, as the group evolves, ensure that everyone remains sensitive to the various needs and interests of group members.

> **EXAMPLE:** Alva and Bobbie decide to go ahead with their carshare; they invite their friend Carolina to join them, too. Alva is doing it to save money. Bobbie is trying to be green and take part in more sustainable transportation practices. Carolina is in it for the free parking in Alva's garage. Without fully understanding the motivations of the other two car-sharers, Bobbie assumes that everyone is doing it to save the planet. She gets an estimate from a local mechanic to convert the car's engine to accommodate biodiesel. Alva protests that this will be too expensive. Carolina is not pleased because the biodiesel station is too far away. Bobbie is shocked and goes on a tirade about offshore oil drilling, and everyone is left feeling bitter. Had the three fully communicated their goals at the outset, they could have made decisions that better accommodated everyone's needs.

Discussing values at the outset might also lead a group to see that its members are incompatible—a discovery that is much easier to make at the beginning of a venture or project than after you are mired in the middle.

If you want, you can put your motivations in writing. Writing down your goals can help you clarify—for yourself and the rest of the group—what you hope to get out of the deal. It also provides a touchstone for later decisions and a context for those who may join the group later. These types of statements are often written in the "recitals" portion of a contract: an introductory paragraph or two that explains how or why the agreement came into being.

> **EXAMPLE:** Five friends rent a house together to create a household with shared values. In their cotenant agreement, they write:
>
> *"We have decided to form a group house in order to create a healthy and supportive living environment. We all value clear and open communication. We also hope to support each other in adopting lifestyles that do less harm to the planet, by sharing resources, using goods that are sustainably produced, and conserving energy, water, and other natural resources."*

2. What Are We Sharing?

Make sure all of you agree on what you are doing and what you are sharing, and, for that matter, what you are *not* doing and what you are *not* sharing. You may be surprised to find that others planned to share more—or less—than you had in mind.

> **EXAMPLE:** Tom and Marilyn are next door neighbors. They decide to remove the fence between their properties to create a large shared yard space that their children can use to play soccer and football. They write down their purpose:
>
> *"Tom and Marilyn agree to remove the fence between their properties to give their children more space to play sports."*
>
> This purpose is limited to sports; it doesn't contemplate other uses of the shared yard. If Tom planted pumpkins in Marilyn's yard or started using the yards to raise goats, Marilyn could object

that this was not within their original agreed-upon purpose. However, if Tom and Marilyn would like to leave open the possibility of using the shared yards for other purposes, they could use broader language, like this:

"Tom and Marilyn agree to remove the fence between their properties. The purpose of removing the fence is to provide the families in both households more space for outdoor activities, including but not limited to playing sports, planting vegetables, and raising goats. Tom and Marilyn must both consent to any use of or activity in the shared yard."

If you will be sharing a lot of things, as is often the case in shared housing or office arrangements, you should make a list of what is being shared and what is not. You can attach the list to your written agreement as an addendum (see Chapter 5). In your agreement, it's also a good idea to describe the shared property in detail ("the HP 1500 Printer") and note its condition ("that's three years old and occasionally jams on large print jobs"). Describing the property in detail will help you determine the value of the item, in case someone breaks it and is asked to compensate the owner(s).

3. Whom Are We Sharing With?

How particular you are about the people you share with will depend on how much interaction, cooperation, and group decision making will take place during the sharing arrangement, as well as how easy it is to leave if things don't work out.

In larger sharing groups, you might not be very concerned about whom you share with. If you join a 15 member tool-sharing group, for example, you may not ever meet some of the other members. The main qualifications for members might be that they are adults, live in a certain town or neighborhood, and take good care of the group's tools.

But if you share a house with someone, you'll undoubtedly want to be much pickier. (See Chapter 2 for qualities you might want to look for in your sharing partners.) Ultimately, most sharing arrangements come down to finding someone you can trust to respect your needs and belongings, and for whom you can do the same.

4. How Many People Are We Sharing With?

If you and your neighbor have decided to share a vacuum cleaner, the potential size of your sharing group is probably not a concern. But if you want to leave open the possibility that the group will grow or shrink, then group size is something you may want to discuss ahead of time.

What should the minimum or maximum group size be? It depends on what you're sharing and how often you'll need to use it, among other things. For example, if you plan to share a car with two other people, and you know that you'll need to use the car several days a week, your group probably can't grow. On the other hand, if you'll need to use the car only a few times a month to do major errands, you could share with a much larger group.

Large and small groups offer different advantages. If you aren't sure what size group will work best for you, consider whether any of these benefits are especially appealing.

Large groups:

- spread costs among more people, which means the group can afford more expensive items, and each person has to pay less
- spread responsibilities and save time
- are more stable; changes to the group, like members leaving, cause less upheaval, and risk is spread among more people
- use less energy and fewer natural resources
- can afford more shared items, which makes it more likely that an item will be available when needed
- allow for more diversity, helping people to feel a greater sense of belonging
- have more power to bargain collectively and negotiate group rates, and
- spare members meeting and administrative time, because they often delegate management to a small board or committee.

On the other hand, small groups:

- are easier to manage and often more flexible
- are easier to start because you don't need as many people
- often involve fewer formalities and less paperwork, and are simpler to form and dissolve

- are more personal
- can tailor their activities to meet the individual needs of members, and
- allow you to make sure all of you are truly compatible. You can really get to know your cosharers to make sure the arrangement will work, which is especially important if you will have to place tremendous trust in your sharing group (to share childcare, for example).

EXAMPLE: A small group of neighbors form a tool and toy sharing group. Together, they buy a shed to put in the backyard of one neighbor, Ubie. Each households has a key to the shed and uses it to store items they are willing to share. They decide to keep their group small, and write this in their sharing agreement:

"We agree to limit the size of our group to six households. By keeping the group small, we will be less likely to lose items and will not worry about lending our belongings to people we don't know. In addition, Ubie prefers to limit the number of people who enter his backyard."

5. How Will the Timing of Our Arrangement Work?

There are a few things you might want to discuss with regard to the timing of your arrangement:

- When does the arrangement begin?
- Is there a set ending date? For example, you might decide to share a car until your graduate school program ends.
- What sorts of events would cause your arrangement to end? For example, if you take down your fence and share a yard with your neighbor, you might want to agree to put the fence back up when one of you sells your house.
- Do you want to start the sharing arrangement on a trial basis? For example, you could agree to start sharing, but reassess after three months.

- Do you want to set any deadlines? For example, you might start sharing your car and agree that your sharing partner will pay you $3,000 in two months to become a co-owner.
- Will your sharing arrangement happen in phases? For example, you might agree in writing to purchase land together, enter into a second agreement when you start construction, and enter into a third agreement when the construction is finished and you begin living together.

EXAMPLE: To save money, Lori, Jeff, and Frank shared Lori's car while they were attending a three-year law school program. They wrote the following in their agreement:

"We will begin sharing the car on the day we sign this agreement and stop sharing the car on May 1, 2011, when we graduate."

6. Who Owns the Shared Items?

If you are sharing a tangible asset, such as a house, car, or appliance, you'll want to be clear about who owns it. The way you own shared items will determine a number of issues, such as who is entitled to the property or the proceeds from selling it if the group disbands, and who is entitled to any tax breaks associated with the property. This will also prevent later confusion about, for example, whether the original owner of the item intended to give it to the group.

Direct or Indirect Ownership

The first choice to make is whether you want to own the shared property directly or indirectly:

- **Direct ownership:** Your group's members can own the shared items themselves, in any combination they choose. Most small groups choose direct ownership because it is relatively simple and straightforward.
- **Indirect ownership:** Alternatively, your group can form a separate entity, such as a nonprofit organization, to own the property.

Creating such an entity has many advantages for large sharing groups. These benefits are discussed in Question 7, below.

Arranging Direct Ownership

There are many ways to share ownership. Imagine, for example, that David, Adrienne, and Nettie decide to share a set of tools. Here are a few different ownership possibilities:

- **Sole ownership:** David owns all the tools and allows the others to use them.
- **Each person owns a divisible part of the property:** Each owns *specific* tools in the set, but may use the entire set; David owns the saw, Adrienne owns the drill, and Nettie owns the wrench set, for example. This is an easy way to determine ownership if each person brings different property to the share. Members continue to own the property they brought into the share and take it with them when they leave the group.
- **Each person owns a fractional share of the property:** David, Adrienne, and Nettie could each own one-third of the toolset (equal shares), or their shares could be unequal, based on how much money they invested in the toolset or how often they plan to use the tools. Fractional shares might be a good option if everyone chips in to buy the property rather than bringing their own property to the share. Fractional shares also make sense for property that can't be easily divided, such as a snow blower or house.

> ### TIP
> **Consider owning property in joint tenancy.** To ensure the continuity and smooth operation of your sharing group, you may want to consider owning shared property in joint tenancy. If one owner dies, the other owners automatically inherit joint tenancy property. This spares the estate administrator and the sharing group from having to divide or sell the shared property upon a co-owner's death. For more information about owning property in joint tenancy, see Chapter 6.

7. Should We Form a Separate Legal Entity?

Some groups create a separate legal entity, such as a cooperative, limited liability company (LLC), or nonprofit corporation, to own shared property or to administer their joint activity. Creating a separate entity makes sense if you co-own assets of significant value, you want to shield members from liability for an activity with substantial risk, or you want to provide structure and continuity for a large group.

If you form a separate entity, each member of the group owns *shares* or has a *membership* in the entity. In this way, members indirectly own the shared property and exercise control over the group's activities. Because creating a separate entity creates an additional layer of ownership (you own the entity that owns the property), this is sometimes referred to as a "mezzanine structure."

There are benefits and drawbacks to forming a separate entity to own and administer a sharing arrangement. One benefit is that people can sell their shares or terminate their membership without the group having to change title to the property or rewrite the sharing agreement. This makes sense if the sharing group is large and its membership may change.

A second advantage to creating a separate entity is that certain structures, such as a nonprofit corporation, cooperative, or LLC, can protect individual members of the sharing group from liability to each other and to outsiders.

> **EXAMPLE:** Mary, a member of a tool-sharing group, takes the group's drill to work at the art museum. The drill spins out of control and pokes a hole in the museum's prized Picasso drawing. The art museum sues Mary and the toolsharing organization, a nonprofit corporation. If the art museum wins, it might take all the assets of the toolsharing organization and it might take Mary's assets, but it probably can't take the assets of the other individual members of the toolsharing group. If there were no intermediate entity, the whole group might be subject to liability for the damage.

Types of Ownership Entities

Here's a quick overview of the options. (You'll find more information on what type of entity is best for particular activities in the chapters that follow.)

- **Unincorporated association.** This is the form that most small sharing groups will likely adopt. It's the simplest type of entity to form, as it requires only that a group of two or more people join by mutual consent for a common purpose. While little or no paperwork is required to form an unincorporated association, most groups will want to create a document describing the group's purpose, structure, governance, procedures, members' responsibilities, and so on. Unlike the incorporated entities described below, unincorporated associations do not usually shield members from liability.

- **Nonprofit public benefit corporation.** This type of entity is used by groups formed to benefit and provide sharing opportunities for the public. Forming a corporation protects individual sharers from liability and, in many cases, provides the benefits of tax exemption under Section 501(c)(3) of the tax code and tax-deductible donations. The disadvantages of forming a public benefit nonprofit stem primarily from the extensive paperwork involved, the strict governance requirements, and limits on the scope of your group's activities.

- **Nonprofit mutual benefit corporation.** The primary goal of a mutual benefit organization is to benefit the group's members, rather than the public as a whole. For example, condominium owners' associations are formed to benefit individual condo owners. This type of organization can obtain tax-exempt status but cannot receive tax-deductible donations.

- **Nonprofit fiscal sponsorship.** An alternative to forming a nonprofit organization is to find an existing tax-exempt organization to sponsor your sharing arrangement. For example, if you are making your yard available to others for a community garden, you could seek fiscal sponsorship from an existing community garden

Types of Ownership Entities (continued)

organization. You will have to relinquish some control over your project, but you will also benefit because the sponsoring organization can accept donations for your project, absorb some of your administrative costs into its existing overhead, and support you in other ways, such as adding you to its insurance coverage.

- **Cooperative corporation.** A cooperative corporation is a business or organization owned and controlled by its members, and operated for the members' benefit. Groups sometimes use cooperative corporations to create resident-owned housing, worker-owned businesses, and cooperative grocery stores, for example. Unlike regular corporations, a cooperative is democratically run. Cooperatives bear some similarities to nonprofit mutual benefit corporations, but one major difference is that a cooperative may pay dividends and distribute surplus assets to its members.

- **For-profit entities.** Your group may want to form a for-profit entity if you intend to make an investment or profit from your sharing arrangement. Many groups who jointly purchase property and develop shared housing choose this option. For-profit entities usually allow the greatest flexibility in ownership, distribution of assets and profits, and governance structure. There are many different considerations when choosing among different entity types, which include different types of LLCs, partnerships, and corporation. It's a good idea to discuss these considerations with a lawyer.

The main disadvantage to forming a mezzanine ownership structure is that it can be complicated and time consuming. The group will have to file some paperwork at the outset, keep careful records throughout, and maybe even file tax returns, sometimes along with an annual fee or tax payment.

The entity structures available to your group will depend on your state's laws and the activities your group will pursue. In Part II, we cover some sharing arrangements that might call for a mezzanine structure, such as sharing multi-unit housing or setting up a large carshare. No matter what type of structure you need, you should consult with a lawyer about your separate entity. A lawyer can help ensure that your group has chosen the right structure, meets all the legal requirements, and includes all necessary information in your documents and agreements.

8. What Should We Call Ourselves?

Do you want to give your group a name? Many sharing groups—especially small groups that don't plan to admit more members—don't bother with a name. But for larger groups that want to endure and grow, choosing a creative, memorable name can help build the group's reputation in the community.

There are a few limits on names you can choose. First, many states restrict groups from using particular words in their names, to avoid confusing the public. Typically, you cannot call yourself "Inc.," "Incorporated," "Cooperative" (in some states), "Ltd.," "Corporation," or "Foundation" unless you are legally incorporated as one of these entities. However, you may freely use the words "Company," "Group," "Associates," "Organization," "Collective," or "Affiliates."

Second, you could be blocked from using a name that's identical or confusingly similar to one already in use by another group or business. This is especially true if the group or business with the same name is located near you or has activities similar to your group. If your group plans to incorporate or register your name with the state, you may also be prevented from using a name that someone else has already registered. To see if the name you want is available, you can do an Internet search and look in your local phone directories. You can look at your state trademark and business name registries and the Federal Trademark Register (www.uspto.gov). You can also find out what fictitious business names are on file locally, usually with the county or city clerk.

Finally, you might want to decide what will happen to the name when the group dissolves. Will any particular person have the right to use it? This is an important consideration if you have chosen a really cute and clever name that your group is attached to, such as "Think Outside the Boss Worker Cooperative."

9. What Do We Get to Do?

Here's the fun part: What does each member get out of the sharing arrangement? Who gets to do and use what, when, and how often? This includes questions such as: Which part of the shared house do each of the sharers get to use? Which area of the garden do they get to cultivate? On what days does each person get to use a shared office? How many days of childcare will each member get for taking part in the child care co-op?

Many sharing groups share and share alike, giving each member the same basic rights to use the shared items. In some sharing groups, however, it makes sense for members to have different rights or privileges. For example, if one member of a carsharing group pays more of the expenses, that person may get the right to use the car more often. In a tool-sharing group, the right to use certain dangerous tools may be assigned only to members with special training.

> EXAMPLE: Jean, Pat, and William are therapists who share an office space to meet with clients. Jean pays $400 per month, and Pat and William each pay $200. Because it is often difficult to coordinate schedules with clients, they created a flexible scheduling system, dividing each day into four three-hour time slots: 7:00 to 10:00am, 10:30 to 1:30pm, 2:00 to 5:00pm, and 5:30 to 8:30pm, thereby creating 28 time slots per week. Because she pays more, Jean chooses 12 slots and Pat and William each chose six slots. The remaining four slots are "floating." Any therapist may use them on a one-time basis or permanently switch one of their slots for one of the floating slots.

10. How Will We Make Decisions?

The way your group discusses and makes major decisions can greatly influence the success of your arrangement and the sense of community you create from it. Because communication and decision making are so important, we've devoted an entire chapter to them (Chapter 4).

Your group might make decisions through a consensus process or by a majority vote. You might decide to give each person an equal say or give some members—for example, those who own the shared property—more voting power. Or, your large group might delegate most decisions to a smaller committee, but reserve major decisions for the whole group.

No matter what decision-making process you decide to use, you'll need to decide whether and how often to meet, how you will set agendas, and what procedures to follow during meetings. Meeting procedures can range from informal conversations to formal procedures such as Robert's Rules of Order. Decision making and meeting procedures are also covered in Chapter 4.

11. What Responsibilities Will Each of Us Have?

You'll need to decide what responsibilities each of you will take for shared property or shared activities. For example, each cohousing resident may agree to take partial responsibility for yard maintenance. In a childcare co-op, each parent may make a commitment to provide childcare for one day each week.

Keeping It Flexible

In many cases, it won't be necessary to come up with a detailed agreement delineating specific responsibilities. Sometimes, you may not know how you want to divide the work until you dive in and really get a feel for what's involved. In this situation, you may want to agree to meet in a few months and discuss the division of labor.

Or, the people in your group may just instinctively pull their own weight and make adjustments to ensure fair distribution of responsibility.

> **EXAMPLE:** Five seniors purchase a five-bedroom house with the intent of creating a supportive community and sharing household expenses and responsibilities. Because they want to keep their division of responsibilities flexible, they write the following in their co-owner agreement:
>
> *"We will share equally the responsibilities and duties related to upkeep and maintenance of the house and yard. From time to time, we will meet to discuss what needs to be done, and decide who will do what. If someone feels that he or she is doing a disproportionate amount of the work, we will discuss ways to distribute responsibilities more equally. We agree to be flexible and willing to compromise regarding our responsibilities and duties, in order to accommodate everyone's personal needs, abilities, and schedules."*

Assigning Roles and Tasks

Other sharing arrangements may require a little more thought, planning, and delegation. It often works well to create different roles and tasks for each person, depending on particular skills or interests. In sharing arrangements where the group keeps records of finances, assets, meetings, and decisions, for example, you might designate one or two people (a secretary and treasurer) to be responsible for these tasks. These are positions that can rotate from time to time. You may also designate someone to be responsible for organizing and facilitating meetings. This is a job that can rotate frequently, even meeting by meeting. Someone else can be the central scheduler—setting the mealsharing or child care schedules. In a carsharing group, a member who is mechanically inclined could be solely responsible for routine car maintenance.

Delegating Responsibilities

In some groups, the majority of responsibilities are delegated to a single member, in lieu of dues or in exchange for greater benefits. The group may also compensate that member for the added duties.

> **CAUTION**
> **Paying a member or providing free membership shares in exchange for services raises some tax and employment law issues.** For example, the IRS may consider the value of what the member receives in exchange for work to be taxable income. A member who works for the group on a regular basis may legally qualify as the group's employee, with all the legal requirements that entails, from payroll withholding to overtime rules, workers' compensation coverage, and more. Talk to a lawyer before you arrange a membership-for-service deal, to see whether you can steer clear of these complications.

Sometimes, the group may want to delegate certain responsibilities to an outside person or group. For example, in many condominium complexes and vacation timeshares, the upkeep and management of shared property is frequently delegated to a management company. For a more detailed discussion of this type of arrangement, see Chapter 6.

12. What Are the Rules for Using Our Shared Property or Meeting Our Shared Responsibilities?

Seasoned sharers advise that setting too many hard and fast rules can have a chilling effect on a group's generous spirit. Of course, you could conceivably come up with rules about everything: No smoking, no singing loudly in the shower at 6 a.m., no incandescent bulbs, no bricks in the washing machine, no iguanas over six feet long. These are all good rules, but do you really need them to be *rules*? Most groups find that setting just a few basic rules is a better approach. Ideally, you can trust the other members of your group to be respectful, make wise decisions, and speak up if the giant iguana doesn't work for them.

Another option is to adopt rules that have some built-in flexibility. You can do this by stating a rule and then adding: "without first discussing it and receiving permission from the group."

> **EXAMPLE:** The owner of an empty lot grants a group of 12 neighboring households the right to install a shared vegetable garden. The neighbors came up with a beautiful layout for the garden, and give each household a plot for which they are solely responsible. They want to maintain the overall look of the garden but still give each household a certain amount of freedom to manage their own plot. So, they make the following rule:
>
> *"Members agree not to make significant changes to the garden and landscape design without first discussing it and receiving permission from the group."*

In addition, the group may want to agree on procedures to follow when a member breaks a rule. When and how should the problem be brought to the attention of the group? What types of restorative measures might the group and the breaching member take to solve the problem? (Chapter 4 provides tips on non-adversarial approaches to problems like this.)

13. How Will We Handle Administrative Matters Like Scheduling, Communication, and Record Keeping?

The intricacies of each sharing arrangement will vary. Two neighbors who share a weekly meal will likely have little to discuss by way of procedures and scheduling. The two households take turns cooking and paying for the food, split the leftovers, and just call or email each other if there is anything to discuss. However, if ten households share meals, they may want to establish some procedures for scheduling, tracking or sharing expenses, dividing leftovers, and so on.

Discussing Administrative Matters

What issues your group needs to discuss will depend, of course, on what you're sharing and how many are in the group. Here are some topics you may want to cover:

- how to come up with a schedule
- how to request changes to the schedule
- where things will be kept
- where certain events will take place
- how shared items will be delivered
- how to keep records
- how to track and share expenses (see Question 14, below, for more information)
- how to make requests for repairs or other things
- how members of the group will communicate, and
- how to give notice of important information to the group.

Methods of Scheduling

Let's use the car shared by Alva and Bobbie, from the beginning of this chapter, as an example. Here are some of the ways they could decide who gets to use the car when:

- **Specifying times.** Each person gets the car on a specific day. Alva gets it Monday, Wednesday, Friday and every other Sunday; Bobbie gets it Tuesday, Thursday, Saturday, and the other Sundays.
- **Signing up.** Alva and Bobbie sign up to use the car when they need it, on a first-come-first-served basis.
- **By agreement from time to time.** Alva and Bobbie agree to talk once a month and decide how they're going to share the car for the next month.
- **Lottery system.** This doesn't work very well for a car on a day-to-day basis, but some vacation timeshare groups use a lottery system to set their schedule. Rather than deciding who gets to use the vacation home on certain holidays, members draw straws or assign use times randomly.

Online Communication and Calendar Tools to Help You Share

The Internet offers innumerable online communication tools, such as discussion groups, listservs, blogs, online shared calendars, and file sharing tools. We don't blame you if you're not excited about the idea of spending more time in front of a screen each day, but some of these online tools can facilitate the sharing process. For example, office sharers can use a Google Calendar to schedule use of the conference room. Also, we have heard of one computer-savvy cohousing resident who designed a computer program to manage shared meals for 30 households. By the time you are reading this book, more tools will have been developed. Here are a few that exist today:

- **Email groups, bulletin boards, and wiki websites.** You have many ways to keep in touch and communicate important information with your fellow sharers. Some sharers use an email group or an online discussion forum, such as Yahoo! Groups or Google Groups. With these same tools, you could also post documents or share simple databases, such as your membership list or a list of shared items. You could also create a whole website for your group and give multiple members the ability to edit the website. This is often known as a "wiki" website. For help creating your own wiki website, go to www.wetpaint.com.

- **Calendars.** With a website such as Google Calendar, you can create a calendar to share with other members of a group, allowing everyone to view it and make additions. If you share a car, for example, a shared online calendar will allow you to check the car's availability and reserve it for the days when you want to use it.

- **Maps.** Some websites, such as Google Maps, allow you to create an interactive map and share it with others. This might be useful if you want to help people in a community come together for a particular purpose. For example, you could make a map with tags on the houses where people have volunteered to share the fruit from their trees. The map could provide contact information for that resident, information on the type of fruit, when it generally ripens, whether a ladder is needed, and so on.

Once you decide how you will schedule use of shared property, you may want to write down the schedule separate from your written sharing agreement. This is because a schedule will likely change from time to time, and you won't want to keep revising your sharing agreement.

14. How Will We Divide Expenses and Manage Money?

Next you should figure out how to apportion costs, obtain money for your project, and keep track of the group's money. In some sharing arrangements, money may never change hands. But in a sharing arrangement where the group owns property, makes purchases, or collects dues, it's important to keep track of the money.

Here we introduce some of the money issues you might face and strategies for handling them. You'll find details on using these methods for particular sharing arrangements in Part II.

Initial Buy-In and Start-Up Contributions

Group members often make some sort of initial contribution, which could take the form of in-kind contributions, a lump sum, monthly installments, contributions of services, and so on. Keep a written record of each person's contributions. You should also decide whether and how people can get a refund, particularly if they leave the group.

Dividing Overhead Expenses

The group may have regular expenses that will be fairly fixed, no matter who uses the shared item and how much it is used. Such expenses could include rent and insurance. In deciding how to apportion these expenses, the group may decide to divide them equally or unequally, depending on ownership percentages or use.

Apportioning Variable Costs

The group might want to assign some variable costs to members based on use of the shared item. For example, a carsharing group may require members to pay for gas based on how much they use the car, either by tracking mileage or by always returning the car with a full tank.

Collecting Regular Dues

Instead of, or in addition to, dividing costs, a group could estimate likely costs and charge each member a regular fixed fee. The group can deposit the fees in a special account from which it pays expenses.

Handling Unexpected Costs

It's always a good idea to expect the unexpected. Your group may either want to create a reserve fund for unexpected costs or decide in advance what to do if the group needs more money in the future.

For example, co-owners of a house might write down the following agreement:

> *"We agree to create a joint savings account and pay $75 each into the account every month. This will create a reserve fund that we can use if we need to make major or unforeseen repairs on the house or one of us is unable to pay his or her share of the mortgage, insurance, or property taxes. We will aim to accumulate and maintain at least $5,000 in the account. As much as possible, we will try to pay for most expenses out of pocket before tapping into the reserve fund. If we tap into the reserve fund to pay one person's portion of the monthly mortgage, taxes, or insurance, that person will be expected to reimburse the reserve account.*
>
> *If the reserve fund isn't adequate to cover an unforeseen expense, we will meet to discuss our options. If one of us is unable to pay for the expense, the other may pay a larger amount. The one who could not make the payment will compensate the other over time."*

Managing Your Finances

Although you won't have to work out all of the details ahead of time, your group will need to create a budget and decide how to keep track of its money. Sloppy bookkeeping can easily lead to disputes over who paid what. In our experience, sharing arrangements go more smoothly when everyone pays a fixed amount on a regular basis, rather than reckoning expenses at the end of each month.

> EXAMPLE: Kristen, Colin, and Mojo share a house. They used to pile up their bills and receipts at the end of each month, figure out who had paid what, and then reckon everyone's payments. The math was often complicated and someone was usually annoyed to find that the bills were higher than anticipated. Furthermore, Mojo was always losing receipts for his purchases of household goods. Then they came up with a better plan: They created a budget and estimated monthly expenses at about $400 per person. They created a joint account, and everyone paid $450 per month (the extra $50 was to meet any budget deficits and build a reserve for unforeseen expenses). Each of them got a debit card to use for household expenses. They also kept some cash in a jar in the kitchen, for spontaneous trips to the corner store.

Loans to the Group

If your group is going to borrow money or property, think carefully about who signs the promissory notes, who is responsible for repayment, and what property is used to secure the loan. If your group can't pay back the loan, the person who signed could be at risk of a lawsuit—and you might lose any property put up for collateral.

When a group member loans money or property to the group, be sure to write down who loaned what, a description of the loaned property, and how the member will be repaid or when the property will be returned.

If a Member Cannot Pay

It's hard to talk about, but you'll need to decide what will happen if a member doesn't make required payments. Do missed payments constitute grounds for kicking the member out of the group? If another member takes up the slack, will the payment automatically be considered a loan from that person to the one who didn't pay? If so, what are the terms for repayment? If someone gets kicked out the group, how will the group collect the missing money?

Using Barter and Sweat Equity

Many sharing groups make use of barter and sweat equity as part of their arrangement. If someone provides goods or services in exchange for other goods or services, with no money changing hands, that is barter. When someone works in exchange for an ownership share or increased value of their share, that is sweat equity.

If your arrangement involves barter or sweat equity, it's a good idea to create a clear agreement about the exchange. If services are being exchanged, how do you plan to measure the services—by hours worked or by the job completed? Likewise, when goods are being exchanged, be sure to describe them in detail. To keep things clear, it's often a good idea to agree on a dollar value for the work performed or goods exchanged, even if you never actually exchange any money.

> **EXAMPLE:** Genevieve, Tim, and Elena are lawyers who share office space in a building Genevieve owns. In lieu of paying rent, Tim and Elena make court appearances on behalf of Genevieve. They put the following into writing:
>
> *"We agree that the market value of the office rent is $600 per month. In lieu of paying rent, Tim and Elena will each make three court appearances on behalf of Genevieve every month."*

Taxes are an important consideration in barter exchanges. Even though no money changes hands when bartering, the IRS may consider the value you receive in exchange for your goods or services to be taxable "bartering income." In the example above, Tim and Elena would have to report the $600 value of the office rental as income. Likewise, Genevieve would have to report the market value of Tim and Elena's services as income. (At the same time, because everyone involved is self-employed, they will each be able to deduct the value they "paid" in the exchange as a business expense.)

You don't have to pay taxes on everything you receive through barter. Casual, one-time, and noncommercial exchanges are not taxed. But if one or both of you are in the business of selling the goods or services exchanged, you'll probably owe tax.

> EXAMPLE: Julie has a peach tree and Rex has an apple tree. In the summer, Julie gives Rex peaches and Rex "pays" Julie back with apples in the fall. Neither Julie nor Rex will need to pay taxes on the value of the fruit they received, because neither of them is in the business of growing and selling fruit.
>
> Now assume Julie grows peaches on a farm and sells her peaches at wholesale prices to small grocery stores. She also has a vegetable stand on her farm. Rex has a similar farm operation with his apples. Julie gives Rex free peaches to sell at his farm stand, and Rex gives Julie free apples to sell at her farm stand. Without the barter arrangement, Rex and Julie would have to buy and sell their fruit, and their sales revenue would become part of their taxable income. With the barter arrangement, Julie and Rex should calculate the fair market value of the fruit they exchange and report that value on their tax returns.

It won't be clear in every case whether you should pay taxes on value you receive through barter. If you aren't sure, consult a tax professional.

15. How Will We Manage Risk and Liability?

One benefit of sharing property is that you also share the risk of loss and liability. This makes co-ownership, in itself, a form of insurance. At the same time, in certain arrangements, you will need to purchase insurance to protect against loss that the group cannot collectively swallow.

What Are Your Risks?

Start by brainstorming about the risks involved in your activity:
- What is the potential for damage to or loss of the group's property?
- What is the potential for damage to or loss of others' property?
- What is the likelihood of injury arising from our activity or use of shared property?

Consider Ways to Avoid or Reduce Risk

Avoiding or reducing risk usually means putting emergency plans in place, taking preventative measures (such as buying fire extinguishers and keeping shared property in good repair), or avoiding certain activities altogether.

Distribute the Risk

Certain risks that arise from a sharing group's activities will already be covered by existing insurance. For example, occasional group activities that occur at members' homes will likely be covered by homeowner's insurance. A casual carpool arrangement is covered by the driver's car insurance. In these situations, the individual home or car owner may be fine with carrying the risk. This is why we have insurance, after all. But in some situations, the person bearing more risk might want other sharers to help pay insurance premiums or to pay for increased premiums resulting from higher liability limits or other coverage enhancements.

If a loss won't be covered by insurance, there are a variety of ways your group might distribute the risk. Typically, who pays for a loss will depend on who was responsible for it. For example, if a shared washing machine breaks unexpectedly, probably the whole group should pay for repairs. If the machine breaks because a member of your group misused it, probably that person should pay for repairs. And if the machine is a goner, you'll have to decide whether the group wants a fancy new model or a cheaper used replacement—and how this cost will be divided. These are all things you and your co-sharers could discuss in advance.

Some sharing arrangements place the burden or risk on one person—often, the owner of the shared property—and that could be a problem. For example, if three neighbors share a lawn mower owned by David, it doesn't seem fair to expect David to bear the full cost of repairing or replacing the mower if it dies after years of shared use. In addition, if one user of David's lawnmower has a bit too much to drink and takes it for a joy ride through another neighbor's prized rose garden, David shouldn't have to pay for that.

One way to deal with worries about where the risk falls is to agree to compensate the person who bears more risk. Lawyers call this "indemnification." For example, the group sharing a lawnmower may write this in their agreement:

> "We agree that if one of us causes the lawnmower to break through negligent use, that person should be responsible for repairing or replacing the lawnmower. If the lawnmower breaks and it's no one's fault, we will each chip in some money to help David pay for repairs or a replacement. If one of us is subject to liability arising from his/her negligent act or misconduct, that user shall hold harmless and indemnify David."

There may also be situations where a group will not want to be held responsible for one group member's stupid or reckless acts. A group that owns property together might use language like this:

> "In the event that a member is subject to liability arising from his/her negligent act or misconduct, that member shall hold harmless and indemnify the group and each of the other group members, to the extent that the amount of liability exceeds applicable insurance carried by the group."

Consider Insurance

If a risk is not entirely avoidable, a group cannot or does not want to bear the risk together, and no one's insurance currently covers the risk, the next step is to look for insurance that covers your activity or shared item. We cover particular types of insurance in Part II.

Limiting Liability Through Group Structure

Some group structures, like LLCs or nonprofit corporations, limit the liability of individuals who are members of the group. If your sharing group is large and will face some risk of lawsuits by outsiders, it might justify investing in a group structure that provides liability protection.

16. Are There Legal Requirements We Need to Follow?

In Part II, we discuss legal rules that apply to different types of sharing activities. At the outset, however, you should consider whether there might be any legal roadblocks to your sharing plan. For example, zoning and building codes may prevent you from running a business out of your home or converting a single-family home into several units. Or, contractual restrictions in a purchase contract for a planned development or in a lease may limit how you may use your property; for instance, your condo complex may not allow you to turn your front yard into a community garden.

You'll also need to follow the applicable laws for your shared activity. For example, a carshare group will have to make sure the vehicle is registered and licensed, and passes smog requirements. A childcare co-op may have to be licensed by the state or local government.

There may also be tax consequences to your sharing arrangement. For example:

- If your state taxes vehicle sales, you and your cosharers may owe taxes if one of you sells a car to the group.
- If real estate changes hands, whether from one member of the group to the group as a whole or from a departing member to an incoming member, taxes may be due.
- If your group sells shared property that has increased in value, members may owe tax on the gain.
- If some members of your group provide services to the group in lieu of paying an initial contribution, the government might treat the value of the contribution as compensation, subject to income tax and employment taxes.

- If there are tax breaks associated with purchasing or owning a certain item (for example, a tax credit for alternative fuel vehicles or tax deductions for property tax and mortgage interest payments), you'll have to decide who gets to take advantage of those benefits.

17. How Will We Resolve Conflicts or Disputes?

In any sharing situation, it's a good idea to come to an agreement about how you will resolve conflicts, *before* a disagreement actually arises. Once you're mired in conflict, hurt feelings and anger can make it hard to agree on anything. Having a process in place for handling disputes will make it much easier to get past potential sticking points. For a detailed discussion of conflict resolution, see Chapter 4.

18. How Will We Bring New People Into the Group?

What happens if your sharing plan is going great and you would like to invite others to join? In the spirit of sharing, some groups have a tendency to grow. Whether your group hopes to take over the whole neighborhood or you simply want to add a member or two, there are a handful of key issues to discuss.

Bringing in New Members

The first topic of discussion is whether your group wants to grow at all. Does everyone agree on how large the group should be? If one member wants to keep the group small and another has plans to include every house on the street, you'll need to come to some agreement before you move on to discuss how to admit new members. (For more information on group size, see Question 4, above).

Once you've resolved the issue of how large you want your group to be, you'll need to consider how you'll choose new members. What criteria, if any, must new members meet? Under what circumstances can new members join? Only when another member leaves? Should the decision to involve new members be unanimous? If it's a small group where people must interact and work together, it's probably best that the decision be unanimous. If the decision requires only the vote of a majority, some people could be left feeling uncomfortable with each other. However, in the case of a large sharing group, where people may never have to see each other or cooperate (like a neighborhood tool sharing group), it's probably fine to have just a majority vote or designate a committee or individual to be responsible for admitting new members.

Requirements for New Members

If your group's members have paid into the group (to buy shared items or cover ongoing costs, for example), you should consider what financial requirements new members will have to meet. Will new members have to make an initial contribution? How much does it cost to join? Will the new member own a portion of the shared item? Will current members have to sell part of their share to the new member?

Other issues are new member orientation, creating handbooks or other written materials for new members, and developing documents for new members to sign.

Temporary Members and Guests

What about temporary members or guests? A sharing group may have a core group of regular members, but also leave open the possibility that guests may take part on an occasional basis. This can help to lessen costs for the group and build community with a broader range of people. For example, Larry, Pam, and Steve have a three-unit condo with a laundry room. They decide to allow friends to come in and use the laundry machines if they pay for each use. Or, a group that has started a community garden might allow other neighbors to join in several times a year.

No matter how you envision allowing nonmembers to participate, your group should discuss the issue and make sure all of you agree on whether and how other people will be included.

19. How Can a Member Leave the Group?

When you are forming a plan to share with friends, it might be hard to imagine anyone wanting to leave or worse, getting kicked out. But the fact is, we live in a society where people move around quite a bit. One member of your group might decide to go back to school or take a job in another state. A member might become too busy to participate or might decide that his or her growing family needs its own car. Things come up. Things also go sour, unfortunately. Because change is inevitable, it's a good idea to plan ahead.

Voluntary Departures

There are a handful of decisions to make pertaining to how members can leave your group: Can someone leave at any time, or will members make some sort of contractual commitment (such as signing a lease agreement)? Does a member who wants to leave have to give notice, so other members can figure out ways to take up the slack? Can members give or sell their share to someone else without the group's permission? Are there responsibilities members must fulfill before they leave?

The answers to these questions will depend on what you're sharing. If you have a shared childcare arrangement, for example, you might want to require enough notice to allow the rest of the group to make sure their childcare needs are covered (and you'll certainly want the remaining group members to be able to choose the person who will take the departing member's place). If you're a member of a large group sharing gardening tools, on the other hand, you might decide that members are free to leave at any time.

Continuing the Group After Someone Leaves

In some situations, if one person leaves, the sharing group will have to disband. This is most obviously the case when one person leaves and only one is left. This can also be the case when the person who leaves has assets or skills the group can't do without.

However, the group can also make provisions that will allow it to continue even after an important member leaves. For example, you could decide to give the remaining members a right of first refusal or a discount on purchasing the departing member's share. Giving sufficient advance notice is also important to allow the remaining members time to find a new member who will work well with the group.

Compensating Departing Members

What a member gets upon leaving the group depends on what you are sharing. For example, if you are sharing responsibilities for elder care and members pay dues annually to cover administrative costs, the departing member could simply stop making contributions for expenses. If the departing member made an initial contribution, you'll need to decide whether to refund the payment, in whole or in part. Some groups decide that the amount of any refund should depend partly on why the member is leaving: Members who leave the group for reasons beyond their control (sickness or disability, for example) receive more compensation than members who leave of their own accord.

If you are sharing property ownership, you should come up with a plan to allow members to buy the departing member's share. The price can be set in advance, determined based on market rates at the time of departure, or expressed as a right of first refusal when the departing member receives an offer from someone outside of the group. If the remaining members aren't able to come up with the money in a lump sum, you can have a provision for monthly payments.

> EXAMPLE: Betsy, Fred, John, and Robin are freelance carpenters who own equal shares of a set of expensive and specialized power tools, worth about $8,000. Knowing that the value of the tools will depreciate over time and that they may acquire additional tools, they meet each year and agree upon an estimate of the tools'

worth. By agreeing on the value of the tools in advance, the group hopes to avoid any disputes when someone leaves. That way, when one member leaves the group, that member will receive a quarter share of the agreed-upon value of the tools.

Involuntary Departures

It's no fun to imagine removing or expelling members from your group, but it might be necessary. For instance, you might ask carsharers to leave the group if they routinely fail to pay their portion of the costs. Or you might ask a family to leave a childcare co-op if their parenting style clashes with the rest of the group. It's a good idea to talk in advance about what constitutes a reason to expel a member; that way, no one can claim to be caught off guard.

You should come up with procedures for removing members, including a policy about providing the member with notice and an opportunity to correct the problem. Also decide on how many votes are required to remove a member. If conflict or disagreement develops over the removal, your dispute resolution procedures should apply.

Expelled members should be compensated for their interest in the group, through the refund of contributions, membership dues, or shares. We recommend erring on the side of extra generosity when it comes to compensating the expelled member, mainly to minimize hard feelings and bitterness.

Keep in mind that removing a member could trigger some legal issues. If the member is a renter in group housing, for example, expelling the member constitutes an eviction, and specific rules and procedures will apply.

20. How Do We End the Sharing Arrangement?

Many good things come to an end, and the same is true of sharing groups. Your group might dissolve when you no longer need to share (your children are old enough to take care of themselves, for example) or members simply decide that the arrangement isn't working well enough to continue. Here are a few decisions to make in advance to ensure a smooth transition if and when your sharing arrangement ends.

- **When will the sharing arrangement end?** What is the duration of the sharing arrangement? Will the group reassess after a certain amount of time or continue indefinitely until everyone or a majority decides to dissolve it? What if some want to end it and others want to keep going?
- **Are there conditions that will terminate the sharing arrangement?** For example, if you and your neighbor are sharing a yard, your agreement will likely terminate when one of you moves out. In this scenario, you might want a written agreement to rebuild the fence when that day comes.
- **What is required to dissolve the group?** Who will prepare any necessary paperwork? Will you create a termination agreement? How will assets be distributed and debts be paid?
- **Who gets the group's assets?** The answer to this question may be determined, in part, by the legal form you chose. For example, by law, nonprofit organizations that are tax-exempt under 501(c)3 must give assets to another nonprofit when they dissolve. LLCs must distribute all assets to members.
- **What if you can't divide the property?** If the shared property cannot be easily divided, who has the first option to buy out other members and at what price? There are many ways to determine this, and deciding in advance can alleviate any worries or conflict that could develop later. For example, in a three-person carshare, members might agree in advance that Alva has first choice to buy out the other members' shares at bluebook value. If Alva doesn't want to buy, then Bobbie may buy. If Bobbie doesn't want to buy, then Carolina may buy. If no one wants to buy the car, they agree to sell the car and divide the money. Another way to do this would be to draw straws; whoever draws the short straw will pay the other members $500 each and keep the car.

Checklist for Discussing the 20 Questions

When you sit down to discuss the details of your sharing arrangement, here's a checklist to guide your conversation:

☐ **1. Why Are We Sharing?**
- What are our personal, practical, financial, or environmental goals?

☐ **2. What Are We Sharing?**
- What are we not sharing?

☐ **3. Whom Are We Sharing With?**
- Do our cosharers need to meet any particular qualifications?

☐ **4. How Many People Are We Sharing With?**
- What are the pros and cons of having a large or small sharing group?

☐ **5. How Will the Timing of Our Arrangement Work?**
- When will it start and stop?
- Will it happen in phases?

☐ **6. Who Owns the Shared Item(s)?**
- Will one person own it and let others use it?
- Will we each own specific items or parts of the property?
- Will we each own a percentage share of the whole property? If so, in what proportions?

☐ **7. Should We Form a Separate Legal Entity?**

☐ **8. What Should We Call Ourselves?**

☐ **9. What Do We Get to Do?**

☐ **10. How Will We Make Decisions?**
- Will we all take part in decision making or delegate decisions to a small group?
- Do we all have equal decision-making power?
- Must all decisions be unanimous or made by majority vote?

☐ 11. **What Responsibilities Will Each of Us Have?**

- Will we assign roles and tasks?
- Will we rotate responsibilities?
- Will anyone receive extra benefits in return for extra responsibilities?

☐ 12. **What Are the Rules for Using Our Shared Property or Meeting Our Shared Responsibilities?**

☐ 13. **How Will We Handle Administrative Matters Like Scheduling, Communication, and Record Keeping?**

☐ 14. **How Will We Divide Expenses?**

- Will there be initial buy-in or start-up contributions? Will we need any loans?
- How will we divide overhead and variable costs?
- How will we collect money? Through regular dues or by reckoning expenses in some other way? Will we start a bank account?
- What kinds of unexpected costs could arise and how will we prepare for them?
- Who will keep track of our money?
- What happens if a member cannot pay?

☐ 15. **How Will We Manage Risk and Liability?**

- What risks are involved in our sharing arrangement and how can we reduce them?
- How is the risk distributed (that is, who could suffer loss or be liable for damages)?
- Do we want to redistribute risk by making agreements with each other or purchasing insurance?

☐ 16. **Are There Legal Requirements We Need to Follow?**

- Are there any required licenses or permits?
- Will this bring up any tax or employment law questions?
- Are there any legal roadblocks arising from zoning laws or private land covenants?
- What steps must we take to become a legal entity?

☐ **17. How Will We Resolve Conflicts or Disputes?**

☐ **18. How Will We Bring New People Into the Group?**

- What procedures will new members follow?
- How will new members be oriented?
- What is our policy on guests?

☐ **19. How Can a Member Leave the Group?**

- What steps must be taken when a member leaves voluntarily?
- Under what circumstances can a member be asked to leave the group?

☐ **20. How Do We End the Sharing Arrangement?**

Thank You For Sharing: Communicating, Making Decisions, and Resolving Conflict

Communication is the key to every successful sharing arrangement. There's no way around it: Sharing is a process that involves other people. To share well, participants must effectively convey information, reach agreements and decisions, discuss their needs and wants, and talk out disagreements and conflicts.

The converse is also true: Communication problems are the primary cause of breakdowns in sharing agreements. There might be a failure to communicate expectations effectively at the outset, a misunderstanding over some part of an agreement, conflicting memories of past events, or confusion about terms that mean different things to different people. The ways that communication can go awry are limitless in their variety. Happily, most of them can be prevented or resolved through careful planning and conscientious interaction with each other. This chapter provides the tools you need to communicate effectively, reach decisions as a group, and, if necessary, tackle conflicts.

Communication Skills for Sharing

Skillful communication is the key ingredient to a successful sharing arrangement. This means not just communicating information accurately, but also conveying it in a way that encourages others to listen openly and communicate honestly in turn. This can be more challenging than it may seem.

Many of our day-to-day communications are fairly simple because they are intended to convey primarily facts. Someone who says, "I will drop the kids off at the south field by 4 for soccer practice," for example, has communicated who, what, where, when, and why, succinctly and effectively. When we integrate sharing into our lives, however, there's a lot more to talk about, spanning all kinds of topics. We need to communicate not just facts, but also topics that can be tough to talk about, like our values, feelings, needs, fears, and personal habits.

Sharing can be a simple transaction, meant to meet our material needs. More often, however, sharing arises from a deeper desire to create community. For example, people who start a neighborhood home repair group certainly want to get help with home improvement projects and may be interested in learning repair skills, but they may be even more motivated by the desire to know their neighbors and enjoy the company and camaraderie of working together.

There are innumerable ways to express ourselves, and the nuances of expression can elicit different emotional responses from listeners. If we want to understand others and be understood by them, we must say what we mean without triggering defensiveness in our listener. To the extent that we can achieve this, we will create durable and successful sharing relationships.

The chart that follows lists some of the qualities inherent in sharing and the communication skills those qualities require, with examples.

Qualities of sharing	Communication Skills Required for Sharing	Examples
Sharing requires give and take.	If a sharer feels that other sharers aren't pulling their weight, it's important to say so before resentment develops.	*"I try to remember to clean the tools before I put them away, but I've noticed that the tools aren't always clean when I take them out to use them. I'm concerned that they won't last as long unless we all clean them after each use. Can we all agree to maintain the tools?"*
Sharing makes sharers interdependent and requires that sharers be sensitive to each other's needs.	Sharers must communicate their needs and listen openly when other sharers express theirs, recognizing that everyone's needs are different.	*"It's very important to me that my dog gets enough exercise every day. Can we talk about how far we plan to walk the dogs each day?"*

Qualities of sharing	Communication Skills Required for Sharing	Examples
Sharers may have different motives for sharing.	Sharers should communicate the values or practical matters that are important to them.	*"I realize that your primary motive for forming this buying club is to help us all afford socially and environmentally sustainable products. I share this goal. At the same time, I'm on a tight budget, and there may be certain things I can't afford, like the organic pecans. Could we visit the option of buying nonorganic foods when prices seem very high?"*
Sharing requires trust.	If something occurs that undermines trust between sharers, it's important to discuss the issue, air hurt feelings, and have everyone take responsibility for their role.	*"I was surprised to see that the kids were still napping at 3:30 when I came to pick Sarah up. It's really important to me that we stick to the schedule we agreed to, including naps ending by 1:30. Otherwise, Sarah stays up late and all of our schedules are thrown off. I'm curious: What made today's schedule different?"*
Sharing relationships are often built on or create a sense of community.	A sharing arrangement can break down if someone doesn't feel like part of the group.	*"I notice that when we get together for work days, you tend to choose tasks that are separate from the rest of the group. What makes you choose these tasks?"*

Qualities of sharing	Communication Skills Required for Sharing	Examples
Sharing can involve unequal power arrangements, where one person has more control or ownership than another.	It's important to talk about how the imbalance could make the sharers feel or how it could affect the arrangement.	*"Although I will remain full owner of the car, I want you to feel free to use it as if it is yours also. On your days, I hope you will consider it to be your car."*
Sharing arrangements may result in people sharing physical space more, such as in carpooling or group housing.	Sharers should feel comfortable asking for space or for quiet.	*"I had to take Johnny to the emergency room last night for his asthma, and he and I are beat. Would it be possible for you to have your Monday night meeting at someone else's house just for today, so we can get some sleep?"*
Sharing can require making decisions in groups.	Sharers should encourage each other to express their personal needs, even when they may initially seem in conflict with that of the group as a whole.	*"I realize that this could create an inconvenience for some folks, but I at least wanted to communicate an idea I had, which is to keep the television off when we are providing child care."*
Sharing is based on overlapping needs.	People's needs evolve over time, so it's important to be willing to reassess a sharing arrangement. It's good to plan to check in with each other periodically.	*"This carshare has been such a great thing for me. But now that I can walk to work, I'd like to get rid of my car altogether and use the City Carshare program for the once or twice a month when I need a car. Maybe the group or one of you would like to buy the car from me; at any rate, I won't change anything for the next month, so you'll have time to figure out what to do."*

Qualities of sharing	Communication Skills Required for Sharing	Examples
Sharing can require more planning than sharers would have to do independently.	Sharers need to talk through the logistics of a sharing arrangement and create routines, schedules, or systems.	*"If we're both going to use the elliptical machine that's in my basement, you'll need a key to my house. I'd like to talk about how we'll allow you as much access as you want and still preserve my privacy."*
Sharers experience both the benefits and losses of a sharing arrangement together.	Sharers should talk in advance about different contingencies.	*"Because the lawnmower belongs to you, you'll be bearing all of the wear and tear. How should we compensate you for this?"*
Sharing requires generosity and gratitude.	Sharers need to express their positive feelings about the arrangement, and remember that everyone is benefiting from it, and giving to it, in different ways.	*"I really appreciate that you open your home to the mealsharing group every week. It's such a beautiful and comfortable space, and it is so nice to all be able to fit around the table!"*

Tips for Effective Communication

People communicate in very different ways. Many communication styles have a cultural basis, and our experiences growing up also form our approach to interacting with others. We communicate best when we acknowledge these differences, accept other people's communication styles without judgment, and commit to bridging gaps by finding common communication ground. Fortunately, there are a lot of concrete, practical skills that can help you do this.

In any communication, you can control only your own side of the interaction. Trying to get the other person to communicate differently or come around to your point of view isn't very productive. Just try not to be defensive or judgmental, and it's likely the other person will follow along. This means trying not to accuse, blame, deflect, or demand. It also means approaching your communications with genuine curiosity about what motivates the other person rather than making assumptions about the other's needs or goals.

Here are some tips and examples of positive ways to bring up concerns or talk about difficult issues.

Concentrate on listening rather than talking. Often, we spend the "quiet" end of a conversation thinking about what we want to say next instead of really listening, and the other person can feel it. When it's our turn to talk, we can expect the other person to return the favor. Try imagining that the most important thing in the world to you is understanding what the other person has to say, and ask questions that allow the other person to explain—and you to understand—more fully. Make sure you're hearing correctly by reflecting back what the other person is saying. Listening is not the same as agreeing: You don't give up anything by providing your full attention.

> **Instead of:** *I understand your concern about spending too much money, but these home improvements will be a good investment.*

> **Try:** *I understand your concern about spending too much money. It sounds to me like you are saying that even though the home improvements might be a good investment, and you don't want to disappoint me, you simply don't believe you have the money to spend right now. Have I understood you completely, or is there anything I missed?*

Don't assume, and do be curious. Don't assume you know what the other person is going to say or why. Instead, make sure you're listening openly, so you can recognize new information. Allow yourself to be surprised. Ask questions about anything you're not completely sure about. Find your genuine curiosity and ask sincere questions that don't assume you already know the answer.

> **Instead of:** *Why have you been grumpy all week?*

Try: *How have you been feeling this week? It seems like you haven't been yourself lately.*

Give the benefit of the doubt. Here's one assumption you can make: that the other person is acting with good will and good intentions. Even if you have been hurt, assume that it wasn't on purpose and ask about what happened and why. There may be an explanation you never considered.

Instead of: *I can't believe you didn't put gas in the car after you used it!*

Try: *What prevented you from fueling up the car yesterday?*

State your intentions at the outset. Say why you're bringing something up—in other words, whether you are simply communicating facts, have a question, or are stating a concern or problem that needs a solution. That way, the other person knows what your expectations are, instead of having to guess how long you want to talk or how involved the conversation might be.

Instead of: *Can we talk?*

Try: *Do you have a few minutes now, or could we plan a time later to talk? I'd like to tell you about some changes in my work life that might require some adjustments to our car-sharing arrangement.*

Be specific and concrete. Say what actually happened or what your concern is—don't beat around the bush or use generalities.

Instead of: *You're inconsiderate.*

Try: *I'm having a difficult time concentrating because of the volume of your music, which I can hear even with my door closed. Could you turn your music down?*

Avoid blaming. Don't make something the other person's fault; just state a problem that exists and work toward fixing it. Also, don't call names or insult the other person. These are ways to end a conversation, not to start one.

Instead of: *You are making no sense! That's absurd!*

Try: *I'm finding this conversation frustrating. I want to understand how you feel about this, but I don't want us to take extreme positions in order to defend ourselves. I'm just not understanding why this happened, and I'm concerned that we might have the same problem again if we don't figure out what's going on.*

Try using "Yes, and" instead of "yes, but." If you agree with part or all of what the other person is saying, and you also have some kind of response you want to make, you'll get a much better response by indicating your agreement clearly, and then using "and" rather than "but" as a bridge to your own point.

Instead of: *Yes, but it isn't just my fault that the convection oven isn't clean. The owner is supposed to have it cleaned once a week.*

Try: *Yes, and I've asked the landlord to make sure the weekly cleaning gets done. I'll also make sure to do my part.*

Never say never. Words like "always" and "never," and especially phrases like "you always" and "you never," are rarely productive. Instead, state what happened in the current situation in concrete terms.

Instead of: *You never listen to me!*

Try: *You are looking out the window and at your watch. It's making me feel like you aren't listening, and I'm wondering if you have time to talk right now.*

State how a situation is affecting you. Instead of judging someone's actions, say how those actions make you feel. People would much rather volunteer to alleviate the problem than feel like they have been unfairly judged. Make "I" statements.

Instead of: *You always take more time than you're allowed in the conference room—it's really unfair.*

Try: *The other day I had to keep a client waiting because you were in the conference room during time I had signed up for, and the* *same thing happened two weeks ago. I like to be on time for my appointments, so it would help me if you would agree to keep to the schedule in the future.*

Try to understand each other's expectations. Differences you have with your sharing partner might be the result of differing expectations from the outset. Even if you feel disrespected or disappointed, your sharing partner might not know it, and might even believe everything's going just as planned.

Instead of: *Why don't you ever want to have dinner with me?*

Try: *I feel sad that we don't share many meals, which is one of the things I was looking forward to when we first moved in together. I am wondering whether we have different expectations about sharing meals together.*

Hold back on solutions. Often, there's a particular way we'd like to see a concern or problem resolved. But there may be a variety of ways to solve the problem, and your solution might not take all of the facts into account. Try to maintain an open mind and don't present your solution along with the problem at the outset.

Instead of: *You're going to have to start doing the dishes in the morning before you go to work, so that they're not sitting in the sink when I get home.*

Try: *I really like having a clean kitchen to cook in when I come home. Any ideas about what we can do to make sure that happens?*

Acknowledge how the other person feels. If you have hurt someone's feelings, it's often tempting to defend yourself. But offering a sincere apology is the best way to make sure that you have an honest conversation about what happened, rather than an argument.

Instead of: *But it's not my fault I was late!*

Try: *I'm sorry that I was late.*

> **RESOURCE**
>
> **Want more information on effective communication?** For a full description of a very effective communication method called "Powerful Non-Defensive Communication," see *Taking the War Out of our Words: The Art of Non-Defensive Communication*, by Sharon Ellison (Bay Tree Publishing), most easily available on Ellison's website, www.pndc.com.

Setting Limits and Asking for What You Need

Sharing arrangements usually require you to communicate something about your personal preferences, needs, expectations, abilities, or worries. The carpool driver may like quiet, while the passengers want music. One parent may prefer that the nanny never give the kids sweet snacks, while the other may believe that a cookie or an ice cream cone once in a while is fine.

In Part II, which covers specific sharing arrangements, we encourage you to communicate clearly at the outset, so you know each other's preferences and concerns when you make your sharing agreement. It's easy to hesitate to bring up topics pertaining to needs or concerns, feeling that it might kill the mood or cause resentment. At the same time, successful sharing requires that the arrangement work for diverse people with diverse needs. Addressing concerns early prevents them from seeping in later in the form of tensions or conflict.

One key is to phrase your concerns in a way that doesn't sound judgmental or untrusting of your cosharers. We've provided some examples below, based on real situations we've heard about in sharing arrangements.

If you have started a carpool but don't want to feel obligated to make conversation all the time: *"I just want to give you a heads-up that I often use my commute time to unwind or let my mind wander, so I may not always join in the conversation. I'll let you know when that's the case."*

If you are sharing a house with your friend and don't want to feel obligated to always invite him to your dinner gatherings: *"I would like it if we could talk about giving each other social space. To me this means recognizing that there are times we may want to be alone with certain* *friends. For example, I like to have small dinner gatherings, and I enjoy the opportunity to spend time just with my guests. I want to make sure we both feel comfortable to ask for social space or to not invite each other to join the dinner party, for example."*

If there is someone you do not want to join your sharing group: *"I think it's important that this child care co-op be composed of people who we get along with and fully trust. I understand the urge to bring more members into the fold; at the same time, I don't feel entirely comfortable having Shoshana and her family join us. It wouldn't be fair for me to elaborate on why, since many of you have a good relationship with her. I just don't think I would work well with her."*

If you have formed a child care co-op and you worry about your child eating unhealthy food at other people's houses: *"We try to limit the amount of processed and sugary foods Sylvester eats. I'm wondering what would be the best way to approach this if he will be eating different snacks than other kids."*

If you are worried about committing to a sharing arrangement that you may want to get out of later: *"Can we make a plan to check in and assess how our sharing arrangement is going after two months? Before we take the significant step of transferring title to the car into both of our names, I'd like to share use of it for a couple months and make sure this is going to work for both of us."*

If you have a tighter financial situation than your co-sharers and you worry that they will make expensive decisions: *"I'd like to talk about our individual financial situations with respect to our cohousing. How should we handle situations where some of us want to invest in something and the others can't afford it? I just want to put it out there that money is a concern for me and I try to keep a careful reign on my finances."*

If you are sharing a yard with another family and worry about having to watch their child: *"Our children will be spending a lot of time in each other's yards, and I'd think it would help to come up with a system for alerting each other when the other's child needs supervision. That way, neither of us will feel responsible for caring for the other's child."*

If you are sharing a kitchen, but don't want to share your nice knives and expensive frying pan: *"Do you have any kitchen items that you would like to* *reserve for your own use? There are certain kitchen items that I try to take meticulous care of, so I would prefer to have those be for my own use."*

If you are worried about being bowled over by louder and bossier people: *"I often have difficulties speaking up in a group setting. It would help me if we came up with a format for communicating that would ensure that everyone always has a chance to speak."*

> **TIP**
>
> **Take communication training.** Many of the sharers we interviewed for this book emphasized the value of having a training session in communication. It's especially effective if your whole group goes together to training, or at least takes the same kind of training so you can work from a common set of guidelines for communication. You'll find training resources we recommend in Appendix A.

Making Decisions as a Group

One of the most important communication issues a sharing group must decide is how you'll make decisions together. Your choice will depend on how large your group is and what types of decisions you'll need to make, as well as how you'd like your group to function. Here are some of the most common ways that groups make decisions.

Consensus Process

In the spirit of sharing and cooperation, many sharing groups adopt consensus decision making. The actual process of consensus decision making varies, but the ultimate goal is to arrive at decisions everyone can accept and support. Group members discuss a proposal and try to reach unanimous agreement. If everyone is not able to agree, the group discusses the suggestions and reservations of those who aren't on board, then adapts and modifies the proposal. Through this process, the proposal continues to evolve until it satisfies all group members. If even one member doesn't agree, consensus hasn't been reached.

Generally, consensus requires that members agree not to withhold their agreement (called "blocking consensus") without a very good reason—often, because the proposal violates their ethics, values, or beliefs in an important way. Consensus doesn't require enthusiasm from all group members. Some may be lukewarm about the proposal, but not feel strongly enough against it to actually block the group from moving forward.

Consensus process can be challenging. It works best in groups where there is mutual trust and a commitment to taking the time necessary to engage in the process. The benefits are enhanced trust and understanding and a greater likelihood that agreements reached will be implemented without problems, because everyone supports—and fully understands—what's been decided. Also, when more people take part in the decision-making process, it creates fertile ground for creative ideas and allows for more effective reality-testing for ideas that are presented. It's the old "two heads are better than one" theory, multiplied by the number of members in your group.

How Consensus Works

What does consensus actually look like? First, it usually involves meeting in person, at least for major decisions. Consensus on simple decisions between meetings can be achieved via email or conference call. Second, a consensus process almost always must be facilitated, which means one person leads the group in coming to a decision. The group might choose one facilitator for a period of time or rotate the task among group members so that everyone takes a turn running the meetings. Small groups sometimes use an informal process without a facilitator.

Here's a quick and general description of what the consensus process actually looks like. This flowchart is borrowed with gratitude from www.seedsforchange.org.uk, which has an "anti-copyright" policy.

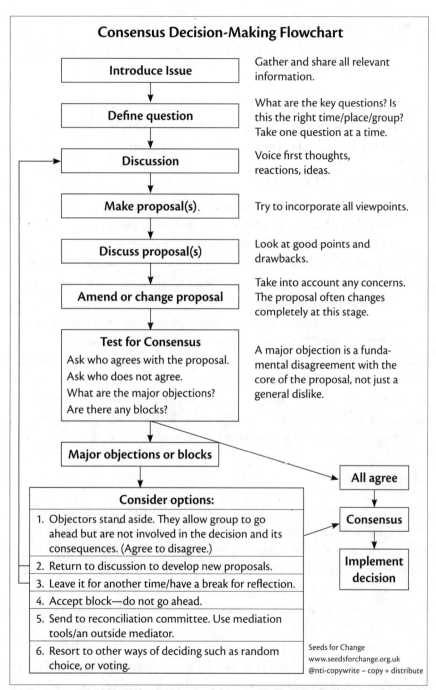

Consensus Decision-Making Flowchart

Introduce Issue
Gather and share all relevant information.

Define question
What are the key questions? Is this the right time/place/group? Take one question at a time.

Discussion
Voice first thoughts, reactions, ideas.

Make proposal(s).
Try to incorporate all viewpoints.

Discuss proposal(s)
Look at good points and drawbacks.

Amend or change proposal
Take into account any concerns. The proposal often changes completely at this stage.

Test for Consensus
Ask who agrees with the proposal.
Ask who does not agree.
What are the major objections?
Are there any blocks?

A major objection is a fundamental disagreement with the core of the proposal, not just a general dislike.

Major objections or blocks

All agree

Consensus

Consider options:

1. Objectors stand aside. They allow group to go ahead but are not involved in the decision and its consequences. (Agree to disagree.)
2. Return to discussion to develop new proposals.
3. Leave it for another time/have a break for reflection.
4. Accept block—do not go ahead.
5. Send to reconciliation committee. Use mediation tools/an outside mediator.
6. Resort to other ways of deciding such as random choice, or voting.

Implement decision

Seeds for Change
www.seedsforchange.org.uk
@nti-copywrite – copy + distribute

This chart was created by Seeds for Change and may be reproduced under the conditions established at their website (http://seedsforchange.org.uk/free/resources). Nolo makes no claim as to copyright.

Modified Consensus

There are some ways to modify consensus process, typically to require less than full agreement while still encouraging discussion and modification of the proposal. One is called "consensus minus one," in which one dissenting member is not enough to block consensus if the rest of the group agrees. Another is to allow decisions by a supermajority vote (80% is common) if consensus can't be reached.

Pros and Cons of Consensus

The benefits of consensus are many. It provides a great opportunity for full participation by all members of the group; the group gets the benefit of every member's best thinking; it's egalitarian and prevents the formation of voting blocs, cliques, or special interests; people are more likely to implement decisions that they truly agree to; and it's respectful of each member's contributions.

What are the disadvantages of consensus decision-making? It can be cumbersome and time-consuming, especially if the group has a lot of members. It requires a facilitator who is both strong and inclusive, skills that your group will have to cultivate in as many members as is practical. It's possible for a single naysayer to prevent the group from making important decisions. It can sometimes be difficult to bring the entire group together for meetings, which can delay decision making.

Majority Rule

The most basic definition of majority rule is selecting the one option out of two that has the support of more than half of the group. Often, the two options are to either accept or reject a proposal, such as whether to serve only organic food in a mealsharing group or whether to purchase a new sofa in a group house. It's simple because it requires nothing but a vote, although your sharing group is likely to want to engage in some discussion before voting.

The term "majority" doesn't always mean just one more than half. Your group can decide that decisions must have the approval of two-thirds of the members or an even higher percentage. You may decide that certain types of decisions require unanimity. (For example:

"Decisions of the following nature may be made only by unanimous consent of the members: (1) borrowing money in the group's name, (2) writing a check or making a purchase for more than $1,000, (3) admitting a new member, or (4) expelling an existing member.")

In contrast to consensus, majority voting creates a group of "winners" and a group of "losers," and those who lose the vote may find it hard to support the proposal they didn't favor. On the other hand, voting is generally efficient and always results in a decision being made, which is not always true of a consensus process.

A majority is different from a plurality, which is the group that has the most votes, whether or not it's more than half of the group. A plurality vote is often used to make a decision among more than two options. The option that gets the most votes wins.

RESOURCE

Want more information on majority rule voting? For resources to help you craft a majority rule decision-making process for your group, look for books on decision making, majority rule, or parliamentary procedure. Many groups adopt a traditional meeting and decision-making process known as Robert's Rules of Order, which are set out in various books on the topic, available at any bookstore. (You can get anything from the original *Robert's Rules of Order* by Henry M. Robert, to *Robert's Rules for Dummies.*)

Weighted Voting

Weighted voting systems are somewhat more nuanced than majority rule, although in some instances they work pretty much the same. In a weighted voting system, certain votes count for more than others, either because certain voters have more power than others (at least, in making particular decisions) or because voters can weight their votes to support a particular proposal more strongly.

Weighting Votes Differently

One method of weighted voting allows some voters to have more of a say than other voters. For example, you might have a sharing group with 15 members, including a leadership committee of three people. In voting on a proposal, you might give each of the leadership committee members three votes, and everyone else one vote. If the leadership committee votes as a block, the rest of the members will have to oppose that option overwhelmingly if they want to defeat it.

This type of weighted voting might make sense if one group member owns the property you're sharing. For example, if you share your car with two neighbors but you are the original owner of the car and the one on the title, you might want the final say on decisions to make major repairs to the car. You could agree that each member will have an equal vote on most issues, but that you alone decide when major repairs are necessary.

Weighted Voting for Multiple Options

Another system of weighted voting works well if a group is choosing among multiple options (rather than voting yes or no on one proposal). Each member gets a certain number of votes to distribute among the various options. For example, let's say you and 11 friends have joined together to purchase a vacation home and you've decided to install a hot tub on the deck, but you need to decide which of three different models you're going to choose. Each person gets three votes to distribute among the three options. If you feel strongly about one option, you can give it all three of your votes; if you like two of them, you can split your votes between them; and if you don't care, you can give one vote to each option. Weighted voting shows clearly not only which option is the most popular, but also how strongly people feel about their choice.

Dotmocracy: Weighted Voting for Multiple Options

If you have a large group and want to organize the discussion, gather information and ideas, and prioritize solutions, you might want to give "dotmocracy" a try. Dotmocracy is a facilitation method for decision making in large groups that uses a weighted voting system involving colored dots. For the office-supply lovers among us, it's heaven. Find out more at www.dotmocracy.org.

Tips for Effective Meetings

Regardless of what decision-making process you choose, your sharing group will probably have meetings, either on a regular schedule or on an as-needed basis. Meetings are important for sharing groups: They create a time and structure for making decisions, talking about concerns and developments, and checking in with one another about how things are going. Even if your group is just you and your neighbor, you and a couple of co-workers, or any other small group of people you see regularly, you should still set aside time specifically for discussing how your sharing arrangement is working out.

Although meetings play an important role in keeping a sharing group functioning well, you may be hesitant to schedule them (or eager to cancel meetings already on the calendar). Perhaps a meeting seems too formal, or you're not sure you have anything to discuss. Maybe you've sat through too many dull meetings at work or for charitable or political causes, and you aren't eager to have more of them with your friends and neighbors. But meetings don't have to be stilted or boring: You can have productive, interesting, and yes, even fun meetings by following some of these guidelines.

Keep meetings as short as possible. These days, free time seems to be many folks' most valuable commodity, and few of us look forward to spending any of our free time in a meeting. One way to keep things short is to have a tight agenda and set a time limit for each agenda item. Also, it helps to reserve meetings for important deliberation or decisions only. Less important decisions can take place outside of meetings or by email. For example, if possible, don't put "Report on last week's gardening class" on the agenda if there is nothing that needs to be discussed or decided about that event; write up your notes and circulate them by email instead.

Do something fun at the start of each meeting. Meeting time is valuable, but you should spend a bit of it lightening up a little. Starting with a fun activity can break the ice, perk people up, get their attention, lighten the mood, and help people feel more connected. For ideas, see *The Big Book of Meeting Games*, by Marlene Caroselli (McGraw Hill).

Designate a meeting facilitator. The purpose of having a meeting facilitator is to ensure that the group moves through the agenda, to keep the discussion on track, to ensure that everyone's input is taken into account, and to guide the group to a vote when appropriate. (See "Tips for Facilitators," below.) Take turns facilitating the meetings, to give each member a turn at being the leader and guiding the group.

Keep track of time. If you're expecting to have a lot of people speaking and you want to make sure the meeting stays on track, have a timekeeper and allow only a certain amount of time for each speaker. Ask them not to repeat things others have said, but only to offer new thoughts, ideas, and opinions.

Designate someone other than the facilitator to take notes or write on a flip-chart. A facilitator juggles many tasks: calling on people, following the agenda, restating parts of the discussion, moderating votes, and most importantly, listening to what is being said and how. Taking notes might add one too many balls to juggle. Let a separate notetaker be responsible for writing on the flip-chart and figuring out how to spell "cooperatively." A notetaker can serve as an extra ear and help organize information, serving as an aid to the facilitator.

If a decision can be delegated, delegate it! If the group decides to hold a potluck on a certain date, it can appoint a person or committee to take care of the rest of the details. There is no point in wasting meeting time sorting out the details if people are happy to delegate.

Send out meeting notes ASAP. Meetings can build a lot of momentum in a group. Decisions are made and people commit to taking on certain tasks … which they may promptly forget as soon as they leave the room. To keep the group from losing momentum, have someone take notes on the discussions and decisions. When someone commits to doing something, underline and bold that person's name in the notes so they can easily see what they committed to. Send out those notes right away.

Serve a meal or snacks during the meeting. Often, the biggest challenge is getting people to fit a meeting into their busy schedule. But the promise of coffee, bagels, and fruit salad can improve attendance dramatically.

Arrange seats in a circle when practical. This allows everyone to make eye contact with each other and prevents a feeling of hierarchy in the meeting.

Tips for Facilitators

Facilitating a meeting isn't easy, but it's an important job and a satisfying one. There are lots of resources on how to do it, and lots of ways to run a meeting. Your group will have to decide on the role of the facilitator, and then make sure there are enough members with the requisite skills so that the job doesn't always fall to the same person. Here are a few basic tips for facilitating discussion and decision making:

- Paraphrase comments and, from time to time, summarize what has been said.
- Ask clarifying questions and questions that will draw out the quieter participants.
- Gently intervene when the group gets off on a tangent or belabors an unhelpful point.
- Help to welcome and introduce new people.
- Try to maintain a certain amount of neutrality, to ensure that you aren't using your authority as facilitator to guide a discussion in the direction you prefer. Stay open to everyone's perspective.
- If the discussion seems to be heading for a roadblock, stay optimistic that a solution can be reached. Your tone and attitude can make a big difference.
- Observe not only the content of what is being said, but also the form, process, and tone that the meeting takes. For example, if a few people are dominating the discussion, you might call that to the group's attention.
- When the group appears to be arriving at a decision, restate what has been said and test for consensus or call for a vote.

RESOURCE

Want more information on being a facilitator? A great book on facilitation and decision making is *The Facilitator's Guide to Participatory Decision-Making*, by Sam Kaner, et al (New Society Publishers).

Delegating Decisions

Most large organizations delegate decision making to boards of directors, committees, officers, or some other person or small group. Practically speaking, an organization with 40 members cannot easily gather for a consensus discussion or vote whenever an important decision must be made. For everyone's ease, the members of a large group generally elect a smaller group to whom they delegate decisions. This group can be on the less formal side, and might be called a steering committee, leadership circle, or whatever suits your group's fancy. If you have formed a nonprofit, your board of directors is the most likely choice to make decisions.

If your sharing group decides to have a smaller group or committee make decisions, here are some issues to decide:

- How will that committee be elected?
- How long will members serve?
- How many members will there be?
- What are the powers and duties of members?
- What kinds of decisions will the committee make, and what decisions will be reserved for the membership?
- How and when will the committee meet?
- How can the committee keep members informed of meeting agendas and minutes?
- How can members give input on decisions?
- What if members do not agree with the committee's decisions?

Handling Disputes

Many groups create their agreement and go on to share happily ever after. Following the suggestions in "Communication Skills for Sharing," above, will prevent many conflicts from arising and nip others in the bud. Still, it's possible that you may find yourself in a dispute with others in your sharing group—or standing by while others in your sharing group have issues with each other. A variety of issues can arise, including disputes about:

- interpersonal problems (such as communication styles, privacy, or personal boundaries)
- property (such as use or care of shared property, repairs, and maintenance)
- financial issues (for example, paying dues, how much to spend on particular items, and how to divide costs), and
- agreements and expectations (such as conflict over what terms in the agreement mean or what each member is obligated to do).

Addressing Concerns or Conflicts Without Outside Help

The starting place for resolving any dispute should be direct communication between the people involved. If your group is small, your first step should be to sit down together and have an open, non-defensive conversation about what's going on.

Start by making sure all of you have the time and attention to devote to the conversation. Turn off cell phones and other distracting little buddies, and choose a neutral environment where you have privacy and adequate space.

Spend a few moments at the start affirming your shared commitment to resolution and to a non-defensive, open-hearted conversation. Agree not to interrupt each other, and try to use the communication techniques described in "Communication Skills for Sharing," above.

Define the problem at the outset, so everyone begins the conversation in the same place. Of course, it may turn out that the heart of the problem lies elsewhere, which will require you to expand the conversation accordingly. Make agreements if you want to, such as not to interrupt or to use a "yes, and" instead of a "yes, but" structure for responding to others.

If only some members are involved in the conflict, the others should find out what the best role for them is—helping to facilitate communication, making suggestions when it comes time for considering solutions, helping to reality-test ideas for resolution, or simply being there to show their support for the group and the members who are in conflict.

Ask someone to take notes (preferably one of those people who isn't involved in the dispute).

If an agreement is reached, write it down and make sure it meets with everyone's approval. If a discussion doesn't lead to a resolution, the next step is to look outside your sharing group for some help with the dispute.

Mediation

We believe that mediation is the method of dispute resolution best suited to sharing groups, because it can actually enhance ongoing relationships by building better communication skills and allowing everyone to have their full say. In mediation, a neutral third party (the mediator) sits down with the people in conflict and works with them, through a structured process, to reach a solution that will work for everyone.

One of the many great features of mediation is that it allows participants to discuss any topic that is important to them, including issues that couldn't be raised in a courtroom setting. You can also fashion creative solutions to your dispute, because you're not limited by what the law can provide (usually, money). In a mediation, for example, people might agree to follow a particular schedule, offer an apology for past hurtful behavior, or plan to attend an anger management or communication skills class together.

Finding a Mediator

There are lots of different types of mediators, with different skills and styles (and fees). Most cities and counties have community mediation organizations that provide mediation services at a reasonable cost. These groups rely on volunteer mediators, who usually work in panels. Some provide free services; others charge a nominal fee, such as $25 per person.

To locate a community mediation service, just look in your local phone book under "mediation" or "conflict resolution." You can also ask a small claims court clerk, the county law librarian, or even a police officer—they almost always know about mediation services because they refer neighbor disputes to mediation with some frequency.

You can also hire a private mediator to work with your sharing group. Many mediators are either therapists or lawyers, and their services will be significantly more expensive. But if your dispute is intractable, involves a significant amount of money, or threatens the very existence of your group, you might want to make the investment to hire someone with extensive training and experience.

Getting Help From a Third Party (Informal Mediation)

If there are no community mediation programs or professional mediators available, or if you really just need help talking to each other, another option is to ask someone outside the dispute—a friend or acquaintance—to step in and help you communicate. You might refer to this as "informal mediation," or you might just call it "asking someone to help us talk." This person should not have an interest in the outcome of the dispute, so that everyone can feel sure the mediator is impartial. This person doesn't need formal mediation training, but should be fair-minded, a good listener, and naturally good at seeing both sides of a conflict.

This kind of informal mediation is often the most immediately available option when discussions break down. During conflict, people can become frustrated, feel that they are constantly being interrupted, feel that they have repeated themselves over and over without being heard, and so on. A third party can help guide people out of this situation by facilitating the conversation, creating some neutral ground, ensuring that everyone involved has a turn to speak, and reframing what each person says in order to help everyone feel understood. The third party could also talk to each person separately, to try to understand any unspoken feelings that may be affecting the dispute. If a third party is able to understand and empathize with both sides, the dispute is much more likely to be resolved.

What a Mediation Looks Like

While different mediators have different styles, and a community-based (or informal) mediation process will look somewhat different than a mediation you attend in a lawyer's or therapist's office, there are some common features and a basic process that many mediators follow.

First, the mediator will get things started by making introductions, explaining what you can expect, and setting some ground rules about things like the order in which you'll speak, how you should speak to each other (for example, no interrupting), and the time frame for the mediation.

Next, each person involved in the conflict has a chance to state the problem from that person's perspective. Often, you'll be asked to talk about only how you view the conflict, not how you think the other person sees it or what solutions you are willing to accept. The mediator may ask clarifying questions and might repeat back the gist of what you said to make sure that everyone hears and understands both sides.

After everyone has had an initial chance to speak, the mediator facilitates a discussion among you. Here's where mediators employ very different styles. Some will simply get you going and then observe the process, possibly asking questions, reframing, or offering suggestions for productive interactions. Others will structure the process more formally, having each of you speak in turn and then asking the other person to reflect back what's been said until the speaker feels the listener has fully understood. This will be the longest part of the process, when you get to the real roots of the problem.

Often, the discussion process leads very naturally to a solution that will work for everyone. Other times, you'll need to propose and discuss possible solutions to reach a compromise that's acceptable to all. Sometimes, you may need to circle back for more discussion of the conflict, and then return to problem solving. In this stage the mediator will probably be very active, working with you to craft possible solutions and then reality-testing them to be sure they're workable for everyone.

If an agreement is reached, the mediator usually writes the agreement down for you, and everyone will sign it. In some cases, you'll later need to produce a more formal, legally binding agreement.

The Mediator's Toolkit

When people are knee deep in a conflict, it can be hard to imagine how a third party could possibly move the situation forward. By being neutral and impartial in a conflict, however, mediators are uniquely situated to help people resolve disputes. Mediators use a set of communication strategies to help the people in conflict see things from each other's point of view and work together more productively toward a solution. These explanations may help if you are acting as an informal mediator for others in your sharing group and want to understand a bit about how you can move the process forward.

- **Reframing.** A mediator can often "reframe" a judgment or accusation into an issue that's simply on the table for both people to solve. For example, Susan might frame a problem as Mike's fault: *"Mike always leaves a mess in the kitchen."* A mediator might reframe the problem as a difference in expectations: *"Susan is frustrated by the situation in the kitchen. It sounds like we should discuss each of your expectations about cleanliness."*

- **Creating space for discussion.** Conflicts escalate when people interrupt each other and negate each other's statements. The mediator might ask participants to take turns speaking and possibly even to repeat back what the other has said, to ensure that everyone has a chance to be heard. A mediator can also intervene if participants become intentionally hurtful.

- **Helping everyone feel understood.** Often, people in conflict will not budge until they are satisfied that the other person understands their point of view. Someone may repeat the same point, hoping that the other party will eventually "get it." A mediator can break people out of this unhelpful cycle by restating someone's point or by asking the other person to restate it. This can create instant relief for the person who is trying to be understood.

- **Seeing both sides.** Because they are neutral in the conflict, mediators can often see how the same incident might have affected the participants differently, and help them communicate their different experiences to each other.

- **Getting at underlying issues.** Seasoned mediators say that the "real" cause of a conflict is rarely the problem the participants are arguing about, and that the foundation of a dispute is often laid long before a particular argument arises. For example, long-time neighbors might go to mediation over a parking dispute that has escalated into hurt and anger. But underneath the disagreement about parking, there might be hurt feelings arising from the fact that the two neighbors, over the years, had gone from being friends to barely saying hello to each other. This problem was somewhat intangible until the parking dispute fanned the flames.
- **Keeping the process on track.** A mediator can help participants set an agenda and stick to it. Mediators keep an eye out for unhelpful tangents, bringing everyone back to the topic at hand.
- **Maintaining optimism.** Frustration levels can run high in the midst of a conflict, and participants are often tempted to just give up. Mediators can help point out where people may have already made progress, help them to identify their common ground, and so on.
- **Eliciting ideas.** Sometimes, participants may become attached to a specific outcome, which prevents them from coming up with creative solutions. A mediator might be able to help develop other options to try.
- **Conferencing individually with parties.** People in a dispute sometimes feel that they will lose the argument if they give even a little ground. They may even try to "hide the ball" by keeping certain facts to themselves in order to maintain a perceived advantage in a conflict. A person who can speak confidentially with a mediator might be more willing to discuss areas of potential negotiation. A mediator can work with this information, gaining insight into possible solutions that aren't yet on the table, and encouraging parties to reveal certain information if and when it makes sense.
- **Confidentiality.** Mediation is confidential. Participants can feel more comfortable expressing their feelings and disclosing relevant information because they know that everyone—including the mediator—must refrain from discussing any of the mediation

proceedings outside of the mediation. This extends to the courtroom, in that the mediator may not be required to testify about the mediation, nor may the participants testify about it.

- **Setting the tone.** Some mediators can help resolve a dispute simply through the subtle expectations they set through their words and demeanor. Even in a room where tempers are running high, good mediators can maintain a genuine atmosphere of calm, respect, kindness, and honesty, which often become contagious.

Arbitration

Mediation has a very high success rate, and in a sharing situation where all of you are committed to the best interests of the group, it's even more likely to work. If it doesn't, however, there are other options for dispute resolution, short of going to court.

One is to hold an arbitration: an out-of-court trial with a decision maker who listens to all sides of the issue and then makes a ruling about what should happen. The decision maker could be a lawyer or even a retired judge if you wish, but you could also choose any arbitrator who's acceptable to everyone involved. The arbitrator doesn't necessarily need any special skills, only the willingness to listen with an open mind and render a decision based on principles of fairness. Neither the process nor the decision must be based on legal rules.

You could also choose a panel of arbitrators—for example, if there are two of you in conflict, you each choose an arbitrator, then the two arbitrators together choose a third person, and the panel listens to the arguments and makes a decision together. You'll make a choice at the beginning of the process as to whether your arbitration will be binding—which means the decision is final and you can't ask a court to overrule it later—or non-binding.

Arbitration is more cumbersome than mediation, because it requires you to prepare evidence and a presentation for the arbitrator to base a decision on. It also takes the decision-making power out of your hands, in contrast to mediation, where the participants make the decisions. But if you're not able to come to a compromise on your own, it can be a good solution.

Collaborative Process

There's also a process called "collaborative practice" that is catching on with lawyers and clients alike. In a collaborative process, both people retain a lawyer, and then both of the lawyers and the clients sign an agreement saying that they will work to resolve the case without going to court. If anyone does initiate court proceedings, the lawyers must withdraw from the case and the clients must find new lawyers for the court process. In the meantime, everyone agrees to have four-way meetings at which information is shared freely and solutions are considered all together.

Collaborative process is different from mediation in that there's no single mediator working as a neutral go-between. It's also different from hiring a lawyer to represent you in negotiations, because you get to be involved directly. You have an advocate in the room, but you also have the opportunity to speak for yourself. This combination can work well when communication needs to be highly structured and you need the support and expertise of a lawyer.

Using Lawyers for Conflict Resolution

If things really escalate, you may need to hire a lawyer to advise you and negotiate on your behalf. A lawyer can be a big help in negotiating if communication has broken down entirely—especially if you hire the right lawyer. Make sure you find someone who is dedicated to negotiation and settlement, not someone who wants to take every case to trial.

A lawyer can negotiate with the other person or the other person's lawyer on your behalf, while you stay out of it. This can help ease tensions and relieve you of the stress of negotiating directly, while still allowing you the final say on any resolution.

A Last Resort: Going to Court

It's rare to have a conflict that can't be resolved using any of the methods described above—and that's worth fighting out in court—but it may happen. Courts are most helpful if there is valuable property or money at stake, or if you and another party have reached an impasse due to disagreement about the terms of your contract.

For example, if you need to terminate a carsharing arrangement, and your sharing partner refuses to either give up the car or pay you for your share, you might sue your cosharer in small claims court. Every state has a small claims court of some kind, where cases within a certain dollar limit can be heard quickly and inexpensively. Each state has a different upper limit on how much a small claims case can be worth; states also have different rules about things like whether you can have a lawyer in small claims court, and what types of cases can be brought.

The small claims court judge will make a decision that is binding on everyone. For example, in the carsharing dispute described above, the judge might require that the car be sold and you split the proceeds, or that your sharing partner pay you half its value. Courts will consider any written or oral agreements between you and your cosharer. For example, you and your cosharer may have made a written carsharing agreement when you began sharing. If the court considers your agreement a valid contract, the judge must interpret and enforce it.

If your dispute is for more than the small claims court limit, you'll have to use a different court, often called a "superior" court. This will require you to follow many more rules, pay much higher filing fees, and put in a lot more time and effort. There aren't many sharing disputes that would be worth this kind of trouble or conflict, but if there's a lot of money or an important piece of property at stake, it's possible you'll need to go that route.

RESOURCE

Want to know more about going to court? For more about small claims court, see *Everybody's Guide to Small Claims Court,* by Ralph Warner (Nolo). California residents can use *Everybody's Guide to Small Claims Court in California,* by Ralph Warner (Nolo). For disputes that are worth more than the small claims limit, you'll need to either hire a lawyer or represent yourself. For those who choose to go it alone, *Represent Yourself in Court,* by Paul Bergman (Nolo) explains the ins and outs of dealing with litigation. California filers can check out *Win your Lawsuit: A Judge's Guide to Representing Yourself in California Superior Court,* by Judge Roderic Duncan (Nolo).

Communication Checklist

Here's a handy checklist for you and your cosharers to review:

☐ Have we talked through the logistics of our arrangement (for example, the 20 questions in Chapter 3)?

☐ Have we discussed each of our concerns or worries regarding the sharing arrangement?

☐ Do we all feel comfortable voicing our needs?

☐ Do we each feel that our needs and values are understood by other sharers?

☐ Do we have a plan for checking in with each other periodically?

☐ Are any of us interested in taking a communication training class? (See Appendix A for training resources.)

☐ Have we chosen a decision-making process?

☐ Have we decided what conflict resolution methods we will use?

☐ Do we want to choose a mediator in advance?

☐ Do we all feel prepared to approach difficult conversation in a constructive, non-judgmental, and non-defensive manner?

Putting Your Arrangement in Writing

Once you've decided what to share, found your fellow sharers, and decided how you're going to manage your sharing arrangement, you have another decision to make: Do you need a written contract?

Sometimes, you won't really have a choice. Certain agreements will not be enforceable unless they're documented, such as agreements to buy, sell, or otherwise change ownership of land and real estate, or agreements that cannot be completed within a year (such as an agreement to share a camper for the next three summers). These rules differ from state to state and topic to topic, and we'll address them more in later chapters.

But for many sharing arrangements, no law requires a written agreement. As long as the arrangement is fairly simple, your sharing group is small, and you know your sharing partner(s) well and trust them completely, you may reasonably decide not to put the details in writing. For example, if your sister lets you plant a vegetable garden in her back yard, you could sensibly do without a written agreement. You know each other well, there aren't any liability or ownership issues, and it will be easy to discuss any questions that come up.

Generally, however, it's a good idea to put your sharing arrangements in writing. This chapter explains why, explains the documents you might need for various types of arrangements, and discusses how to prepare written agreements that will work for your group and arrangement.

The Benefits of a Written Agreement

There are lots of good reasons to get your sharing agreement in writing. A written sharing agreement:

Helps prevent amnesia. Putting information and decisions on paper means keeping less of it in your head; there's a limit to how many details we can keep organized in our brains. Even with people whom you trust completely, you may have had the experience of remembering the same event or conversation differently. Making a written agreement is an easy way to avoid confusion and potential conflict. You won't have to figure out (or argue over) whose memory is accurate, because you have the answer in writing.

Provides a handy reference. If anyone in the group has a question, you can just look up the answer. Having documents on hand also provides a quick and easy way to orient people who join an existing sharing group.

Leads to a well-thought-out plan. Putting ideas in writing helps a group think through details that might not have been ironed out during discussions. Plans that seem really great over a glass of wine don't always make as much sense when you lay them out on paper.

Encourages consistency. Having a written agreement provides one set of procedures for everyone to follow. For example, if a group rotates its secretary and treasurer, each person might track money and keep records a little differently, which could create an administrative muddle. Providing the secretary and treasurer with written procedures will help prevent that problem.

Promotes group harmony. Documents keep everyone "on the same page" and prevent disputes from arising. And if disputes do arise, the documents serve as a good reference for sorting them out. The documents may also provide set guidelines for how to resolve a dispute (see Chapter 4).

Seals the deal. Some people are more comfortable committing their time, money, and energy to something if they are sure that everyone else is committed. People want to feel protected and assured that the other member(s) of the group won't bow out suddenly and leave them in a bad spot. Written agreements can also help weed out people who aren't completely committed. Having to actually sign an agreement creates a moment of truth that can help someone realize he or she isn't really ready—or willing—to take on the responsibilities the sharing arrangement will require.

Creates group recognition and legitimacy. If you will be dealing with people or institutions outside of your group (for example, if your group will enter into contracts, hire an accountant or lawyer, apply for a loan, or open a bank account), a signed agreement will encourage outsiders to recognize you as a group. For groups that plan to borrow money, a signed agreement will ensure the lender that members have made a financial commitment to that group. In fact, some lenders will require a written agreement to approve a loan.

Lets YOU make the rules. If you don't have a written agreement, local and state law may dictate some of the rules for your group, especially if a dispute arises. For example, if Horton and Babar own a house as tenants in common and do not make an agreement about how one of them could later sell his share, a dispute could arise that winds up in court—where a judge gets to decide how the property will be handled. The judge might force a sale of the whole property and decide how to distribute the proceeds. If Horton and Babar had made their own agreement, they would have been able to decide this issue for themselves (and possibly avoid the problem entirely).

Lets you share your sharing agreement. One really good reason to put your decisions in writing is that people are going to come and say to you: "Wow!! How did you arrange your awesome dog walking co-op? I'd like to do the same with my neighbors." Then you will proudly whip out your agreement and procedures and send them off on their wagging way.

Makes for easier enforcement if you want it. A written agreement is much easier to enforce than an oral agreement. This is a benefit of writing things down, but it can also lead to anxiety. Maybe your group wants to put things in writing just to make sure your plan is sound and everyone's on the same page, but doesn't want to create a legally enforceable contract. In that case, you can write at the end: "We do not intend for this to be a legally binding agreement. We have written this agreement in the spirit of cooperation and to help clarify our plans related to sharing dog walking responsibilities."

Documents Your Group Might Need

Depending on what you're doing, you may need just one written document, or you may decide—or be required—to have more than one. There are two types of paperwork your group might have: Documents to be used only among yourselves (such as house rules for a shared home or an agreement to share a car) and documents that are legally required (such as articles of incorporation for a nonprofit or a bill of sale showing that your sharing partner purchased half of your car).

Documents for the Group's Use Only

Simple sharing arrangements require only a basic agreement. Larger groups or arrangements that involve more "moving parts," such as fluctuating activities and schedules, and members who come and go, might be better served by creating a few internal agreements.

The Basic Agreement

For all the reasons above, we think most sharing arrangements will benefit from a basic written agreement. In simple sharing arrangements, like a small tool sharing group, probably one basic agreement will suffice. This document should explain how your group will work, covering as many of the topics in Chapter 3 as are relevant to your arrangement (see "What Your Basic Agreement Should Include," below, for more information).

You may supplement the basic agreement with other documents, such as a list of shared items, a schedule for using shared items, a member list, fee information, instructions for using shared property, information for new members, and so on.

When to Use Multiple Agreements

For some sharing agreements, and especially for groups whose activities, membership, or schedules change frequently, it may make sense to use more than one agreement. Multiple agreements help you maintain continuity and flexibility as your group changes or grows. Some agreements will be relatively stable, while other agreements may change on a regular basis. (Our government works in a similar fashion. We have a Constitution that is rarely amended, statutes (laws) that change sometimes, and many sets of administrative rules and procedures that are updated quite often.)

There are some agreements that you will rarely, if ever, need to change. These documents usually describe the basic purpose and nature of your group, the way the group is structured and governed, and how ownership rights are distributed. Examples include bylaws (often the basic governing document used by nonprofits and corporations) or a tenancy-in-common (TIC) agreement, which describes the property rights and responsibilities of owners in a co-owned building. These documents are designed to change infrequently, often requiring unanimous agreement or a two-thirds majority of members to approve a change. As such, they preserve certain basic qualities of the group or ownership rights, even when the group's activities or membership may fluctuate.

Other agreements are designed to be more flexible and evolve along with the group. In a shared housing arrangement, for example, the TIC agreement may be supplemented by a "cohousing agreement" detailing day-to-day matters, such as rules about pets, smoking, sharing expenses for the garden, rules for construction and remodeling jobs, and so on.

You might also want different agreements for different phases of your project, such as one agreement to purchase land and construct housing, and a second agreement about your living arrangements once the shared housing is finished.

Documents Required by Law

Your group might be required by law to have certain documents. For example, to create a nonprofit to administer a car sharing program, you will have to file a document, typically called "articles of incorporation," with the secretary of state's office in your state. Or, if you are going to share real estate, you will have to file a deed specifying, among other things, how you are taking title (for example, as joint tenants or tenants in common) with the land records office in the county where the property is located.

In addition to any documents you're legally required to file, your group might want or need to create additional documents dictated by the type of group you form and what you plan to do. For example, if you form a nonprofit to run a carsharing program, you will probably want to apply for tax-exempt status with the IRS and your state tax agency, a process that requires you to file additional paperwork. You will want to adopt bylaws, which establish the rules for how your group will elect directors, hold meetings, make decisions, and so on. You'll need to document the group's decisions, most likely by taking minutes of meetings. For the cars themselves, you'll need title documents, proof of insurance coverage, perhaps smog certificates, and so on. As you can see, the list of documents your group might need—in addition to the basic agreements and other paperwork you use amongst yourselves—can get pretty long.

If you're forming a separate legal entity, purchasing real estate, or starting a large group, it's a good idea to talk to a lawyer about the documents your group will be legally required to prepare.

Preparing Your Documents

Your sharing agreement does not have to be on fancy paper or include lots of "heretofores" and "parties of the first part." Instead, you should write your agreement in plain language, so everyone signing it—and anyone who has to read or agree to it later, like new members, a mediator, or even a judge or arbitrator, if you have a dispute—understands exactly what it means.

Creating a Binding Contract

As explained in "The Benefits of a Written Agreement," above, your group may—or may not—want your agreement to be legally binding. If your group chooses not to create an enforceable agreement, you can simply write down your shared understanding of how your group will work and the rules members will follow, then sign your names.

If, however, your group wants a binding enforceable agreement (in other words, a contract), you will need to agree to exchange something of value (for example, to provide goods or services, pay money, and so on). From a legal perspective, this is called "consideration." This requirement prevents people from enforcing one-sided promises. For example, if someone promises to pay you $500 without you promising to do anything in return, and then the other person doesn't follow through, there isn't a contract and you can't sue to get the money. On the other hand, if someone promises to pay you $500 to landscape a yard, and you do the work, you have a binding contract that you can enforce to get paid.

It's a good idea to type your agreement, though it's not legally required. And everyone who's involved in the agreement should date and sign it. For simple sharing arrangements, you won't need to have your signatures notarized. For anything involving real estate, however, notarization will probably be required. And some states have their own requirements about notarization—for example, a few have laws saying that any transfer of a vehicle must have notarized signatures, and others require fingerprints if you're transferring real estate. If you're transferring property of any kind, check your state's laws.

> **SEE AN EXPERT**
>
> **If you're dealing with real estate, have a lawyer draft or at least review your documents.** While we're all for doing it yourself, the paperwork involved in transferring and owning real estate can be complex and subject to lots of state rules. Even if you draft your own documents, make sure you ask a lawyer to review them before you sign, seal, and deliver them. You'll find more information about hiring a lawyer below.

What Your Basic Agreement Should Include

What kinds of things might you want to put in your agreement? Chapter 3 lists the most important 20 questions you and your fellow sharers may want to consider, from what you will share to how your arrangement will end. Once you've discussed those questions and made decisions on all of the issues that apply to your group, you're ready to write them down as your sharing agreement.

Sample Sharing Agreement

Here is a sample sharing agreement for a fairly simple arrangement among people who work in the same building to share a bicycle. As you'll see, the agreement incorporates most of the 20 questions covered in Chapter 3; some of the questions weren't relevant to this particular sharing set-up, and aren't included in the agreement. You'll also see that the agreement is written in straightforward language that's easy to understand, and runs only a couple of pages.

Sample Form: Basic Sharing Agreement

Sharing Agreement

This agreement is between all members of the Grayson Street Bike Sharing Group ("Group"), who all work together at 1010 Grayson Street. We have decided to share the use of an office bicycle. By signing this agreement, each member agrees as follows:

Purpose: We agree to share a bicycle for the purpose of occasional use by members, in order to save money and reduce our use of energy and natural resources.

Shared Property: The shared item is described as follows: blue Trek bicycle, 13 speeds, "Trek" logo on bar, "One Less Car" sticker on back fender.

Initial Members: Initial members of the Group are Sarabeth Johnson, Martin Carver, Joe Nathanson, and Flora Jiminez. The Group may choose to add new members at a later date, as detailed below.

Number of Members: We agree that the Group should have no more than five members, and that all members must be tenants at 1010 Grayson Street.

Timeline: We will begin sharing on July 15, 2009 and will continue until the group chooses to dissolve.

Ownership: The bicycle is and will remain the separate property of Martin Carver.

Structure: We are a loose association of individuals. We do not intend to enter into a partnership or form an incorporated entity.

Benefits: Each member of the Group may use the bicycle when needed, but for no more than 10 trips per week, unless the Group agrees to allow a member more trips.

Decisions: Important decisions of the Group will be made by consensus. Important decisions include those relating to the schedule of use of the bicycle. We will discuss decisions over email using our Yahoo group. If the group cannot reach an agreement, Martin will be the decision maker.

Responsibilities: Each member is responsible for complying with the Group's rules, maintaining the schedule of use, and treating the bicycle well. This Group won't have an administrator as our administrative needs are simple.

Rules: Members agree to use the bicycle only at times they sign up for, ride it with care, return it on time, and always lock it carefully.

Procedures: Members will communicate with each other in the following manner: We'll set up a Yahoo group and a calendar for use of the bicycle. Everyone in the Group can sign up to use the bicycle any time within the limits stated above.

Costs: We don't anticipate any significant costs. Flora agrees to keep the bicycle in good working order with maintenance and tune-ups, at no cost to the rest of the group members. If parts or supplies are needed, Joe and Sarabeth will share the costs equally up to $50 per year, in exchange for Martin's allowing use of the bicycle and Flora performing the maintenance work. If repairs or parts are needed that cost more than $50, we'll discuss what to do.

Loss and Liability: Each of us has health insurance. We all agree to hold one another harmless for any injuries or damages that we incur while riding the bicycle. We all agree to wear a bike helmet at all times when riding the bicycle.

Dispute Resolution: If a conflict or dispute arises that we are unable to solve through discussion, we agree to use SEEDS Community Resolution Center to help us resolve our dispute, and to share the minimal cost equally, regardless of who asks for the mediation.

New Members: Membership is limited to tenants at 1010 Grayson Street, and new tenants are welcome to join the Group.

Procedure for Withdrawing from the Group or Expelling Members: Anyone can leave the Group at any time, and Martin is free to stop allowing use of the bicycle whenever he wishes. If anyone feels that another member isn't following the rules, we'll have an in-person meeting to discuss what to do.

Dissolving the Group: There's no formal procedure for dissolving the Group. We'll end it when there are no longer at least two people who want to participate.

Print Name: _____ Date: _____

Signature: _____

Address: _____

_____

Print Name: _____ Date: _____

Signature: _____

Address: _____

_____

Print Name: _____ Date: _____

Signature: _____

Address: _____

_____

Print Name: _____ Date: _____

Signature: _____

Address: _____

_____

Understanding Contract Boilerplate

Many sharing groups will draft their own agreement in plain English, like the samples we provide in this book, and be on their way. Sometimes, however, it might make sense to use a standard contract document. For example, you may need to complete official paperwork for your local government, or you might want to use a standard form for your covenants, conditions, and restrictions (CC&Rs), so they can be easily understood by lenders, title companies, and future purchasers of property.

If you use a form contract, you'll quickly run into "boilerplate": standard provisions that appear in many contracts. Here are some examples:

- **Entire Agreement.** What you might include: *"This document contains the entire agreement of the parties. Any modifications to the agreement must be in writing and attached to this document."* Why you might include it: The language makes clear that you don't have any side agreements that aren't included in the written document, and also that you can't make changes without putting them in writing.
- **Successors Bound.** What you might include: *"This document is binding on the heirs, successors, and assigns of the parties."* Why you might include it: You probably would use this provision only if the property you're sharing is valuable and you want to be sure that if someone dies and his or her share passes to a family member, the family member will comply with the agreement.
- **Amendments.** What you might include: *"This agreement may be amended only by a writing that is signed by all of the parties."* Why you might include it: Include this provision if you want to prevent oral changes to the agreement. An agreement could otherwise become muddled over time if you make multiple oral changes and never write them down.
- **Validity.** What you might include: *"If any portion of this agreement is held by a court to be invalid, it shall be severed and the remaining provisions of the agreement shall remain in full force and effect."*

> ## Understanding Contract Boilerplate (continued)
>
> Why you might include it: It protects your agreement in case you
> inadvertently included a provision that your state considers illegal,
> by making sure the entire agreement isn't doomed by the one bad
> provision.
> - **Choice of Law.** What you might include: *"This agreement will be
>   interpreted under the laws of the State of _____."*
>   Why you might include it: It's unlikely you need this provision, but
>   if the law in your state relating to the subject of your agreement
>   is very different from another state's laws, and there's a chance
>   anyone in your group might move away at some point, including
>   this provision and naming the state you live in could protect you
>   from having to go elsewhere for a court fight.

In later chapters in this book, we provide sample language for various
types of sharing arrangements. You can use elements from all of these
examples to come up with an arrangement that will work for your group.

Attachments to Your Agreement

Some basic agreements will need attachments, either prepared at the
same time as the basic agreement or added later. There are a few different
kinds of attachment you might decide to use.

Amendment. An amendment is a later change to the original
agreement.

> **EXAMPLE:** Darren and David share childcare; each has one child
> and pays half the cost of a nanny, who alternates between their
> homes. Darren will soon adopt a second child. Although they
> want to continue their arrangement, Darren and David want to
> make some changes. They write down those changes, including
> that they will pay the nanny more, that Darren will chip in a
> larger share of the cost, and that the nanny will spend more time
> providing care in Darren's home than in David's. At the top of
> this document, they write:

"This agreement amends the Sharing Agreement dated _____ between Darren and David. This amendment is hereby incorporated into the original Sharing Agreement."

They both sign the amendment, make copies, and keep it with the original agreement in their files.

Addendum. An addendum is something you add to a contract when it is made. You might use an addendum if you are using a standard contract and want to add a provision that isn't included, or if you want to attach lengthy material but don't want to put in the contract itself.

> EXAMPLE: Darren and David have a long list of things they've agreed upon in terms of how care is provided to their children—foods the children can and can't eat, limits on television watching while the nanny is there, and the like. They put a reference to the addendum in the agreement, and then make a document that begins: *"The following information is a part of the Sharing Agreement Contract dated _____ between Darren and David,"* and list the rules for care.

Attachment. An attachment is something that doesn't change the terms of the contract, but contains a list, schedule, or visual representation. A membership list or a schedule for use of an item can be attached to the agreement, with a provision in the agreement that says the attachment can be changed and that, if the new attachment is signed (or even initialed) by all the parties to the agreement, it becomes part of the original agreement.

> EXAMPLE: Darren and David have a list of information about their kids with things like allergies, doctors' contact information, and their current favorite games. They expect this list to change as the kids grow, so they make it an attachment that can easily be replaced when facts change.

Getting Legal Assistance

Most of us share all the time, and we rarely need advice from a lawyer. You'll definitely be able to write your own simple agreements. You can even handle somewhat complicated sharing agreements yourself, using the material we provide in this book. However, this book can't fully prepare you to write every type of sharing contract on your own. If you need help from a lawyer, here are some good ways to find one:

- **Personal referrals.** If you know any lawyers, start by asking them for referrals to the type of lawyers you need. Most lawyers specialize in one area of the law, so unless your friend is an expert in the field you need, you're better off getting a referral from that person to a specialist. If you don't know any lawyers, maybe someone you know—a friend or family member—knows a lawyer or has used one in the past. A personal referral is often a good way to find a lawyer, but make sure you interview the lawyer yourself before signing on. It's important that you feel comfortable with the lawyer's skills and demeanor.

- **Lawyer directories.** There are a number of lawyer directories available on the Internet. Nolo's Lawyer Directory, at http://lawyers.nolo.com, offers comprehensive profiles of the lawyers who advertise there, including each attorney's education, background, areas of expertise, and philosophy. Other lawyer directories include www.findlaw.com, www.avvo.com, and www.martindale.com. These allow you to search by geographical area and specialty, but often provide limited information in their listings. Many attorneys also have websites that can be a rich source of information.

- **Lawyer referral services.** Many local bar associations operate lawyer referral services, which do some of the searching for you, but leave you with less choice about the lawyer you connect with. Also, bar associations do very little screening of the attorneys on their lists, so a lawyer's experience level can be a hit-or-miss proposition.

Interview the lawyer before you agree to hire him or her. Once you decide to hire someone, get a clear written agreement about the work the lawyer will do and how much you will pay.

If you'd like to do some legal research on your own, pick up a copy of *Legal Research: How to Find & Understand the Law,* by Stephen Elias and Susan Levinkind (Nolo). It explains how to look up statutes, cases, and regulations, and how to make sense of what you find.

Part II:
Sharing Solutions

Sharing Housing

S hared housing might sound like a big step—and in many ways, it is. At the same time, it's something all of us have done, for much of our lives. When you think about it, sharing living space—with parents and siblings in our childhood home, cabin mates at camp, roommates at school and beyond, and partners, spouses, and our own children later—is the rule rather than the exception.

And for good reason: Sharing a home is economical, sustainable, convenient, and just plain fun. We can benefit from shared housing in countless ways:

- **Shared housing saves money.** Whether you co-own a house, live in a cohousing complex, or share a group house, you share more than the rent or mortgage. You may share the cost of utilities, maintenance, insurance, landscaping, property taxes, and major repairs. Shared housing also makes it easier to share services (such as childcare) and material things that most households own alone, such as laundry facilities or a tools. It also allows for volume discounts through bulk buying.

- **Shared housing is a gateway to homeownership.** Splitting the cost can make homeownership a real possibility for people who couldn't otherwise afford a large down payment.

- **Shared housing can get you more for your money.** When you share housing, you can also share the cost of amenities that you couldn't afford on your own, such as a hot tub, swimming pool, or large yard.

- **Shared housing helps seniors and people with disabilities.** The interdependence that comes with shared housing can ultimately bring a great deal of independence. Shared housing reduces the cost of living and allows residents to share the cost of in-home care and other services.

- **Shared housing creates community.** Shared housing brings all the benefits of having more people around. For single parents, shared housing can provide added support. For only children, there are playmates. For the elderly or people with disabilities, there is less isolation.

- **Shared housing facilitates convenience.** In shared housing, there's probably someone who can lend you that missing ingredient for your dinner, let you in when you are locked out, or provide one of those teeny-tiny screw drivers when your sunglasses break.

- **Shared housing saves the planet, affordably.** Three-fourths of the lumber consumed in the United States goes into homebuilding. The construction of new housing also causes suburban sprawl and takes over former wetlands, deserts, and forests. Once built, a house continues to tax the planet through energy costs and material use. When we share, we use less energy and less stuff, and we can better afford sustainable materials and energy sources, such as solar panels, better insulation, or a grey water system.

There are countless ways to arrange shared housing, each involving a different degree of sharing. Shared housing usually includes a combination of private and common spaces. People may share a single dwelling unit or share common spaces bordered by multiple units. Some shared housing also entails cooperative activities, such as mealsharing, and the sharing of household goods and services.

What's a Dwelling Unit?

By "dwelling unit," we mean a living space that includes at least one sleeping/living area, one kitchen, and one bathroom. A dwelling unit may also include other amenities—a dining room, multiple bedrooms, a living room—but, in essence, a dwelling unit is comprised of the basic necessities that a household requires to live independently.

Identify Your Housing Needs

Choosing a form of shared housing has much to do with your wants, needs, and resources. Some factors to consider include:

- How much personal space do you need? Do you want your own unit?
- Do you want to own property or rent?

- Would you prefer to form a new shared housing arrangement or join an existing one?
- Will you move into existing structures, retrofit to accommodate shared housing, or build new housing?
- Do you want to create a community of people with shared interests or needs, such as senior housing?

The worksheet below will help you identify the issues most important to you. You can share this worksheet with the people you plan to live with. It can help you get to know each other, determine your compatibility, and choose a housing arrangement.

Legal Issues to Consider When Sharing a Home

When you buy or lease a home with others, you're not just entering into a living arrangement: You're entering a legal relationship as well. How you own a home together determines how you can get financing, what your rights and responsibilities are, how and to whom you can each sell or leave your share of the property, and more.

Your legal relationship won't extend only to the people with whom you share housing. When you lease a home, for example, you'll have legal obligations not only to each other, but also to your landlord. If you live in a planned community (for example, a condominium or cohousing complex), you'll have to follow its rules and restrictions. You'll also have to follow the zoning laws and building codes of your local government.

Ways of Owning Shared Housing

There are a number of ways to own real estate in shared housing arrangements. Here, we provide a brief overview of the most common arrangements for different types of shared housing, to help you start thinking about how you'll own and finance your shared home.

Worksheet: Rate Your Housing Priorities

Rate each of the following priorities by circling a number
(1 = least important; 5 = most important).

The Space:

1 2 3 4 5 I would like to have my own unit.

1 2 3 4 5 I would prefer my own bathroom.

1 2 3 4 5 I would like to have a large kitchen.

1 2 3 4 5 I would like access to a yard.

1 2 3 4 5 I would like to be able to garden.

1 2 3 4 5 I would like on-site laundry facilities.

1 2 3 4 5 I would like on-site parking.

1 2 3 4 5 I would like a large storage space.

1 2 3 4 5 I would like other amenities, such as (*a hot tub,*
_____ *swimming pool, etc.* _____)

Material Needs and Long Range Plans:

1 2 3 4 5 I would like to own my residence and build equity.

1 2 3 4 5 I prefer to rent my residence.

1 2 3 4 5 I hope to save money from this arrangement.

1 2 3 4 5 I am looking for a place that I can live in for a long time.

1 2 3 4 5 I am looking for a short-term arrangement.

1 2 3 4 5 I would like to share furnishings.

Furnishings I own and could share include: _____
_____
_____

Furnishings I need or would like to have include: _____
_____
_____

Home Environment, People, and Lifestyle:

1   2   3   4   5   I want to live in a way that is environmentally sustainable.

1   2   3   4   5   I want to feel free to have social events where I live.

1   2   3   4   5   I want to live in a nonsmoking home.

1   2   3   4   5   I would like to have some rules about drug and alcohol use.

1   2   3   4   5   I want to be able to have overnight guests.

1   2   3   4   5   I would like a quiet space (or quiet times).

1   2   3   4   5   I need space to practice trumpet (or other loud activity).

1   2   3   4   5   I want to share housing with someone who can help care for my child/pet.

1   2   3   4   5   I am open to caring for others and/or their children and pets.

1   2   3   4   5   I hope to feel a sense of community with people I live with.

1   2   3   4   5   I want to live with like-minded people. This means:

_____

_____

1   2   3   4   5   I would like to do activities with my cosharers, such as: _____

_____

1   2   3   4   5   I would like to do mealsharing and collective food buying.

Other wants and needs: _____

_____

_____

_____

_____

_____

> **SEE AN EXPERT**
>
> **You'll need a lawyer to draw up the documents.** Because real estate ownership is governed by state and local laws, we can't cover all the legal ins and outs of various ownership arrangements. For this, and to draft and review the necessary legal documents (such as a tenancy-in-common agreement), your group should definitely consult a lawyer.

Tenancy in Common (TIC)

When you own property as tenants in common (TIC), you each own an undivided share. For example, if you own a duplex with another person as tenants in common, you each own a portion of the *whole* building, even though each of you may live in and maintain one of the units. TICs are customarily used when two or more unrelated people own a home together, and are also frequently used in multiunit residential buildings, such as a duplex or triplex.

If you take title to property as a TIC, you and your co-owner(s) will want to draft a written agreement covering each owner's rights and responsibilities. For multiunit property, the TIC agreement gives each owner rights to, and responsibility for, one unit, which creates a feeling of separate ownership. You'll also have to figure out financing. Until recently, owners of TICs usually financed their property with a single mortgage secured by the whole property. This arrangement creates some problems, however: All owners must qualify together for the loan, for example, and all owners are at risk if one gets behind on the mortgage. Although the single-mortgage approach is still used for sharing a single-family home, many lenders now offer fractional mortgages for TIC properties that are easier to divide into separate units. For a fractional mortgage, each owner signs a separate promissory note and deed of trust. Each must qualify for the loan separately and can select different loan terms. Each fractional mortgage is secured only by that owner's interest in the property.

Joint Tenancy

Joint tenancy is a form of ownership that includes a right of survivorship. When one owner dies, that person's share of the property passes automatically to the other owner(s); in contrast, a TIC share goes to the owner's heirs at death. Joint tenancy is most often used by couples and families, but it could also work well for unrelated owners in a small shared housing arrangement who want the security of knowing that their interests in the property will be protected if another owner dies.

Forming a joint tenancy usually requires that all owners have equal interests in the property, and that they acquired title at the same time, on the same title document. Most joint tenancies are financed with a single shared mortgage.

Condominiums

Condominiums are legally divided so that portions of the property can be separately owned. Condominium ownership typically involves owning both an individual unit and a share of ownership in common areas, often called "common elements." Multiunit properties that were not built as condominiums can often be converted to condos; this usually requires the assistance of an attorney and professional surveyor, and the process depends greatly on local laws and regulations.

A condominium form of ownership is often used in housing where residents own separate units. A condominium complex can be as small as a duplex or as large as a multi-story apartment building. Cohousing groups frequently use the condominium form because it facilitates both individual autonomy *and* sharing. Condominiums are much easier to finance than undivided property, such as TICs.

Condominium ownership typically requires membership in a community association that governs and manages the common elements and enforces restrictions on the use of units. These associations collect monthly dues, often called "assessments," from each owner to pay for the costs of upkeep, taxes, insurances, and other expenses.

Housing Cooperatives

In a housing cooperative, residents own shares or a membership in a corporation, which, in turn, owns the entire property, including the individual units. Cooperatives can be formed as for-profit or nonprofit entities. Housing cooperatives are most common in the northeastern United States, but the cooperative form is also used throughout the country to create affordable housing. Because co-ops exist to benefit their owners or members, and there is no landlord seeking to profit from tenants, the cost of living in a cooperative can be kept relatively low.

RESOURCE

Want to know more about the philosophy of cooperatives?
Many modern cooperatives are guided by a core set of values and principles associated with a pioneering cooperative from the 1840s in Rochdale, England. The Rochdale Principles espouse democracy, economic participation, autonomy, and community—goals shared by co-ops formed centuries later. You can find the Rochdale Principles at the website of the International Cooperative Alliance, www.ica.coop.

A resident buys into a housing cooperative by purchasing shares and signing a "proprietary lease" that entitles the resident to occupy a particular residential unit. Unlike typical leases, a proprietary lease has no fixed term. It lasts as long as the resident is an owner in the cooperative and doesn't violate important lease terms. The cooperative corporation typically holds a single blanket mortgage on the property, and resident shareholders sometimes take out loans to finance their purchase of shares in the cooperative. In addition, residents pay regular fees to cover property taxes, management expenses, mortgage payments on the building, and so on.

Even though residents don't own the real estate directly, they still enjoy some of the tax benefits of home ownership. For example, although the corporation makes the mortgage and property tax payments, residents may still deduct their portion of these expenses from their income taxes. If residents take out a loan to purchase shares, however, the loan is usually treated as a personal loan, so the interest isn't deductible.

Cooperatives are typically governed by a board of directors elected by the resident shareholders. The board of directors has the duty to act in the interest of all resident shareholders of the cooperative, and is usually empowered to approve or deny new owners and to respond when members fail to pay dues.

Limited Liability Company (LLC)

In the process of developing shared housing, such as cohousing, many groups form a limited liability company (LLC) that holds title to the property. By forming an LLC, the group becomes a legal entity and can enter into contracts, which allows it to purchase land and partner with developers and contractors. The LLC form of ownership also provides liability protection to individual group members, should anything go wrong during the development process.

When the shared housing project is developed, the LLC transfers title to the land and individual units to the members, usually in the form of a TIC or condominium. Once the project is complete, continuing to hold the land as an LLC creates certain disadvantages to the owners. For example, owning property through an LLC means that owners cannot deduct mortgage interest and property tax payments, and can't claim the $250,000 capital gains tax exclusion if they sell their residence.

Legal Restrictions on Shared Housing

Municipal laws may impose some restrictions on whether and how you may share housing in a particular neighborhood. If you move into a planned community, its rules may also limit your shared housing options.

Zoning Rules

Each city or county has a planning agency that enacts zoning ordinances controlling how particular neighborhoods are used. Typically, planning agencies divide residential neighborhoods into different zones. Some zones allow only single-family homes; other zones allow multiunit dwellings; others allow commercial or light manufacturing activities, and so on. The intent of these laws is to control the atmosphere and quality of neighborhoods and to control population density.

Zoning rules can conflict with shared housing in several ways:

- **Restrictions on number of residents.** Some zoning ordinances limit how many people can live in a home and how many unrelated people can live together. For example, in Cobb County, Georgia, every single-family house must provide at least 390 square feet of living space per adult, and no more than two unrelated people may live in the house.

- **Laws allowing only one "household" per house.** Some zoning laws restrict houses to one "household," usually defined as residents who are related to each other or have shared finances.
- **Restrictions on the number of dwelling units on a parcel.** Zoning ordinances usually define a "dwelling unit" and limit how many units are allowed on a parcel. For example, an ordinance might provide that a dwelling unit contains a kitchen, bathing facilities, and sleeping accommodations. Thus, if you wanted to add a second "kitchenette" to your house to create a separate living space for someone, you might run into zoning hurdles.
- **Limits on building sizes.** Zoning laws often restrict the size of buildings and the number of buildings you can have on each lot, as well as building height and proximity to the property line.
- **Extra requirements for multiunit housing.** Your zoning law might impose additional obligations on multiunit housing, such as requiring a certain number of off-street parking spaces.

To find out how your neighborhood is zoned, look at your city's general plan, ask someone at the planning agency, or check your city's website. If you find a law that could pose a barrier to your sharing arrangement, don't despair. You may be able get a special permit or request an exception to the zoning rules (called a "variance"). Although the application process varies, you'll probably have better luck if you get the support of your neighbors. Often, the planning agency's biggest concern is whether your plan will adversely affect the neighborhood's character, livability, or development.

Building Codes

When you share housing, and particularly if you remodel, you may have to comply with building codes. Generally, residential buildings with multiple units have stricter safety and access requirements than single-family homes. For example, multifamily housing may require increased fire safety mechanisms, such as sprinklers and access roads, and swimming pools in multifamily housing are more carefully inspected and regulated than pools at private homes. Sometimes, stricter building codes are triggered when you expand your home. For example, in Marin County, California, homes that expand to more than 4,000 square feet must fill out a green building checklist and get a certain number of "green points" to pass inspection.

Building laws vary from city to city, but most derive from a uniform set of laws. If you are building a shared housing project from the ground up, your contractor and architect should know the rules.

Contractual Restrictions

In addition to legal restrictions, you should also check for privately imposed restrictions on your home, in a lease or the written rules for a planned community.

Leases and Rental Agreements

If you decide to rent shared housing, your state and local laws will determine many of your rights and obligations vis-à-vis each other and your landlord, from how much a landlord can charge as a security deposit, to when and why a landlord can enter your home, to what happens if one of you doesn't pay your share of the rent. (You can find detailed information on these rights—including state-specific information on a variety of topics—in *Every Tenant's Legal Guide*, by Janet Portman and Marcia Stewart (Nolo).)

Your lease or rental agreement will also establish the rules of your relationship to the landlord—such as how much rent you must pay, whether you can have pets, and how the tenancy can be ended. Certain lease provisions could prevent you from sharing rental housing as you'd like. For example, a lease might limit how many people can live in the house or prohibit subletting.

Planned Community Restrictions

Common interest developments (CIDs) are planned communities comprised of individually owned houses or condominiums, along with commonly owned areas, such as streets, a swimming pool, or a golf course. By some estimates, 25% of people in the United States live in such communities.

When these communities are created, a set of covenants, conditions, and restrictions ("CC&Rs") are developed, which residents must follow. The intent of the rules is, in part, to preserve the character of the community and protect property values for all owners. Typically, a property owners association has the right to make more rules and enforce them. Even when you own your home, you could still be subject to use restrictions that could limit your shared housing options, such as rules about how many people can live in a home and whether and how houses may be remodeled.

Solution 1: The Co-Owned House

For many, owning a home is a hallmark of financial success and stability. At the same time, taking the leap from renting to owning can be expensive. Not only will you have to come up with the down payment, but you'll also have to pay expenses like insurance, property taxes, home repairs and maintenance, and utilities. It can be a hard leap to take alone, which is why some people choose to buy a home with someone else.

Here are some people we know of who came together to buy a house:

- **Two young couples,** all just starting careers, agreed to share a three-bedroom, two bathroom house.
- **Two single moms** paired up to share not only the costs and responsibilities of homeownership, but also childcare and meals.
- **Two friends** became co-owners shortly after one bought a home on her own and then lost her job. Rather than risk foreclosure, she asked her friend to move in with her and take over the mortgage payments in exchange for a share of ownership that would increase over time.
- **Two brothers and a friend** realized they could save a lot by moving out of their apartments and buying a small three-bedroom house together. One brother couldn't afford much of a down payment, but made up for it by doing work on the house.
- **Four unrelated older adults** bought a house together to cut their expenses, share household responsibilities, reduce their living space, and create a supportive community while they age.

- **A woman and her parents** bought a house for the daughter to live in; the parents made the down payment and their daughter pays the mortgage and other expenses.

Buying a house is a big decision; sharing ownership of a house with someone else brings additional considerations into play. In addition to reviewing and discussing the questions for any sharing arrangement from Chapter 3, you must make decisions about how you will own and finance the house, share the space, and handle expenses.

Typically, two or three people who buy a single-family home together take title as tenants in common, or sometimes as joint tenants. (See "Ways of Owning Shared Housing," above, for more information.) A larger group of buyers might form a cooperative or LLC; for a small group, however, this rarely makes sense. In this section, we assume you'll own your home as tenants in common or joint tenants.

Buying the House

If you plan to buy a house with someone else, you might go house hunting and buy a house together. But this isn't your only option; if one of you already owns a home, the other might buy an ownership share of that home. For example:

- The new owner can pay the original owner a lump sum to assume a percentage ownership in the equity (the value of the home less what the owner owes on it), and the co-owners will share mortgage payments in the same percentage. For example, Jackie has $100,000 of equity in her home. Tom pays her $40,000 in a lump sum, then pays 40% of the mortgage payments going forward, to own 40% of the house.
- The new owner can start making all or part of the monthly mortgage payments, thereby acquiring ownership gradually. Here's an example using some round numbers. Jamaal bought a house for $250,000, on which he made a $50,000 down payment and paid off $50,000 of the $200,000 mortgage, leaving $150,000 to be paid. Because the current market value of the house is about $300,000, he has about $150,000 of equity in the home. He quits his job to start a business, and needs to reduce

his monthly expenses. He offers to let his friend Merritt move in to the back part of the house and take over the $1,500 monthly mortgage payments. Merritt's ownership in the home will grow by 0.5% with every mortgage payment she makes. They agree that Merritt will own half the home if she makes all mortgage payments for 100 months.

No matter how you decide to let the new owner buy in, make sure you add his or her name to the deed at the outset. You'll also need a clear written agreement about ownership shares and how you will divide payments and responsibility for the house.

Determining Ownership Percentages

When you purchase a house with someone, you can use a handful of different criteria to decide who will own how much of the house. One simple method is to allot ownership based on the amount of the purchase price each person paid, no matter how much of the property each person uses. For example, if Peggy and Bill buy a house together, they might agree that Peggy will own 60% and Bill will own 40%, because that is how much each of them can afford to chip in for the down payment and mortgage.

Sometimes, ownership shares change gradually as the owners take on more or less financial responsibility for the home. For example, one person might start paying a larger share of the mortgage or agree to underwrite significant improvements on the property. In this situation, the owners might decide to change their ownership percentages to reflect that one is paying more.

Owners who will divide use of the house unequally might base ownership percentages on the value of the area that each owner occupies.

EXAMPLE: Caroline and Julia buy a three-bedroom house together. They agree that Caroline will use a small bedroom and bathroom. Julia will use the master bedroom and bath, plus the third bedroom as a home office. Julia will also use the garage for parking; Caroline doesn't own a car. They will share the living room and kitchen. In this scenario, clearly Julia is getting more space out of the deal. If an appraiser determines that the space allotted to Julia is worth $350,000, while the space allotted to Caroline is worth only $150,000, they might decide that Julia will pay for—and own—70% of the house and Caroline will pay for and own the remaining 30%, in direct proportion to how they will use the property.

Caroline and Julia might also decide to simply split the ownership and mortgage payments 50/50, even though Caroline occupies a smaller area. Caroline will still benefit from the real estate investment, because she'll be entitled to half of the profit when they sell the house. They could make up for the unequal use of the house in other ways, such as by giving Julia full responsibility for all yard care and having her pay a larger portion of the property taxes and utilities.

Financing Options

If you purchase a single-family home, you and your co-owner will likely have to take out one mortgage loan. As discussed above, fractional financing is difficult to obtain for a shared single-family house.

When you sign a mortgage with someone else, you become "jointly and severally liable" for the mortgage, which means that both of you are liable for the full amount. If one owner doesn't pay, the other will have to pick up the slack to avoid a delinquency on the account, penalties, or even foreclosure. Before signing on to a shared mortgage, you and your co-owner should have a serious talk about your financial situations and how you'll handle it if one owner can't keep up with the payments. You might decide that one owner can make the other owner's missed payments and either be reimbursed or obtain a higher percentage of ownership in exchange. Of course, the best way to avoid problems is to buy a house in your price range, make sure both of you can comfortably afford the mortgage and other expenses, and create an emergency fund (or get insurance) for unexpected events like a job layoff or medical problem.

What is Equity Sharing?

In an equity sharing arrangement, home ownership is shared, but not all owners live in the home. For example, Diane and Teo buy a house together for $200,000. Diane will live in the house, but Teo will not; he is looking for a real estate investment. Teo makes a $30,000 down payment and Diane takes out a mortgage for the remaining $170,000, for which she will make the entire monthly payment. When they purchased the house, Diane and Teo made an agreement to end their arrangement in five years, at which time either they will sell the house or Diane will buy Teo's share by refinancing. They agreed that Teo would be entitled to the $30,000 he paid, plus half of the remaining equity.In this way, Teo earns a return on his investment, and Diane can use her earnings to finance the purchase of an entire house.

There are many ways to arrange an equity share, but the example above is fairly typical. Equity sharing works best when the buyers are family members, such as parents who make a down payment on a house for their grown child. This helps ensure that the buyers have a common interest. Otherwise, an investor who is motivated solely by profit might want to sell out when the market is ripe, which could put the resident homeowner in a tough spot. Likewise, a resident who wants to sell and move out puts the investor in a tough spot of having to find a new partial owner. That's why mom and pop are your best co-investors. Their goal is likely the same as yours: to give you a home.

You should also think about how you'll make mortgage payments if one of you dies. One strategy is to take out life insurance policies on each other, so that if one owner dies, the other will be able to keep up the payments.

There are many ways to divide your responsibility for financing. This is one of the wonderful things about sharing: You can agree to handle things in whatever way suits your needs best. Although you will be jointly and severally liable for the mortgage, you might decide that one of you will pay a larger share to reflect ownership of a larger percentage of the house, to reflect use of more of the shared space, or simply because that person can afford to pay more. Also, you don't have to split your down payment and ongoing mortgage payments the same way. For example, Alice might have significant savings but a low monthly income. Linda might have very little savings, but a high paying job. In this situation, Alice could pay 75% of the down payment but assume a smaller portion of the mortgage payments.

No matter how you approach equity sharing, you'll need a lawyer to draft an agreement for you. The agreement will dictate how and when you sell the house, what happens if one owner wants out of the arrangement early, how one owner can buy out another, and how to share profits. For more information about equity sharing, see www. homeequityshare.com.

Sharing Expenses

Owning a home comes with a lot of expenses renters don't need to pay, such as property taxes, repairs and maintenance, higher insurance costs, and often higher utility payments. Like your mortgage payments, down payment, and ownership percentage, you can share these expenses in any way that works for everyone. You might decide to split everything right down the middle or come up with another system of dividing expenses, based on ownership percentages, use of the property, financial status of the owners, or any other factors that make sense for you.

> EXAMPLE: Jeri and Camila own a house together, with 75% and 25% ownership, respectively, but they share use of the house fairly equally. They split most day-to-day expenses, such as utilities, phone, water, and small repairs. Any major improvements on the house they divide according to their ownership percentage. For insurance and property taxes, Jeri pays 60% and Camila 40%. This division was based not on a careful calculation, but on a desire to even out the expenses and benefits of homeownership. Because they use the house equally, they felt that it would be unfair for Jeri to pay 75% of these expenses, but also unfair to split them when Jeri will benefit much more from an eventual sale of the house. The 60/40 split just seemed more equitable.

Sharing the Space

Unlike sharing a duplex, sharing a single-family home means that you will be using the same space. It's important to talk about who has a right to use particular rooms, storage areas, parking spaces, and so on, and in what ways. Does one of you want to use the garage as an art studio? Turn the yard into a dog run? Have a party every weekend to watch football games on a big-screen television? These are all things you should air in advance. You should also talk about whether you can have overnight visitors or long-term guests, or sublet your share of the space.

Sharing living space can sometimes lead to disagreements and frustrations. One of the best ways to avoid problems is to start with a home that's easy to share. An easily shared house means one that creates a feeling of separate space for each sharer, whether through layout, size, soundproofing, or other features, and has enough room for sharers to enjoy common spaces together. Here are some of the qualities that make a house shareable:

- a layout that gives the feel of semi-private entrances, or at least doesn't require one person to enter the house too close to the other person's private space
- at least two full bathrooms
- no unnecessary noise, whether from poor soundproofing, creaky floors and doors, or common spaces that are too close to the bedrooms
- enough room for all of the cooks to use the kitchen at once, and
- adequate closets, storage space, and parking areas.

Your Co-Ownership or TIC Agreement

You absolutely must put your co-ownership plans in writing. If you don't have a written agreement and a problem develops that you can't resolve on your own, a court might wind up making important decisions for you, or even ordering the property sold. Because the legal requirements for TIC agreements vary by state—and because your shared home represents a big economic and emotional investment—you should hire a lawyer to help you prepare an agreement that meets your needs.

Here are the topics your TIC agreement should cover:
- Who will buy the house?
- When will the owners buy the house?
- How will owners take title?
- What are the ownership percentages?
- What is the purchase cost?
- How will the down payment be divided?
- How will the mortgage payments be divided?
- What happens if one person is unable to make mortgage payments?
- What if one owner wants to refinance or borrow against equity?
- How will other costs be divided (taxes, insurance, utilities, maintenance), and what happens if someone can't pay?
- Who gets to use what part(s) of the house?
- What are each owner's responsibilities for upkeep, maintenance, and cleaning?
- What about subletting and guests?
- What if one owner wants to leave? Will the other owner have a right to buy that person's share before it's offered to someone else? How will you determine the value of that owner's share for purposes of the buyout?
- What if both owners decide to end the arrangement? Who has the right to buy the other out?
- How will costs and profits be divided if the house is sold?
- What happens if one owner dies?
- How will the owners resolve disputes?

Solution 2: The Retrofit House

If you're ready to get creative and make more space for sharing, you can remodel an existing house to fit more than one household. One disadvantage of sharing a single-family house is that the space was designed with one household in mind. But what if you could remodel a house to have two entrances and living spaces, plus a shared kitchen, deck, and garage? Or what if you'd like to build an addition to your

Two Households Join Forces and Resources

Regina and Joel, a young couple with a child, wanted a long-term living arrangement. They loved where they lived—Bonny Doon, a tiny town in the Santa Cruz Mountains—but the cost of housing there is high, and they wanted to own, not rent, a home. They began house-sitting occasionally for Jane, who owned a home in Bonny Doon. Jane lived with her dogs and traveled often; although she sometimes felt isolated living by herself, she loved her home in the woods.

As Jane got to know Regina and Joel, she found that they were pleasant, respectful of Jane and her home, and generally good-natured and trustworthy people. When she heard of their difficulty in finding affordable property, she proposed a radical solution: building a home on her land.

The idea of a separate house was thwarted by a local zoning ordinance that allowed only one house per property. Instead, they built an addition to Jane's home that created a feeling of two separate homes, with a shared kitchen in the middle. They also share a hot tub, laundry facilities, and tools and kitchen items, as well as shopping trips, spurred by the fact that their home is a 30-minute drive from the nearest grocery store. There is an ongoing shopping tab posted in the kitchen that tracks what each has spent on the other's groceries.

The arrangement works because everyone benefits: Regina and Joel have a beautiful home at an affordable price, and occasional help with childcare. Jane has more company, fewer expenses, and occasional dog care. Everyone understands that they are benefiting in different ways, and thus don't always expect all things to even out. Jane gave us a great tip, which we think applies well to any sharing arrangement: "As soon as you develop an attitude of 'he never [*takes out the trash*] and she always [*eats my bananas*],' then you are headed down a bad road." Jane says that an attitude of generosity is the most important ingredient of successful sharing.

house so that your mother-in-law can move in but live somewhat independently from you?

There are plenty of ways to outfit existing spaces for shared housing, and there are lots of types of spaces to work with. We've all seen large developments filled with 5,000-square-foot "McMansions" with half a dozen bedrooms and bathrooms and "Garage-Mahals" with space for a fleet of vehicles. The average house size has more than doubled since the 1950s, from just under 1,000 square feet in 1950 to roughly 2,500 square feet in 2008. And there are fewer people sharing that extra square footage: The average number of people living in a house has decreased from 3.7 to 2.6 since 1940. But recently, the growth in home size has finally leveled off. City and county governments are imposing restrictions to discourage huge home developments, and people are learning that they just don't need that much space. This leaves plenty of houses with enough space to accommodate two households; they just need some reconfiguring.

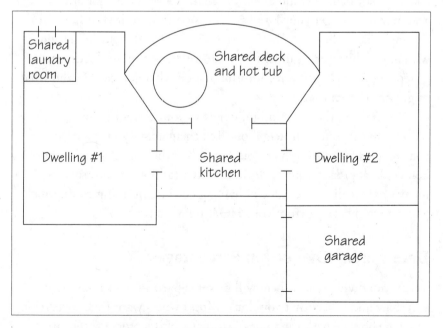

Solution #2: The Retrofit House

Building and Zoning Issues

Almost any time you change the structure of your house, you'll need a permit from the building department. If you are expanding your house beyond a certain size, stricter building code requirements might apply.

You'll have to make sure your changes meet applicable zoning requirements for setbacks, house-to-lot size ratios, egress (emergency exits), and so on. For example, a "setback" requirement might require at least ten feet between your home and the street or neighboring lot, which could prevent you from expanding your home too far into your front or back yard. If the changes you want to make don't meet the zoning requirements, you might need to request a variance.

Homeowners Associations

If you want to retrofit a house in a planned development, you may be subject to restrictions imposed by a homeowners association (HOA). HOAs often regulate architectural changes to buildings and any other changes they believe could affect the character of the neighborhood. You may need to get your HOA's permission to retrofit your house for sharing. Check the CC&Rs that were recorded with your home, along with any architectural guidelines, HOA rules, and other documents governing your property, for information on what you can do and what might not pass muster.

If you think the HOA might object to your retrofit plans, try to build support from your neighbors. Tell them about your plans and your reasons for sharing; you could even buy them a copy of this book. You could approach your HOA in a similar fashion. As our society increasingly realizes the value of living green and building community, you may find barriers from your HOA are not a problem.

Determining Ownership Percentages

When you divide space, there will be some parts of your house that you share and others that you don't. Most owners want their ownership share to correlate with the value of the parts of the property they use. But determining ownership percentages this way can get tricky, because it means assigning value to separate parts of the house. This requires a highly specialized appraisal. Sometimes, co-owners hire two independent appraisers to make sure they're working from accurate figures. Once you average the appraisers' figures for each share, you can add them together and calculate each sharer's percentage of the total to come up with your ownership percentages, which you can then use to determine how much of the down payment you will each make, how much of the monthly payments and expenses you each will pay, and so on.

When you retrofit and partially divide a house, you are more likely to be able to sell the shares separately than if you were sharing a standard single-family home. If you sell each share separately, the total value may exceed the value of the undivided property. Thus, an appraiser would value each unit as if it were being sold separately. You would then add together the combined values, calculate their relative percentage of their total value, and use that to determine ownership percentages.

Financing Options

As with sharing a regular single-family home, you and your sharing partners will likely also have to share a mortgage. Even though you have created a somewhat divided space, banks will probably be hesitant to provide you with fractional financing. (See "Financing Options" under Solution 1, above.)

Because a partially divided house is more likely to be sold in shares than an undivided house, owners should think in advance about how a partial sale will affect financing. Having a single mortgage means that if one owner wants to sell, the entire property may have to be refinanced. One way to avoid this is to shop for a mortgage that is assumable. This means that the new owner could simply assume the selling owner's portion of the mortgage, and the remaining owner will not have to refinance.

If You Sell the House

When you plan your retrofit housing share, you should consider what you'll do if one of you wants to sell. For co-owners who share some overlapping space, it may not be easy to find a buyer for only one owner's share. If one owner finds a buyer and sells, the other owner may end up sharing a kitchen or other parts of the house with strangers, which is probably not what you envision. Here are some solutions for you and your co-owners to consider:

- Agree that all of you will live in the house for a certain number of years and then sell the entire house or make a new agreement for another period of time. If you go this route, you should also have a backup plan in case someone needs to leave sooner or wants to stay longer.
- Agree on a predetermined price (or a formula to calculate it) for which one owner can buy the other out.
- Give each owner the first right to buy the other's share if the other wants to sell.
- If one owner plans to sell, give the other six months to search for a new co-owner to buy the departing owner's share. You can also come up with a predetermined amount or formula to calculate what the share will cost.

If one owner wants to sell just that owner's share, the price could be determined by the market. However, if you sell the whole property at once, you will need to agree on how you will determine what percentage of the sales price each owner will receive. Even if you've come up with ownership percentages based on an appraisal of the property each owner is using, you may want to reappraise each portion of the property again prior to sale, especially if one owner has spent a lot of money on improvements.

> **EXAMPLE:** Bill and Paul bought a house with two separate living spaces and a shared kitchen and dining room. An appraiser determined that Bill's larger space was worth $300,000 and Paul's smaller space was worth $200,000. Based on those percentages, they divide the purchase costs and expenses 60/40. Ten years later, they sell the entire house. Rather than divide the proceeds 60/40, they had their portions re-appraised. The appraiser determined that each portion was worth $400,000. Paul's share had doubled in value because he had built a back

porch with a hot tub, installed beautiful interior cabinetry and bamboo floors, and made other improvements. Bill's unit had fallen into some disrepair, but still appreciated in value. Based on the appraisal, they split the sale proceeds down the middle to reward Paul for his work on the house.

Solution 3: The Group Rental House

Sharing a group rental can be an attractive option for single adults, single parents, students, and anyone trying to economize on space and living costs. The monthly rent in a group house is usually just a fraction of what you'd pay for your own apartment. And, you can economize further—and build community—by sharing chores, meals, outdoor space, household items, social events, and more.

Some of the issues you'll need to discuss and decide with your renters' group will be the same as for a group that will share an owned home, such as how to divide space and expenses. And, you should review the questions in Chapter 3, as you would for any sharing arrangement. This section details issues of special concern to renters.

Agreements Among the Tenants and With the Landlord

A group that will share a rental should have two written agreements: (1) an agreement among the renters (for example, a cotenant agreement or housemate agreement) and (2) an agreement between the renters and the landlord (the lease or rental agreement).

A renters' group will likely want to control how it runs the house, so it might want to negotiate for certain responsibilities that would otherwise be retained by the landlord to be delegated to the group. For example, the group may want to be responsible for recruiting new housemates, collecting security deposits, and making certain improvements on the property (such as landscaping). If the landlord is willing to allow one tenant to be the "master tenant," who has the right to sublease to others, your group can retain more control; however, the master tenant will be solely responsible for paying rent and meeting the other lease obligations.

Signing a group lease makes all tenants "jointly and severally liable" for rent and other lease provisions. If one person can't pay rent or leaves, the others are responsible for making up the lost rent money. This is why it's so important to have a clear written agreement among the tenants about how the house will operate.

The tenants should agree among themselves, in writing, about the following:

- who will use what parts of the house
- how to divide chores and responsibilities
- how to make group decisions
- when and how to meet to discuss household concerns
- how much rent each person will pay
- how to divide expenses such as utilities
- procedures for collecting rent and expense money and paying bills
- what happens if a tenant can't pay
- when a tenant can be asked to leave and what process the group will use in this situation
- how much notice a tenant should give before moving out
- whether departing tenants are responsible for finding a replacement
- whether to carry renters insurance
- policies about overnight guests, pets, and so on, and
- how to bring in new housemates (for example, will the group use an application; try to maintain some balance of gender, age, or race; or give preference to friends or family members).

Agreement With the Landlord

The landlord will probably present your renters' group with a standard lease or rental agreement that includes at least the following terms:

- the total rent for the property, as well as how and when the rent must be paid (and any late fee the landlord will charge)

- the term of the lease or rental agreement and how it can be terminated
- which expenses the landlord will pay and which the tenants will pay
- the security deposit
- how repairs and maintenance will be handled, and
- rules about pets.

The lease or rental agreement will probably also include terms about who may occupy the property and what happens when a tenant leaves. This is where your group may need to do some negotiating with the landlord. Ordinarily, the landlord will want to list all tenants who will live in the house, by name, and expressly prohibit anyone who isn't in the written agreement from living there. The reason for this is to protect the landlord's investment: Not knowing who's living in the house means the landlord can't screen tenants to make sure the people in the house take good care of the property and are able to pay their rent. Even though all of the tenants are equally liable to the landlord, a sensible landlord would rather have money in the bank and well-cared-for property than a right to sue after something goes wrong.

This means a few things for renter groups that want to decide who they will live with: You will have to come up with some way for the landlord to approve new tenants, for new tenants to be added to the lease (and former tenants to be removed), and for the security deposit to be equitably apportioned among you. Of course, your landlord will have to approve whatever you propose.

- **Choosing new tenants.** When a tenant leaves, you will undoubtedly want to decide who moves in with you. And your landlord will likely want to make sure whoever moves in will be a good tenant. A good solution is to propose that your group find prospective new tenants, subject to the landlord's veto. This makes things easy on the landlord and protects everyone's interests. The landlord may ask prospective tenants to submit certain information to make screening easier, such as a credit report or references. As long as your landlord is reasonable, this arrangement should work well for everyone: After all, neither you nor the landlord wants a new tenant who won't pay the rent or take care of your home.

- **Changing tenants on the lease.** It's in the interest of both your group and the landlord that the lease or rental agreement accurately reflects the tenants who are living in the house at any time. The agreement is a contract, and whoever is named in it is responsible for carrying it out. If you don't keep it up to date, a former tenant who is still named in the lease could be legally liable for damage to the house long after moving out; likewise, the landlord might have no legal recourse against the people actually living in the house who caused the damage. To change tenants on paper, you'll need a couple of agreements: one between the former tenant and the landlord, releasing the former tenant from the lease or rental agreement, and one between the new tenant and the landlord, adding the new tenant to the contract.

- **Handling security deposits.** If you'll have tenants moving in and out, your landlord doesn't want to be bothered with inspecting the property every time, handing over some portion of the deposit to the departing tenant, then collecting that portion from the new tenant. Instead, the landlord will want to charge a security deposit when your group first moves in, then inspect the property and give the deposit back, less any amount withheld for damage to the property, when your group moves out. This means your group will have to decide among yourselves how to manage the deposit—and how to make sure departing tenants pay for any damage they've caused.

Handling Expenses, Security Deposits, and Rent Payments

Both the renter group and the landlord will probably feel at greater ease if the group opens a joint bank account. It shows the landlord that you are organized about your finances and take seriously your responsibilities as a group, and it is convenient because the landlord must process only one rent check per month. The group bank account also allows you to simplify and centralize payment of expenses. You might want to use the account to build a reserve fund for unforeseen expenses, too.

Rent

Deciding how much rent each person pays can sometimes be contentious. What if a house has four big sunny bedrooms and a cave-like bedroom in the basement? Should the person who lives in the cave pay less rent? In some group houses, tenants pay equal rent but allow people to move into nicer rooms as they gain seniority and others move out. How much rent should a couple who share a room pay? And what if one tenant uses a larger or smaller share of the common space than the others— for example, if one tenant uses the whole garage, sets up a desk and computer in the living room, or spends very little time in the house?

Sharing Expenses

In group houses, it often makes sense to share expenses beyond rent and utilities. Some group houses pool resources to buy dry goods, household supplies, food, and appliances. You can track expenses and divvy them up every month, but that might mean a lot of time in front of a calculator. You can simplify expense sharing by estimating monthly expenses and creating a household budget. Each housemate then pays a fixed amount into the group account each month, from which you pay expenses.

Some tricky questions may come up with regard to sharing expenses for things you use unequally. For example, what if most of your housemates use cell phones and only a few share the landline? What if some of you eat most of your meals out? You'll probably have to discuss and work out issues like these after you've lived together for a while and have a sense of each other's habits. And note that the most common advice we hear from people who share housing is this: It works better to overlook minor inequalities, and try not to nickel and dime each other for household expenses. A spirit of trust and generosity is likely the most valuable asset in your household.

Ten Tips for Staying Organized in Shared Housing

1. Keep a calendar on the wall to write down when there will be events and visitors at the house, shared meals, house repair appointments, work days, special trash pickup days, out-of-town trips, and so on.

2. Keep a file box or drawer with all shared bills, as well as a copy of the lease, deed, and/or TIC agreement, and instructions and warranties on all appliances.

3. Open a separate bank account for housing costs and have everyone pay a fixed amount each month. Pay all the bills from this account (and try to build up a reserve fund).

4. Keep a list of who owns what, especially when things are intermingled (in the kitchen, for example). Also keep a list of things that are shared.

5. Keep a pen and paper by the phone for phone messages if residents don't have individual phones.

6. Have a place to sort mail as soon as it comes in.

7. Have a designated space for random junk and clean it out together every three months.

8. Keep bins in the garage or near your garbage cans for thrift store donations, used batteries, broken electronics, and other things that may require special trips to the recycling center or Goodwill.

9. Keep a list of needed food, condiments, and kitchen supplies on the refrigerator, and a running tab of who bought what. Also, keep a pen and stickers near the refrigerator. Make a list or create a space in the fridge of food that is fair game; write suggested "eat-by" dates on things. Cooperate to stock certain condiments. Don't accumulate 15 different salad dressings, for example. Do the same for food cabinets.

10. Consider hiring and paying a housecleaner. Residents in a group house can easily split the cost of hiring someone to clean shared areas—another benefit of shared living. It sounds like a luxury, but it eases tension about differing standards of cleanliness and distribution of chores.

Security Deposits

As mentioned above, your landlord most likely won't want to hassle with changes to the security deposit every time someone moves in or out, so you'll need to come up with your own system. One way to handle it is to have all original tenants pay a share of the initial deposit. A new tenant can pay the departing tenant for the latter's share of the deposit. For this to work, however, your group will have to make sure—typically, by inspecting the property—that the departing tenant deserves the entire deposit share back. Any damage that tenant causes will ultimately be taken out of the group's security deposit, so it's only fair to ask the person who caused it to pay for it.

Insurance

Be sure to think about how you are covered in the event of a loss. It is probably best that both the renters' group and the landlord carry insurance. Usually, the landlord will carry an insurance policy that covers the building and some liability; your renters' insurance will cover your personal property and liability. You may be able to get renters insurance as a group, and it's possible that individuals could get insurance. However, insurance companies sometimes don't want to provide insurance to one renter in a group house unless all renters in the house carry renters' insurance, because a tenant that doesn't have insurance might try to make a claim on someone else's policy.

Solution 4: The Shared Vacation Home

While owning a second home is a luxury that few can afford, 10% of a vacation home might be more in your price range. Through fractional ownership, you can share a home with a larger group of people without actually sharing the space when you go on vacation. Instead, each owner uses the home for a portion of the year.

TIP

Fractionals v. timeshares: Check the fine print. Fractional ownership isn't the same as a timeshare. While timeshares come in many forms, they are typically owned and run by for-profit companies. Rather than having your name on a deed, you sign a contract giving you the right to use vacation property for a certain amount of time. In contrast, if you own part of a fractional vacation property, your name is usually on the deed, and owners exercise more control over the property. Not everyone uses these terms the same way, however. Check the details of any arrangement you're considering very carefully to make sure it offers the rights and protections you want for your shared vacation property.

There are a variety of ways to get into fractional home ownership:
- You could manage the whole process yourself by forming a group of friends, acquaintances, or people you find on the Internet, and buying property together. You can use a website such as www.yours2share.com or even Craigslist to find potential co-owners.
- You could buy a property (or use a property you already own) and sell fractional shares to others. It often helps to have a vacation fractional broker or consultant handle the marketing and sale of the shares. An example of such as service is www.fractionalrealestateconsulting.com.
- You could buy into a vacation fractional or timeshare that has been organized by a private developer or broker. These services are typically based in a particular region of the world. If you do an Internet search for "Fractionals" or "Timeshares" and "Costa Rica," for example, you will likely find a local company that sells fractional vacation homes and timeshares. Also take a look at fractional service websites such as www.dreamslice.com and www.grandshare.com.

TIP

Vacation all over the country. Many timeshare and fractional home ownership programs give you points or credits that you can redeem to use other vacation properties. For example, a timeshare ownership might entitle you to

14 nights per year in vacation properties across the country. With a fractional ownership program, you may own a deeded portion of a property, but that ownership sometimes comes with points you can redeem at other properties in a fractional vacation home network.

Ownership Structure

Fractional vacation homes are typically owned as tenants in common. Every owner's name appears on the deed, along with their respective ownership percentage. Some fractional owners form an intermediate entity, such as an LLC, nonprofit, or for-profit corporation. Rather than owning the property directly, the owners hold shares in the company or a membership in the nonprofit. This limits the group's liability and makes it easier to bring in new owners, but also creates administrative burdens and prevents owners from claiming property tax and mortgage interest deductions. (You'll find more about forming an intermediate ownership entity in Chapter 3.)

Typically, co-owners take out a group mortgage and divide the down payment and monthly payments. However, fractional financing may be available, particularly if your group is relatively small.

Another Vacation Option: Home Swapping

Picture this: You have an apartment in New York City, but dream of exploring the art treasures of Florence, Italy. You find a family from Florence that longs to see the lights of Broadway. You have multiple discussions with them by email, and ultimately swap homes—and perhaps a car, bike, and even ideas for things to do—for a few weeks. Some families we know have even "swapped" friends, babysitters, and more, by hooking their visitors up with people to contact while they're in town. See Appendix A for web resources on home swapping.

Sharing Expenses

It's a good idea to ask every owner to chip in a set amount each month to cover expenses. This is preferable to trying to reckon costs as needed or reconcile bills every month. You can also overestimate costs, which allows the group to build up a reserve fund for major repairs or remodeling. Vacation fractional owners often hire outside management companies to handle scheduling, pay expenses, and do regular cleaning, maintenance, and repairs.

Scheduling and House Rules

Because only one owner uses the home at a time, scheduling is an important issue for a fractional home, particularly if the home is likely to be most popular during one season or time of year (as might be true of a ski cabin or beach house).

Your group can use any system that works for you. A typical scheduling method is to assign certain weeks or months to each owner every year. You can use the same schedule every year—some groups even include these dates in the deed or other recorded real estate document—or you can rotate or otherwise change the dates each year. If you want less formality and more spontaneity, you can simply sign up when you want to use the house, and pay the group based on the number of days you use it. At the end of the year, if the payments exceed the annual costs, then owners divide the surplus. If the amount falls short of the annual costs, each owner chips in extra money to cover the deficit. Of course, this method risks disputes when owners want to use the home at the same time. You could require owners to sign up well in advance, or perhaps rotate the most popular months or weeks, to solve this problem.

Your group should come up with rules about what kinds of alterations can be made on the property, whether there is a fixed decorative scheme, whether pets are allowed, whether there's a limit on the number of guests, and so on.

Resale Issues

Make sure that you can resell your share of a shared vacation home without too many hassles. Some co-owners might want a right of first refusal or even a right to reject a proposed buyer if they can articulate a good reason why.

If you have a shared mortgage on the property, the group may have to refinance if one person sells a share. In some states, selling a share may also mean the property is reassessed for property tax purposes— something your group no doubt wants to avoid.

It can be hard to sell a share of a fractional, which means some owners may eventually feel stuck with a share of a home they no longer use (for example, once their children move out or they hang up their downhill skis for good). To avoid this problem, the group may want to set a future date, in their sharing agreement, when owners who want out can either force a sale of the whole property or require other owners to buy them out at the then-current market price.

Renting the House

One thing to consider before buying into a fractional vacation home is whether you or other owners will be able to rent out the house during the time when it's yours to use. One benefit of fractional ownership, versus individual ownership, is that there is less need to rent out your property. Traditionally, vacation homeowners rent out their property to cover the costs of owning a second home. By dividing the cost of ownership, you can avoid having to rent.

If, however, you want to be able to rent out your fractional share, make sure your agreement allows for it. There will be a number of issues to work out, including how often the house may be rented, how renters will be chosen, how much rent you can charge, what happens if a renter damages the property, and so on. And depending on how many days you rent out the property, there may be some tax implications to consider. (See IRS Publication 527, *Residential Rental Property*, for more information; you can find it at www.irs.gov.)

Regulatory Hurdles

In many states, timeshares and fractionals are subject to approval by a state real estate agency. For example, in California, a vacation home with more than ten owners must be approved by the state Department of Real Estate, to ensure that the property, financing, and agreements between owners are properly arranged. Before buying, your group should talk to an attorney or consultant who can advise you about any regulatory issues that apply in your state.

Also, if your fractional home is primarily an investment vehicle and all owners will share in the rent, the arrangement may be subject to state and federal securities laws. Generally, these laws may apply when ownership shares earn passive income (income from someone else's activities). In this situation, you should consult with an attorney and find out whether you'll have to meet additional legal requirements.

Share Your Couch: The Spread of Hospitality Exchange

Although not an entirely new concept, "hospitality exchange" or "couchsurfing" has recently taken the world by storm. A number of websites (listed in Appendix A) let travelers introduce themselves to people in other parts of the world and arrange to stay in their homes—for free! It's a system that relies on give and take, so travelers are expected to offer a homestay to others once they're back home.

There are more than 750,000 registered members of CouchSurfing, www.couchsurfing.org. Half live in Europe, 30% in North America, and the remaining 20% in nearly every other place on earth, including more than 3,500 in Morocco, more than 500 in Vietnam, and 10 in Papua New Guinea. With a system similar to eBay, CouchSurfers can rate each other and their experiences. Before you crash at a stranger's house, you can read comments that others have posted to make sure the host has provided safe and friendly accommodations. To ensure that people are honest about their identity, the CouchSurfing site also takes their credit card numbers.

> **SEE AN EXPERT**
>
> **Get legal help when purchasing foreign property.** If you want to buy a share of vacation property in another country, you'll need an attorney in that country and one in the United States. Depending on the laws of that country, you may have a difficult time enforcing an ownership agreement and carrying out real estate transactions. One way to solve difficulties with vacation home ownership in other countries is to create an intermediate entity, such as an LLC, in the United States to hold the property. That way, all contracts relating to membership in the LLC are governed by American law, and buying and selling ownership does not involve a real estate transaction in the other country.

Your Fractional Ownership Agreement

It is especially important to have a written agreement to govern fractional ownership. There are likely to be a number of owners who will come and go over the course of the arrangement, and you'll want to ensure that all future owners know the terms of the deal. The documents your group creates will depend on whether you buy into a housing development, whether you create an intermediate entity, and so on.

Solution 5: Cohousing

There are hundreds of cohousing communities in the United States and Canada. Cohousing is often thought of as "cooperative neighborhood," and it typically contains 15 to 30 households, give or take. In cohousing, each household usually owns a complete dwelling unit and shares ownership of extensive common facilities, such as a large commercial-scale kitchen for shared meals, dining and living areas, a guest house, storage for shared household goods, and specialized rooms such as a workshop, music room, hobby room, or kids' play room. Cohousing is typically designed to feel like a neighborhood, focused around common areas and community-oriented outdoor spaces. Residents usually take part in many shared activities, including mealsharing, gardening, game nights, and more.

Shared Housing for Seniors

For seniors, shared housing requires a little interdependence and creates a lot of independence. In many ways, sharing is the new Social Security, because it's a way for communities to come together to meet individual needs. Cohousing or a group house for seniors can create an environment where residents can provide care, or "co-care" for each other. It can facilitate shared purchase of services such as meals-on-wheels, home health care, yard care, home repair, transportation, and so on. Senior cohousing could also include a space for a live-in caretaker to provide care to multiple residents. (For more on sharing care providers, see Chapter 9). Multigenerational shared housing can provide other benefits, such as opportunities to be around young children or to get help from younger, stronger adults.

A handful of communities in the United States were designed specifically as cohousing for seniors. Shared senior housing raises unique questions, such as:

- Should there be age limits or health requirements for new residents?
- How much will the residents be able or willing to do for one another? Help with household chores? Cook for each other when one is sick? What about helping with personal care needs, such as feeding, dressing, or bathing someone who is very ill?
- Under what circumstances should a person leave and move to a home with a higher level of care (if ever)?
- Is there special funding available, such as public or private grants for senior housing?

Characteristics of Cohousing

"Cohousing" is a word brought to the United States in the early 1980s by architects Kathryn McCamant and Charles Durrett, and was inspired by shared housing communities in Denmark. According to McCamant and Durrett, cohousing has these characteristics:

- **Residents participate in community design.** Most cohousing communities are planned, designed, and built by the residents.
- **Intentional neighborhood design.** Although each household has its own space, cohousing intentionally creates community through a centralized design, which often puts parking at the periphery of the properties, and incorporates inviting landscapes and pedestrian pathways.
- **Extensive common facilities.** Residents often share extensive outdoor areas, and a common house that usually has a large kitchen, dining area, and community living space.
- **Complete resident management.** While many condo and apartment complexes are managed by outside companies, cohousing groups manage their own community, typically by forming committees to oversee things like maintenance and repair, landscaping, new resident recruitment, group activities, meals, and environmentally sustainable practices.

Others would add two more defining characteristics to the list:

- **Non-hierarchical structure.** Typically residents make decisions as a group, by consensus (for more on consensus, see Chapter 4). According to cohousing architect and pioneer Charles Durrett, "the single most important attribute in the creation of a cohousing community is a coherent, fair, thoughtful group process."
- **No shared economy.** Cohousing residents have their own jobs and earnings; they don't share income.

Any existing retirement community can adopt many of the sharing mindsets and practices of cohousing communities, and even retrofit buildings to create more shared space. For a wonderful book on forming senior cohousing communities, read *Senior Cohousing: A Community Approach to Independent Living*, by Charles Durrett (Ten Speed Press).

Forming a Cohousing Community

It can take years to form a cohousing community, especially if you are building from the ground up. It's far beyond the scope of this book to describe the process and varieties of cohousing; see Appendix A for resources on creating and joining cohousing communities. Typically, groups follow these basic steps in some form:

- Gather a group of people interested in forming a cohousing community.
- Begin initial planning by meeting, getting to know each other, and discussing hopes, desires, needs, and concerns.
- Form a legal entity, such as an LLC, so your group can sign contracts. (This also ensures member commitment and investment during the planning and building stages.)
- Search for a location; typically, a large, undeveloped piece of land, zoned to allow high-density housing with some open space.
- Consider partnering with a developer that specializes in cohousing, such as Cohousing Partners or Wonderland Hill Development Company. The developer will consult at every stage of the process, and make the development affordable by sharing the investment and risk with your cohousing group.
- Get financing to buy the land and build; this may come from many sources, including future residents, the developer, loans, and grants.
- Purchase land.
- Develop a community design with an architect and contractor.
- Obtain all zoning and building approvals and start building.
- Consult with experts, such as a lawyer, who will help you choose and form an ownership structure (typically, condominiums).
- Recruit additional residents, if necessary.
- Upon completion, each household obtains an individual mortgage and purchases a unit.
- Move in and thrive!

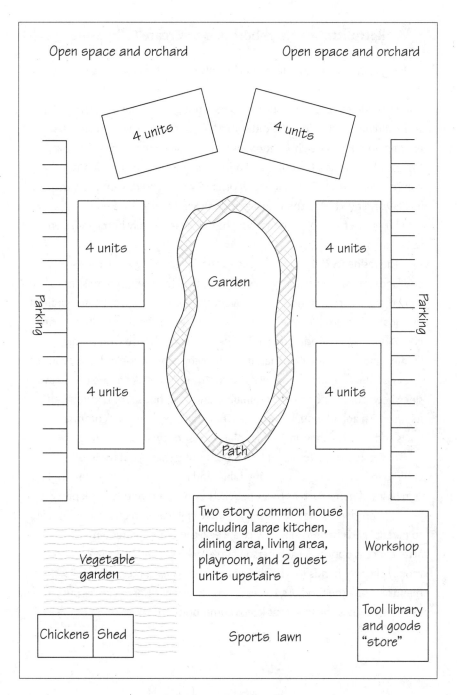

Open space and orchard   Open space and orchard

4 units   4 units

Parking   Parking

4 units   Garden   4 units

4 units   4 units

Path

Two story common house
including large kitchen,
dining area, living area,
playroom, and 2 guest
units upstairs

Workshop

Vegetable
garden

Tool library
and goods
"store"

Chickens | Shed   Sports lawn

Solution #5: Cohousing

Retrofitting a Neighborhood to Create Cohousing

Building from the ground up is not the only option for creating a cohousing community. In Denmark, some groups have successfully renovated factories, school buildings, and row houses into cohousing communities. Here's a story of nine households who did something different: They transformed existing homes in a neighborhood into a cohousing community. Temescal Creek Cohousing is a beautiful and quiet oasis just blocks from a busy commercial district in Oakland, California. Six households came together in 1999 and purchased three adjacent duplexes. Later, the community grew when friends of group members bought two single-family homes adjacent to the duplexes.

The residents did many things together, like sharing a car, meals, and landscaping their enormous yard. Still, they felt they were missing something: a common house. They went through a long process to obtain permits and easements and build a common house straddling the property line of two parcels. Today, they have their common house with a large kitchen and dining area for shared meals, living room area, and guest room. They also built a ninth unit above the common house. All of the units have since been converted to condominiums, and each household "purchased" its unit with an individual mortgage. They share expenses for common areas and maintenance, including solar panels for their community.

The residents of Temescal Creek Cohousing share yard tools, office equipment, a hot tub, a ping pong table, and much more. They make bulk purchases of items such as toilet paper. They hold a monthly work party to keep the properties maintained. They share childcare, an enormous benefit to parents and children alike. Twice a week, the group shares a meal; attendance is optional. Each person cooks once every three weeks or so. No money changes hands for the shared meals: the designated cooks pick the menu and buy the food. As Temescal Creek resident Karen Hester puts it, "Sharing meals is the glue that keeps community together."

Solution 6: Casual Cohousing

Casual cohousing (sometimes called "cohousing light," "cohousing cousins," or "cohousing-inspired") is sort of a scaled-down version of cohousing. A casual cohousing community might have two to five households, each with its own separate dwelling unit, plus shared common spaces. Casual cohousing residents may also share meals, childcare, purchasing goods and services, and so on. Casual cohousing might be set up in a duplex or multiplex, accessory units (such as in-law apartments), or a small condominium project. Housing that isn't officially joined can also be turned into cohousing. For example, neighbors might decide to take down the fence between their houses and share their outdoor space and other common facilities.

Forming Casual Cohousing

If casual cohousing sounds right for you, there are different ways to make it happen:

- Form a group of people you would like to share housing with and buy property together.
- Buy into pre-existing casual cohousing. Others who form casual cohousing occasionally have units to fill, and advertise in places like www.cohousing.org.
- Buy a multiunit property, then find appropriate cohousing partners to fill the units.

This section focuses on the first scenario, where a group forms and purchases property together.

If you and some friends are serious about purchasing property to form casual cohousing, we recommend that you enter into a written agreement ahead of time. The agreement could detail your plans, initial investments, how you collect funds, borrow money, and so on. Having an agreement enables the group to move forward by guaranteeing everyone's commitment and giving individual members the security that their rights and investment will be protected.

A Casual Cohousing Story

Inspired by many wonderful cohousing communities in the San Francisco Bay Area, Berkeley residents Diane Dodge and her friends Cecilie Surasky and Carolyn Hunt, a couple, created their own cohousing community, on a smaller and more casual scale. They purchased a house with a second unit in the back on top of a garage. Cecilie and Carolyn renovated the back house and converted the garage into living space, ultimately creating a beautiful two-bedroom, two-living-room home. With the birth of Teo, a third member joined their household. Diane lived in the front house and rented out two rooms to university students.

The women initially bought the property as tenants in common. They each paid a portion of the purchase cost based on the value of their respective living spaces. They later converted the property into condominiums, which means that Diane owns the front house, Cecilie and Carolyn own the back house, and the three of them comprise an unincorporated "condo association" to manage shared space. The community later expanded when Diane bought a duplex across the street with her friends, a couple with a child. The couple lives in the back unit and Diane rents her half of the duplex to another couple.

Each of the four households is fairly autonomous, though everyone enjoys casual friendships and encounters with each other, as well as many spontaneous conversations and gatherings. At the same time, they have adapted many of the sharing practices typical of cohousing, and the interdependence among the households is much more than you would find in a typical neighborhood. Among the things they share are:

- a yard, garden space, hot tub, grill, and compost heap
- laundry facilities
- household items, such as a bicycle pump, vacuum, extension cords, emergency kit, and inflatable mattress for guests
- a bicycle and, at one time, a pickup truck
- movies and books
- occasional meals and leftovers, and
- help with chores large and small, from childcare to dog walking, moving furniture, and bringing groceries when someone is sick.

Ten Tips on Joining an Existing Shared Housing Arrangement

1. Look at the governing documents, such as the CC&Rs, cohousing agreement, or Community Rules. Look for any restrictions that seem unreasonable to you, such as rules against subletting, painting in particular colors, or having cats.

2. Find out whether the community has much debt, if there is a reserve fund, and whether there are any lawsuits pending against the community. Also find out whether other people in the shared housing arrangement consistently pay their mortgage and monthly fees on time.

3. Find out what kind of improvements people want to make on the buildings, what renovations are planned, and so on.

4. Find out about monthly dues: how much they are, what they cover, how often they rise, and when they are due.

5. Ask what type of upkeep you are responsible for outside of your own living space or unit.

6. Ask about the community decision-making process and governance structure. Look out for situations where one person owns a large portion of the property or units in a community; that person might have a great deal of control over decisions.

7. Explore what kind of financing is available. Will you be able to take over the loan of a departing resident?

8. Find out whether you are expected to assume a previous owner's debts, such as missed dues payments.

9. When you buy in, will the property be reassessed or refinanced? If so, will you be solely responsible for paying the increase in costs to the community?

10. Finally, get to know the residents. Find out how they like living there, what kinds of activities people do together, what types of conflicts have come up and how they were resolved, and so on.

Ownership Structure for Casual Cohousing

The most common ownership structures used in casual cohousing are tenancy in common (TIC) or condominium. Both of these forms are described in more detail in "Ways of Owning Shared Housing," above. Often, multiunit properties are initially purchased by a group as a TIC, because that's the automatic form of ownership created when a group buys property together. The owners can later convert their property into condominiums (which typically requires the help of a lawyer and surveyor). Cohousing owners often prefer condominiums because they are easier to finance and resell than TICs, and may provide a greater feeling of autonomy to residents.

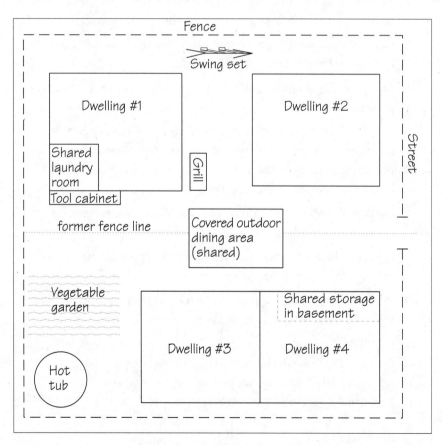

Solution #6: Casual cohousing

At the same time, the TIC form of ownership can be crafted to feel much like a condominium in a multiunit context. To achieve this, TIC units should be appraised, ownership percentages divided carefully, and a TIC agreement should make clear everyone's respective ownership and use rights to the property. In this way, everyone's ownership interests are delineated and protected, banks are more likely to provide fractional financing, and owners can more easily resell their units. In sum, it will feel like condo ownership.

Sharing Expenses in Casual Cohousing

No matter how you own the units, your group will share ownership of and responsibility for common areas and property. It's important to come up with agreements about some of the following money issues:

- How will you divide expenses such as property taxes? Will you split the property taxes or divide them based on ownership percentages?
- How will you share insurance costs? In a TIC, each unit owner has separate personal property and liability insurance policies, and the group collectively purchases a policy to insure the building(s) and protect against liability in common areas. You'll have to decide how to divide the common insurance expenses. Insurance is handled somewhat differently with condos, depending on whether each owner owns the structure of their unit or just the air space within it.
- How will your group manage finances? It's often good to have a group account into which each member makes a monthly payment, and from which you pay all common bills. And how will you create a budget and determine how much each member must pay each month?
- Will your cohousing group have a reserve fund to pay major unforeseen expenses or cover a member who fails to pay monthly expenses?
- How will you share utilities? If utilities are metered separately for each unit, there will not be much to talk about. But if there's

one meter, how will you divide costs? Will you charge more for households with larger spaces and more family members?

- How will you share any increases in property taxes that result from reassessment, or a rise in mortgage payments as a result of refinancing? If, for example, one owner makes an improvement on his or her portion of the property that triggers a tax reassessment, should that owner bear the cost of the raised taxes? If so, for how long?

The Bigger Picture: Shared Housing

Here are some ways that businesses, nonprofits, community leaders, developers, lawmakers, and others can help make shared housing an option for everyone:

- Increase public funding—loans, grants, and tax incentives—for cooperative housing and cohousing, especially for seniors, low-income households, and people with disabilities.
- Banks and lenders: Increase fractional finance options for people who purchase homes and tenancies in common (TICs) together.
- Residential real estate developers and architects: Partner with community groups to design and develop more community-oriented housing, such as planned developments, condos, and cohousing with shared space and common houses.
- Increase funding for and creation of community land trusts to buy and develop properties that serve as shared housing and limited equity housing.
- Revise local zoning ordinances to encourage shared housing and cohousing developments, raise number of allowable residents per household, and allow conversion of single-family homes to multi-family homes.
- Owners of multiunit rental properties: Consider conversion to resident ownership.

What's an Ecovillage?

Ecovillages are residential communities built around ideals of ecological, social, and economic sustainability. There are nearly 100 self-identified ecovillages in the United States, and many more around the world. Examples of what you might find at an ecovillage include:

- green building practices, including energy efficient buildings, non-toxic materials, and construction with renewable resources, such as straw bales or bamboo
- renewable energy sources, such as solar or wind power
- grey water systems for water recycling, onsite wastewater treatment, and extensive composting
- food production through vegetable gardening, fruit orchards, and animal husbandry
- carsharing
- democratic and non-hierarchical decision-making processes, and
- community social activities.

Your Casual Cohousing Documents

Depending on your ownership arrangement, your casual cohousing will likely be governed by multiple tiers of documents. If you own the property together as tenants in common (TIC), your primary governing document will be a TIC agreement, (and possibly a "cohousing agreement," described below).

If you have formed a four-unit condominium, your first tier of documents will be the deeds, which declare ownership of certain units as well as partial ownership of common areas. Your second tier document will be the CC&Rs, which include many of the basic agreements about how your property is divided and shared, such as:

- the location and description of the property
- descriptions of the units and their boundaries
- a description of commonly owned portions of the property, also known as "common elements"

- a description of the areas that are owned by the group, but reserved for the use of individual unit owners, also known as "limited common elements"
- details on the creation of a condo owners association or other organizational entity to govern the shared property, including a provision requiring that unit owners be members in the association
- allocation of voting rights of unit owners
- how the association will handle finances and allocate expenses between unit owners
- how the association will enforce rules and payments
- a framework for regulating use and architectural design of the property
- who is responsible for maintaining common areas, and
- attached maps and floorplans.

Your third tier of documents may govern the specifics of how your cohousing is managed and how your group makes decisions. This is often included in a document called the bylaws. If your community association is formed as a nonprofit corporation (which provides the benefit of liability protection), you will also have articles of incorporation, a short document you file with the state to create your nonprofit.

All of the documents in the first three tiers should be drafted by a lawyer who is familiar with state and local real estate law.

Finally, you will likely have a fourth tier of documents, which you can draft yourself and change as often as necessary. The primary document, often called a "community agreement," "community rules," or a "cohousing agreement," lists many of the day-to-day details of how your cohousing group operates, including:

- how residents may use shared areas of the property
- what kinds of alterations residents can make to their units or the landscaping
- policies on guests and subletting
- rules about pets, smoking, noise, parties, and so on
- parking arrangements
- decisions about common expenses and how they will be shared

- what household goods are owned by the cohousing community and how residents may use them, and
- residents' responsibilities with regard to the yard, garbage, recycling, composting, newspaper, mail, and so on.

For the sake of education and sharing, many ecovillages welcome outside guests to take tours and stay overnight. For example, the ecovillage in Ithaca, New York, offers weekend and weeklong stays. For more information on ecovillages, see the resources in Appendix A.

The Triple Bottom Line: The Benefits of Shared Housing

Social and Personal Benefits

- Get more living space than you could afford on your own. For example, in cohousing, you might have a 1,000 square foot personal unit, but share a 3,000 square foot common house. That quadruples your indoor space, and offers shared outdoor spaces, gardens, and luxuries such as a hot tub.
- Sharing housing with others could make you healthier and happier, and probably will help you live longer. Studies have found that having a strong sense of connection and nurturing with others can contribute to longevity.
- Shared housing creates safer places to live.
- Shared housing helps meet other day-to-day needs, as it facilitates mealsharing, sharing household goods, childcare, adult care, and household chores.

Environmental Benefits

- Shared spaces or units with shared walls are more energy efficient and cost less to heat and cool.
- Sharing housing reduces suburban sprawl. It also means less logging and less waste created in the construction process.

- Sharing housing can make renewable energy and green building practices more affordable to residents.

Financial Benefits

- Shared housing can make homeownership affordable for those who team up with others to make the purchase.
- Pay as little as $150 per month for rent in a group house.
- Save on monthly expenses beyond rent or mortgage payments.
- Shared housing facilitates the sharing of food, cars, goods, childcare, and much more.

Sharing Household Goods, Purchases, Tasks, and Space

Sharing household goods and tasks has benefits that speak to some of the most persistent challenges in our lives, like clutter, procrastination, money worries, and waste. It also helps us address broader concerns, such as our impact on the environment, our patterns of consumption, and material inequities. There are countless ways to meet your household and personal needs by sharing chores, tasks, goods, purchases, services, space, and more.

Solution 1: Share Household Items

"First job is to prepare the soil. The best tool for this is your neighbor's motorized garden tiller. If your neighbor does not own a garden tiller, suggest that he buy one."

—Dave Barry

There are many creative ways and good reasons to share household goods. In particular, those who don't have basic household goods benefit greatly from these arrangements. Young adults living alone for the first time, recent divorcees, returning veterans or travelers, and low-income households might not otherwise have access to a vacuum, tools, laundry facilities, and other amenities a sharing group can provide.

For people who already own these basics, there are still many benefits to sharing household goods, including:

- access to items that might break (for example, the opportunity to use a neighbor's washing machine if yours conks out), items that you need only occasionally (such as a bread machine or extra folding chairs or tables for a large party), and items that are rare (a karaoke machine or slide projector, for example)
- opportunities to build trust and community with your neighbors, which can lead to other sharing arrangements
- helping the planet by reducing everyone's need to manufacture and buy consumer goods, and
- elimination of household clutter and duplication.

Sharing at Home:
Household Goods, Purchases, Tasks, and Space

Home Maintenance

Neighborhood home improvement groups

Collective purchasing of services such as small removal, gutter cleaning, and carpet and upholstery cleaning.

Energy/Water

Community supported energy

Collective bargaining for renewable energy

Group firewood buying

Home energy saving group

Shared water testing and purification

Household Supplies

Buying Clubs

Neighborhood dry goods "store"

Neighborhood emergency kits

Sharing appliances and other household goods

Yard

Take down a fence and share a yard

Collective purchasing of landscaping or tree services

Clothes

Sharing a laundry room

Sharing formal wear, business attire, specialized sportswear, accessories, jewelry, and costumes

Tools

Tool lending libraries

Neighborhood toolsharing groups

Waste

Compost cooperative

Recycling and reuse group

Shared grey water systems

Fun/Hobbies/Sports

Sharing season tickets

Sharing sports gear, entertainment equipment, and hobby supplies

Book sharing groups

Sharing fitness equipment, sportswear, kayaks, etc.

Other

Skill sharing

Credit unions

Sharing wall space for murals

Sharing Consumer Goods: An Alternative to Landfills

These days, it's not hard to furnish a whole house on a small budget. Cheap plastic goods made overseas always seem to be on sale at the local big box store. A $10 toaster, a $20 stereo, a $30 vacuum cleaner, and you're all set! But all too quickly, this cheap stuff breaks. Because it usually costs less to buy a new item than to get the old one fixed, much of this stuff goes to landfills.

Beyond feeding landfills, the manufacture, transport, consumption, and disposal of consumer goods are major sources of pollution, extraction of natural resources, exploited labor, and countless other societal and environmental woes. As consumers, we have the power to reduce our reliance on cheap and disposable consumer goods, and help shift to an economy based on more sustainable industries.

Sharing goods is one solution. For example, with the money you save when you buy a new vacuum with your upstairs neighbor, you could probably invest in something that will last longer, preferably with a long warranty. By sharing the investment in a durable and repairable item, you not only help the planet, but you may also save on your overall lifetime expenditures on new vacuum cleaners. You also help create jobs for people who can fix things and help to support the artisans and manufacturers who care about quality. All just by being willing to walk upstairs to get the vacuum!

For more information about the impact of consumer goods on the planet and society, go online and watch the wonderful 20-minute cartoon "The Story of Stuff," www.storyofstuff.org, or read the book *Affluenza*, by de Graaf, et al (Berrett Koehler Publishers).

Ways of Sharing Goods

It's easy and convenient for each of us to buy our own cheap consumer goods and gadgets and have them on hand when we need them. Ice cream makers, leaf blowers, and electric screwdrivers are all useful from time to time. But especially for things we need only occasionally, sharing is much less costly—and more environmentally friendly—than buying our own.

Sharing household goods can happen in many ways. It can mean that you and a friend buy a video camera together and each use it when you need it. Or, it can entail an organized system of borrowing and lending goods, like a neighborhood toolsharing group.

It's possible to share almost anything, especially:

- items you don't use every day
- items you don't tend to need on a moment's notice (for example, as infrequently as you might need it, we don't recommend that you share a fire extinguisher with your neighbor down the street)
- items that can be easily moved from one home to another, and
- items that are kept in a space that all sharers can access.

Most of the time, it's easiest to share household goods with people who live nearby, such as neighbors or fellow residents in your apartment complex or cohousing. But you can also share goods with anyone you see regularly, such as at work, school, or church, where you can easily hand off a shared item. You could even share something like a kayak with someone who lives across town, and drive by to pick it up before you head to the lake.

No matter what you share, who you share with, and how you arrange to share it, we recommend that you and your cosharers review and discuss the questions covered in Chapter 3. This will help you think through important issues such as what happens if the item breaks, how to schedule use, and so on.

Forming a Goods Sharing Group with Neighbors

A neighborhood goods sharing group is primarily a system of borrowing and lending, in which participants allow others to use their stuff but actual ownership of the items doesn't change hands. To get started, you'll need to know what everyone has and needs. Use the form below to find out what each participant is willing to lend, willing to let others use, and looking to borrow. (You'll find a blank copy in Appendix B; the version below includes sample entries.) Once these forms are filled out, you could either copy them all and give a set to each sharer or compile them into a master list organized by category. Because the list will change as people and items come and go, it may be good to post an updateable list online or have someone print out the list and distribute it every few months.

Where to Keep Shared Goods

Where you store shared goods will depend on what they are and how often you need them:

- **With their owners.** If sharers will be borrowing and lending individually owned items, it may make the most sense for owners to keep their own things. Someone who wants to use an item can make arrangements with the owner to pick it up and return it.

- **In an accessible place.** You can also keep shared items in a place that everyone can access (the "sharing shed" or "stuff library," for example). This might be a shed that everyone can open with a combination lock or key, or someone's garage or basement that has a separate entrance. It could even be a room or closet in a staffed office at an apartment or condominium complex. If you keep everything together, make sure you keep a detailed list of who owns what, label each item with the name of its owner, and come up with a system for signing out and returning items. Have sharers write down what time they expect to return the item, so others will know when it will be available. For certain items, you may want to set a time limit on borrowing.

- **Immobile items.** You may want to share items that cannot be easily moved, such as a washer and dryer, rowing machine, or ping-pong table. One way to do this is to keep these items in a part of the house that can be accessed without disturbing the residents, such as a garage or laundry room with a separate entrance.

Goods to Lend and Borrow

Name: _____

Address: _____

Phone: _____

Email: _____

Please list all items you are willing to lend, as well as items you would be interested in obtaining by sharing or borrowing them from others. If an item cannot be moved, but you are willing to let people use it in your house or yard, please list this in the second column. For items that you would be willing to lend, please note any limitations. For example, if you will lend your vacuum cleaner only for an hour at a time, or if you will lend your ceramics wheel only to experienced users, please note this.

Categories of Goods	Items to Lend	Immobile Items Others May Use	Items I'd Like to Borrow or Buy With Others
Tools	Allen wrenches, ladder		Electric screwdriver, drill
Cleaning	Vacuum cleaner		Carpet cleaning machine
Cooking	High power blender, espresso maker, ice cream maker, popcorn machine, bread maker, yogurt maker, food dehydrater, juicer, a large cooler, BBQ (on wheels)		Beer-making supplies, coffee roaster, deep fryer, slow cooker

Categories of Goods	Items to Lend	Immobile Items Others May Use	Items I'd Like to Borrow or Buy With Others
Yard	Leaf blower, snow shovel, rake, hoe, shovels, trowels, wheelbarrow		Lawn mower
Sports/Fitness/ Outdoor	Camping gear, small inflatable raft	Elliptical machine (in my garage; you could arrange to get a key from me). Basketball hoop (in my driveway; let me know if you'd like to use it and I'll park my car on the street)	Surfboard, fishing gear, trampoline
Fun/ Entertainment	Lots of DVDs	Pool table (also in my garage)	Karaoke machine
Clothing/ Accessories	Ski clothes, Elvis costume, gorilla costume	Washer and dryer (also in my garage)	Wetsuit
Hobbies/Arts/ Crafts	Sewing machine	Ceramics wheel and kiln (also in my garage)	

Categories of Goods	Items to Lend	Immobile Items Others May Use	Items I'd Like to Borrow or Buy With Others
Travel	Giant rolling suitcase, travel guides for most of South America		
Furniture	Inflatable mattress, folding chairs, 6-foot folding table, card table, lawn furniture		
Electronics	Record player, digital video camera		Copier
Health	Humidifier, massage chair, massage table		Water purifier
Other	Postage scale, typewriter, slide projector, realistic rubber cockroach (great for gags)		Emergency preparedness kit, hot tub, binoculars, generator

Tool Lending Libraries

When it comes to smart sharing ideas, tool lending libraries hit the nail on the head! The Tool Lending Library in Berkeley, California was a major source of inspiration for this book. When the author needed to cut a metal bike lock (after losing the key), she checked out a power metal-cutting saw and goggles and received some instructions from the friendly library staff. Within the hour, she victoriously freed her bicycle and returned the tools.

Tool lending libraries can be useful for those times when you need a rare or specialized tool, or even if you are just having a gardening party and need extra shovels and wheelbarrows. The word "tool" can be broadly construed to include other kinds of useful items and gadgets, too. For example, in Ottawa, Canada, the public library lends pedometers to encourage exercise and help people measure physical activity, and "Kill-a-Watt" meters that measure the energy use of household appliances.

There are at least 20 tool lending libraries in the United States. Often, tool lending libraries are affiliated with local public libraries; some are sponsored by local housing departments or nonprofits.

Owning Items as a Group

Your group may own some items together. For example, a member of your group may move to Florida and give the group his snow blower. Someone may find a free blender and put it in the sharing shed for others to use. Or perhaps some neighbors decide to buy a volleyball net together, each chipping in $5 to cover the cost. If you will own items collectively, especially if they are expensive, be sure you agree on how they may be used, whether members will be bought out by the others if they move, and so on.

If Something Breaks

Stuff happens. Think in advance about what your sharing group will do if a shared item is damaged or lost. If you own items as a group, then the impact of the loss is spread to the whole group. But if the damaged item is owned by one person, what is the role of the member who damaged it or of the group in fixing or replacing the item? Does it matter what caused the damage or who is at fault?

One option is for the group to create a reserve fund, which can act as insurance. If one member breaks something, the group can agree to reimburse the owner by paying all or part of the lost value or replacement cost. To keep things simpler, some groups may just want the owner and borrower to sort it out between themselves.

For groups who pool their things in one location, such as a shared shed, members should decide how to share the losses if things are stolen. Should the losses be borne by individual owners or should the group find a way to compensate those who lose valuable items? If the owner of the property where items are stored has insurance that covers the loss, should members kick in for the cost of the insurance?

Goods Sharing Group Member Agreement

If you start a neighborhood goods sharing group, it's a good idea to have a written member agreement, to make sure that everyone understands how the arrangement works. The agreement also clarifies what will happen if property is damaged or a member is injured. Because group members will probably come and go, having a written agreement encourages consistency and continuity in how your group operates.

Sample Goods Sharing Group
Member Agreement

This agreement is between all members of the East Lilburn Stuff Share Group ("the Group"). By signing this agreement, each member agrees to the terms of this agreement, as follows:

Purpose: We have formed this Group to help neighborhood residents save money, meet their household needs, and consume less by providing an easy way for people to share household goods, otherwise known as "stuff."

Definition of "stuff": "Stuff" includes many kinds of useful items, including appliances, clothes, books, tools, electronics, toys, and so on.

Shared property: The shared stuff is described in the attached Stuff Master List and on the Group's password-protected website. Upon joining the Group, each member will fill out the "Personal Stuff List" where the member will list all items that member is willing to share, any limitations related to borrowing or using item, and items that member is interested in borrowing or acquiring with others.

Ownership: All stuff is and will remain the separate property of its owner. No item will be owned collectively by the Group, unless it is specifically given to the Group or acquired by the Group for the purpose of collective ownership.

Member qualifications: Membership is open to anyone who is at least 13 years old and lives within the section of East Lilburn bordered on the north by Precita Avenue, on the south by Ward Road, on the east by Clemonsville Road and on the west by Abby Road. This encompasses approximately 80 households. At our annual meeting, we may consider whether to expand.

Structure: We are an unincorporated association. We do not intend to enter into a partnership or form an incorporated entity.

Decisions: We will hold an annual meeting and block party in the summer. All members will be invited to the meeting, to be held during the hour prior to the start of the block party. At each annual meeting, members present will elect a Stuff Share board of five members. Major decisions regarding the structure and size of the Group will be thoroughly discussed and decided by a majority vote of the membership. Decisions about minor and day-to-day issues, such as how to organize stuff, will be made by the board.

Stuff share board member responsibilities: Members of the Stuff Share board will be responsible for recruiting new members, processing member agreements and personal stuff lists, and updating the Stuff Master List and website at least once every three months. Board members will also be responsible for planning the annual party.

Member responsibilities: Members are responsible for updating their personal stuff lists as necessary and treating borrowed stuff with care.

Procedures: To borrow an item, the borrowing member should find the item on the Stuff Master List and contact the member that is offering the item. The borrowing member should describe how the item will be used. The offering member may agree to or decline the loan. The borrowing and offering members may decide together the length of the loan and any other terms of the loan, including appropriate and inappropriate uses of the item.

Costs: There is no cost to join the Group, although members may be asked to make a small contribution to pay for the party. Members do not enter into this agreement with the intent to profit. As a general rule, members will not charge for the use of items they lend. However, if use of an item will entail an expense for the owner (such as gasoline for the leafblower), the borrower and lender may agree on a way to compensate the lender.

Damaged or lost items: In the event than an item is lost or damaged while in possession by a borrower, the borrower and lender will decide together on an appropriate remedy or compensation. As a general rule, borrowers should be expected to compensate lenders for the value of the item lost or damaged, not necessarily the replacement value.

Indemnification and release of liability: All borrowing members, as consideration for borrowing an item from an offering member, agree not to make a claim against or sue an offering member for injury, loss, or damage that results from borrowing and/or using the item, including injury, loss, or damage arising from the negligence of the offering member. Borrowing members agree to indemnify, hold harmless, and defend offering members from all claims, liability, or demands that the borrowing member or any third party may have or in the future make against the offering member for injury, loss, or damage arising from the borrowing member's use of the offering member's property.

Dispute resolution: If a conflict or dispute arises between members and they are unable to resolve it through discussion, members agree to use mediation to attempt to resolve the dispute. All mediation services will be paid for by the members involved in the dispute.

Procedure for withdrawing from the group or expelling members: Anyone can withdraw from the Group at any time by providing written or email notice to the board. Within a reasonable amount of time, board members will remove that member's name from the member list and will remove that member's items from the Stuff Master List. Members may be involuntarily removed from the group by a three-fourths vote of membership.

Dissolving the group: The Group will remain in operation as long as there are members interested in keeping it going. We may decide to dissolve the Group by a unanimous vote of active members or by a unanimous minus one vote. If, at the time of dissolution, the Group owns items collectively, we will decide how to distribute those items. We may decide to sell these items and split the proceeds, or simply give those items to individual members, if at least two-thirds of the Group agrees.

Signature	Date
Signature	Date
Signature	Date
Signature	Date
Signature	Date
Signature	Date
Signature	Date
Signature	Date

Agreements Between Borrower and Lender

Some sharers may want to enter into separate agreements with each other, especially for valuable items. For example, if Maxine lends Dave an expensive video camera, Maxine may want some extra protection, such as a receipt from Dave and an agreement about liability and compensation for damage. Here's an example of a brief agreement that you can adapt for your own use:

Sample Receipt and Liability Waiver for Shared Item

I, Dave Postle, acknowledge that on July 29, 2009, I borrowed Maxine Dryden's Sony High Definition Camcorder. Maxine has lent me her camera for my trip to Malaysia. I will return the camera on or before September 30, 2009.

In consideration for letting me use her camera, I agree to hold Maxine harmless from any claims resulting from my use of it. I understand that Maxine has made no warranties or representations as to the condition of the camera or its safety or suitability for any use.

I will return the camera to Maxine in the same condition it was in when I borrowed it. If the camera is damaged while in my possession, whether it's my fault or not, I will pay for the repairs or will pay Maxine its current value, which we agree is $900.

Dave Postle
_____
Dave Postle

July 29, 2009
_____
Date

Neighborhood Emergency Preparedness Kits

The Red Cross recommends that neighborhoods work together for disaster preparedness. Some local fire departments and other city agencies offer free disaster plan classes and kits to neighborhood groups who organize and plan for disasters together. Even if you pair up with just one neighbor to create an emergency kit, you will save a lot of money and resources. Neighbors could make a shared investment in disaster kits, bottled water, power generators, and other emergency items, and store them in an accessible location.

In addition to preparing and sharing supplies, neighbors can cooperate to create a disaster plan. This could include:

- sharing personal and emergency contact information with each other
- making a list of household pets and coming up with a plan for checking on or evacuating them during an emergency
- discussing evacuation routes and possible carpooling
- designating an emergency meeting spot to ensure that everyone is accounted for
- planning to gather at homes with basements in the event of a tornado, and so on.

For more information on preparing for an emergency, see the Red Cross website, www.redcross.org.

Sharing Clothing and Accessories

Initially, it might sound strange to share something as personal as clothing or jewelry, but there are ways to do it that work well and make a lot of sense.

Sharing Jewelry and Accessories

Sharing accessories is becoming increasingly common among those who appreciate, but cannot always afford, high-end designer items. Small groups can share accessories in any way they choose. A group of friends might buy an item together, or one person might post an online ad looking for others to go in on a purchase. One example is described in Cheryl Jarvis' 2008 book *The Necklace*, a true story about the adventures and sisterhood that developed between 13 women who shared a $37,000 diamond necklace. Each woman chipped in to purchase the necklace and got to use it for four weeks out of the year.

There are also jewelry and designer handbag lending websites, such as From Bags to Riches (www.frombagstoriches.com) and Bag Borrow or Steal (www.bagborroworsteal.com), which also has jewelry, sunglasses, and watches to borrow. With these programs, members select an item online, receive it in the mail a few days later, and return it when they are finished using it.

Sharing Clothing

Clothing is often passed from one person to another, via hand-me-downs, second-hand stores, or clothes-swapping parties. It's not as common for two people to own clothing simultaneously, but it makes sense for a variety of clothing items that are expensive, specialized, or worn infrequently, such as:

- **Professional clothing.** Business suits can eat a hole in your wallet. Consider sharing, especially if you use a suit only for occasional job interviews, conferences, or important meetings. Some college career centers, such as at Barnard College, maintain a set of professional clothes for students to borrow. Workplaces could "follow suit" by making suits available to employees.

- **Tuxedos and evening gowns.** Renting a tuxedo or other formal wear costs about a quarter of the purchase price. If you share the purchase with a friend, it won't be long before you wear your money's worth.

- **Ski clothing, wetsuits, or other specialized sports attire.** If you don't already own the necessary outfit, you could find that buying ski clothing will be more expensive than your ski trip itself. Sharing specialized sports wear is a good way to go, especially for clothes used infrequently.

- **Maternity clothes.** If you join a group of expecting mothers (for example, a birthing class), suggest sharing maternity clothes.

- **Costumes.** If you have a particularly festive group of friends, actors, role-players, Elvis impersonators, pranksters, or sci-fi convention goers, you may have the ideal ingredients for forming a costume-sharing group. It's the best way to ensure that your gorilla suit is put to good use.

Sharing in the Fun

There are plenty of ways that people can cooperate to maximize leisure, fun, recreation, and entertainment:

- Form a group of friends or neighbors to create a shared library of DVDs, videos, music, books, board games, video games, and audio-visual and gaming equipment. Each person could make a list of what they have to lend, or everyone can pool their things in one place.
- Start a family book sharing and reading group. Here's a great resource: *Family Book Sharing Groups: Start One in Your Neighborhood*, by Marjorie R. Simic and Eleanor C. Macfarlane (Family Literacy Center).
- Organize neighborhood board game or movie nights.
- Give neighbors access to yards for use of a pool, trampoline, basketball hoop, and so on. (See Solution 5, below, on sharing spaces.)

Sharing Season Tickets

Groups can save a great deal of money by sharing season tickets for sporting events, theme parks, and music and theater performances. Especially for major sporting events, tickets can be prohibitively expensive—and not everyone wants to go to every home game in a season.

Ticket-sharing consortia are very common in sports. There are a number of ways to do this. At AT&T Park in San Francisco, for example, one four-person group shares two season tickets under one person's name. The owner gets all the informational notices from the team and receives and pays for the tickets. At the start of the season, the participants get together and choose the games for which they want tickets.

Another two friends have a different sharing arrangement. Each "owns" one seat, next to the other. This means each pays for her own seat and receives information—and sometimes promotional items—from the team. However, they consider the two seats shared, and they decide together how they'll use them. Each month they decide which games they'll attend together, and then each one takes both tickets for certain games. The leftover tickets are sold through an email list maintained by one of the seat partners, who sends out a notice each month listing the available games and sells them at face value.

> **TIP**
>
> **Take someone out to the ball game.** Parking at an arena or stadium can be very expensive, and traffic to and from the game can also be a hassle. Save money—and have some companionship for the ride—by setting up a carpool. (See Chapter 10 for more.)

Solution 2: Purchase Supplies and Goods Together

In addition to sharing ownership or use of goods, people can also cooperate in purchasing staples and other supplies. Group buying has many benefits. Of course, it helps you save money through volume discounts, wholesale pricing, and consolidated shipping costs. But it also saves packaging and transportation costs (and energy); gives you greater access to products that might be otherwise hard to find or too expensive, like organic or fair-trade products; makes it affordable to support local and small businesses; and saves shopping time. It's also a lot of fun: You will learn a lot about how others live, what they buy, and why.

Chapter 8 covers grocery cooperatives and food-buying clubs. Here we talk about all the other household items you could cooperate with others to buy.

Goods to Purchase

You can collectively purchase just about anything your group wants in large quantities.

Household Goods That Are Regularly Replenished

Here are some goods that consumers can cooperate to purchase regularly:
- firewood
- propane
- paper products, such as toilet paper
- bath and hair products
- personal and dental hygiene products
- baby care products, such as diapers
- laundry detergent, dish soap, and sponges
- cleaning supplies
- over-the-counter medicines and supplements
- school and office supplies
- batteries
- light bulbs (LED or CFLs to save energy, of course), and
- gardening supplies, such as soil, mulch, and plant food.

Infrequent or One-Time Purchases

It might also make sense to join forces to buy items that you don't need regularly. If enough people want something, you can probably save money by buying together. For example, if you have a number of neighbors landscaping in the spring, you might all go in on a couple of tons of gravel, to be distributed among your walkways. You could also bargain collectively to get a discount on things like furniture or other large items.

> **EXAMPLE:** Charles approached his friend Olive, a furniture-maker, to buy two Adirondack chairs. Charles wanted to support Olive's furniture business, but he couldn't afford the chairs at $200 apiece. Charles asked Olive whether she would give him a discount if he found more people who would buy the chairs at the same time. He talked up the idea to friends and neighbors, and

even posted an ad online. Charles found eight other people who wanted to buy the chairs, and everyone paid $130 per chair. As a result, Olive was able to buy wood for, make, and sell 16 chairs all at once, and she got amazing free marketing from Charles. By cooperating with other buyers and coordinating it with the furniture maker, it was a great deal for everyone.

How to Form a Buying Club

If you'd like to purchase goods with others, follow these steps to form a basic buying club.

1. **Get your group together.** Form a group of people interested in doing group buying. The group does not have to include only neighbors; because your purchases will be relatively infrequent, coworkers, friends, and family members who don't live nearby will probably be willing to come to you every few months to share in the bounty. Larger groups require more administrative work, but they are also better able to leverage the benefits of group buying.

2. **Decide what to buy.** Once you have enough people, hold your first meeting and plan your purchases. What criteria will you use in choosing products—do you want only the cheapest, the greenest, the most socially responsible? How flexible are people willing to be about brands? For example, most people aren't too picky about toilet paper, but some only use a certain type of shampoo. Your first meeting might be long—listening to everyone talk about what products they want and why—but it could be interesting, educational, and even fun.

RESOURCE

Is your group interested in buying environmentally and socially responsible products? Take a look at the Good Guide: www.goodguide.com. This online consumer research tool ranks thousands of products based on more than 600 criteria, including health hazards, environmental sustainability of production methods, labor and human rights practices of the producing company, use of animal testing, and so on.

3. **Decide on a schedule.** Unless your buying club is ordering perishable food, you'll probably want to order only once every month or two, or even once every quarter. You can always adjust the schedule if you need to.

4. **Choose shipping and distribution locations.** You will need a place where you can receive large quantities of items. This could be a single location—like someone's workplace, especially if it's staffed during the day—or more than one. For example, you could have your shipment divided and delivered to four homes, to make sure no one is stuck with piles of stuff. Choose a place where everyone can meet and divide up the goods.

5. **Research your options.** Have each person research purchasing options for a different type of product. For example, if your group decided to buy three brands of shampoo, someone needs to research whether you can buy directly from the shampoo company or from distributors, prices, minimum order requirements, shipping options, and so on.

6. **Meet and plan your order.** Once everyone has finished their research, get together to share your findings. Decide which companies or distributors you will order from and figure out the price per unit, such as how much members will have to pay for 16 ounces of dishwashing liquid or a roll of toilet paper. Decide how much of each product to order. This may require some negotiation, because you may have to meet minimum order requirements or unit requirements. For example, you might have to order toilet paper in units of 120 rolls. Keep track of how much people agree to buy, preferably on a spreadsheet that does the math for you.

7. **Create a group bank account and make the first orders.** Have everyone make an initial deposit and prepay the estimated cost of their order. Use the account to pay for all orders.

8. **Have a distribution party.** After all orders have been received, meet to divide everything up. You can make it fun by having a potluck.

9. **Decide what to do with any excess.** If you come out with surplus goods, you could divide them up, store them, or ask members to buy them from the group.

10. **Decide on your next round of orders.** You can plan your next round of orders at the distribution party or handle it later, perhaps by email.

TIP

Bring your own containers. Some buying clubs order things in large containers and redistribute them into smaller containers. For example, you might order shampoo in one-gallon bottles, and then have everyone bring empty individual-size bottles for refill. This saves an enormous amount of plastic and money, too.

Neighborhood Dry Goods "Store"

Instead of a buying club, you could create a dry goods "store" for you and your neighbors. This is a convenient way to meet basic household supply needs. And, because there's no owner, staff, or overhead, it can help you save money, too.

Here's one way to do it: Choose a place where goods can be stored and easily accessed, such as shelves in someone's garage or in the common space of a cohousing community. Have everyone deposit $100 into a bank account to build initial inventory, for which they will receive 400 tickets, worth 25 cents each. After canvassing the group to find out what the store should carry, order supplies in bulk and determine a unit price for each item (preferably divisible by 25 cents). Post the price list in the store. You will probably want to designate volunteers to coordinate ordering, stocking, and accounting.

Members who need supplies may go to the store, retrieve a toothbrush for three tickets, a role of toilet paper for two tickets, a light bulb for 14 tickets, and so on. When they are low on tickets, they can make another deposit into the account and receive more.

Solution 3: Share Services and Utilities

Purchasing services and utilities together offers some of the same benefits as collective purchasing of goods: lower cost and greater choice of services. If you gather a group of friends or neighbors interested in purchasing services, you have greater bargaining power, which gives you better options and prices. It's a good deal for service providers, too: They get free marketing and a significant source of work.

Sharing Services

If you are jointly purchasing service or utilities with others, it's a good idea to talk through the 20 questions we list in Chapter 3. Talk about how to divide costs, what happens if someone isn't happy with the services, and so on.

Here are some examples of services you might share:
- **Landscaping and yard work.** You and your neighbors may be able to get a group rate if you have a gardener provide services to a group of you on the same day.
- **Cleaning.** Similarly, a housecleaner, carpet cleaner, upholstery cleaner, or window washer could efficiently visit a number of houses on a block in one day and give you a group rate.
- **Maintenance and repairs.** Do your neighbors need a chimney sweep, piano tuner, gutter cleanout, tree trimming, carpet cleaning, pool or hot tub service, or other regular maintenance? Service providers may offer a lower price for a significant chunk of work.
- **Wireless Internet.** Sharing your Internet connection with neighbors may be illegal or violate the contract you sign with the provider. But some providers allow and even encourage shared service, so ask around.
- **Diapers.** Reusable diapers can be much cheaper than disposables, not to mention less wasteful and healthier for babies. Services that pick up used diapers and drop off clean ones provide significant discounts based on quantity. If your neighbors have a

baby, talk to them about partnering with you in subscribing to a diaper service.

- **Snow removal.** Some people hire services to remove snow from their driveways after major snowfalls. You could probably save money if you bargain collectively with your neighbors and have your snow removed all at once.

Credit Unions

Here's one more way to introduce more sharing into your life: Join a community-based credit union. Credit unions are cooperatively owned financial institutions that perform many of the same services provided by banks. They are democratically controlled and usually governed by a volunteer board of directors. A credit union's purpose is to provide members with at-cost banking services, encourage savings, and provide the cheapest loans and credit possible. Credit unions make decisions based on what will most benefit members and their communities. As a result, putting your money into a credit union is a way to share an investment in your own community. To read more about credit unions, go to the website for the World Council on Credit Unions, www.woccu.org.

Sharing Renewable Energy

Solar and wind power and other sources of renewable energy are the wave of the future, but remain unaffordable for the average household. While renewable energy systems pay for themselves in the long run, they require large initial investments. There are at least a few ways people can cooperate to gain access to and increase local renewable energy sources.

Collective Solar Energy Bargaining

Home and business owners who would like to go solar have recently started forming bargaining collectives to gain an edge on pricing. By forming groups and seeking bids from solar panel installation companies, individuals have managed to cut their solarizing costs in half or more. An example of a group helping form these collectives is One Block Off the Grid, www.1BOG.org.

Cooperative and Community Supported Energy

Solar and wind energy projects have been implemented in some areas by large utility companies and by individual home or business owners. Somewhere in between these large- and small-scale options is a third and relatively new option: community supported energy.

Community supported energy (CSE) is a model inspired by community supported agriculture, described in Chapter 8. Through a CSE, citizens collectively pay the costs of building medium-scale energy projects—a solar array or wind turbine, for example—and share the energy and income it produces. One example of a CSE is MinWind, in Minnesota, which began as two wind turbines owned by 66 local investors, primarily farmers. The project has since grown to include nine turbines. CSEs are an excellent way to produce energy locally and efficiently and keep income from the project in the community.

A major obstacle to building medium-scale, community-based renewable energy projects is the regulation of the energy industry. The approval process for energy projects is extremely costly. Green energy advocates want to encourage lawmakers to loosen regulation of small-scale projects, and even provide incentives for community-based energy programs. In the meantime, one way that community groups can overcome this barrier is to partner with an existing utility company for such projects.

Utility Cooperatives

Utility cooperatives have long helped people meet their telephone, electricity, gas, and water needs, especially in rural areas where for-profit utility companies have been unwilling to expand service. Utility cooperatives are owned and governed by the consumers. Because they operate for the sole benefit of members, utility cooperatives often keep prices low.

Many utility cooperatives have chosen to invest in alternative and renewable sources of energy at the request of members. If you are a member of an energy cooperative, you can exercise your power by voting for green energy.

Sharing Water

Through cooperation, there are many ways we can cut our water use and increase our access to clean water:

- **Share a water purification system:** Water purification systems can be costly. You could invest collectively in a good system, set it up in one person's yard, and allow everyone to fill up jugs of drinking water.
- **Catch rain water:** Especially in asphalt covered urban areas, a lot of rain water flows into street gutters and storm drains. By catching this water, you could facilitate urban food growing or help water a garden. Form a group of people interested in harvesting rain water, research different methods, and set up rainwater barrels around your neighborhood.
- **Grey water:** Form a group to learn about and build water recycling and grey water systems in your neighborhood. Be sure to check your state and local laws; most grey water systems require permits. For a helpful resource about grey water and applicable laws, see www.oasisdesign.net.
- **Water testing:** Testing for contaminants is expensive but important, especially if you have a private water supply or share an aquifer with others. You can save money by sharing the cost of lab testing or sharing the cost of a home water testing kit.

For resources on calculating your water "footprint" and conserving water, see www.waterfootprint.org or www.H2Oconserve.org.

Solution 4: Form a Work Group for Home Projects

A neighborhood home improvement group is one of the most cost-effective sharing investments you can make, in terms of both time and resources. The concept is simple: A group of neighbors gets together on a regular basis and rotates among their homes, working together on projects designated by the household of the moment. Each household receives the benefit of the old adage "Many hands make light work," often finishing in a single day projects that the household would have spent weeks—or significant labor costs—to complete.

The only limits to what you can do in a neighborhood work group are group members' skills and willingness to work hard. One group we know taught themselves how to do all kinds of things; they installed an irrigation system, built fences and gates, refinished wood paneling, and put a new roof on a shed. They also made quick work of big tasks, like painting members' houses and landscaping whole yards.

Sharing for Art's Sake

Mural painting is a great way to beautify neighborhoods. And murals almost always involve sharing: They require at least one person to provide a wall, fence, or garage door, and an artist or group of artists to do the painting. If you share your wall or paint on someone else's, it's important to have a written agreement covering questions such as who may alter the mural, who will maintain it, what happens if the mural is to be removed or the building demolished, and whether the artist may relocate the artwork (by moving or replacing the entire fence or door, for example). It's also good to be familiar with the Visual Artists' Rights Act and comparable state statutes that govern ownership of works of art. These may sound like drab details, but they ultimately help us create a more colorful landscape.

Organize a Skillshare

A skillshare is an event that usually involves a series of classes and workshops taught by those with practical skills to share. It's a fun way to learn new skills and see a different side of your friends, coworkers, and neighbors. Plan an afternoon or a whole day and invite people to teach short classes on a topic of their choice, such as How to Make Mozzarella, How to Build with Bamboo, How to Change Your Bike Tire, How to Make Soap, or How to Knit. For more ideas, check out the annual Boston Skillshare (www.bostonskillshare.org).

Starting a Neighborhood Work Group

How should you go about forming a neighborhood work group? Here's how one neighborhood work group, in the Maxwell Park area of Oakland, got started. First, the organizer posted a message on the neighborhood listserve, which consisted of a few hundred households. (If your neighborhood doesn't have a listserv, you could go door to door or start with the neighbors you already know; see Chapter 2 for tips on getting sharing started with neighbors.) The message explained what a neighborhood work group is and what would be expected, and asked people to respond if they were interested. The organizer asked everyone who responded to complete the Tools and Skills Assessment form shown below.

The organizer got 17 completed forms back that showed a wide range of skills and tools. She knew that was too many for one group. Oakland's climate is temperate, but it does rain and get chilly in the winter, so most work projects get done from April to October. At one project per month, that meant each group should have six or seven households, so she created three groups with a balance of skills and resources. She asked each group to identify a leader, to whom she sent the letter shown below.

Home Improvement Group: Tools and Skills Assessment

Name(s): _____

Address: _____

Phone: _____ Email: _____

Preferred Work Day (check one): ☐ Saturday ☐ Sunday

Skills			
Skills	Seen It Done	Done Some	Done a Lot
Carpentry			
Plumbing			
Electrical			
Masonry			
Tile work			
Painting (exterior)			
Painting (interior)			
Gardening			
Demolition			
Basic wiring			
Other (list)			

Tools I Have for the Group to Use:

☐ Basic garden tools

☐ Basic hand tools

☐ Saw(s)

☐ Drill

☐ Ladder(s)

☐ _____

☐ _____

Comfort Level				
Tool or Activity	**Expert**	**Fine**	**Willing**	**Rather Not**
Power tools				
Lifting				
Heights/Ladders				
Attics/Basements				
Managing logistics				
Other (list)				

Possible Projects for Our Household

1. _____

2. _____

3. _____

Maxwell Park Home Improvement Project

Hello Fearless Leaders. You've volunteered for a dangerous and wonderful mission.

Attached are the forms that we have for the people in your group. The coordinators to start with for each group are as follows.

Group A	Luan	luan@aol.com	555-8888
Group B	Lisbeth	lissyb@gmail.com	555-0000
Group C	Jose	jdorado@earthlink.net	555-1111

Here's what you need to do next:

1. Contact your people to meet and talk about projects and calendaring them.

2. Get skills forms from those who didn't complete one.

3. Make copies so everyone has a packet of contact info.

4. Good grief, make up a name for your group. This ABC thing is boring.

Let's all coordinate if there are people who want/need to switch groups, or if there are more people interested. You're on your own to keep this going, but I'll help if I can.

Some basic points:

• Everyone agrees to work at all the other projects in return for having their house worked on. You can play that as you like. One person from the household might be sufficient, or someone may want to make up the day by working before or after—helping with prep or finish work—if they can't make it. Again, it's up to what your group feels comfortable with.

• The homeowner serves lunch to the group and should provide water. It's only nice.

- The hours are up to you, but 9 to 12 or 12:30, a half hour or 45 minute lunch break, and then working until 4 is usually a good guideline. Mornings will be most productive.
- Pay attention to where the sun is going to be for outdoor projects.
- The homeowner should have all projects clearly outlined and any materials needed already at the house before the work day. Know how many people are attending so you can assign the appropriate number of people to jobs. If people will need to bring gloves, tools, or anything else, let them know ahead of time.
- Encourage people to take pictures before big jobs like painting or landscaping. It's fun to see, and we can start a Yahoo group and post them there.

That's it for now. Let's all keep in contact and see what's going on.

Luan
Luan

One of the groups is still going strong into its fourth season. Over the years, they have done exterior painting, built a stone staircase outside a home, refinished furniture, rewired a kitchen, installed crown molding, rototilled a backyard, built and repaired gates, dug a trench, replaced a roof, and installed a beautiful outdoor mosaic path. The group gets together in the spring for a scheduling brunch and plans the projects for the year. At least one person from each household must show up at each work day. If a household needs to cancel its work day, the group tries to trade days or reschedule. If it doesn't work out, the group slots that household into an early month in the following year. Everyone in the group is proud of the work they've done to help each other and improve their neighborhood.

Set the Home Improvement Group Loose in the Neighborhood

While there never seems to be a shortage of home repair projects, a neighborhood home improvement group could also beautify community spaces in your neighborhood. Here are some ideas:

- Plant gardens on sidewalk and median strips.
- Remove unnecessary pavement to create more green space. (For example, see www.depave.org.)
- Offer to help neighbors remove or replace chain-link fences.
- Help out with the local school or community garden.
- Care for neighborhood trees.
- Contact owners of empty lots and ask if you could plant a community garden (see Chapter 8).
- Restore habitats and creeks.

The streets, sidewalks, and other areas may be owned by the city, so you may need a permit if your group takes on public projects.

Form a Home Energy Saving ("Energy Raising") Group

You may have heard all the advice about ways to save home energy: caulk your windows, seal air ducts, insulate your water heater, and so on. These are all great ideas, but who has time to learn how to do them, much less actually get them done?

That's why many people are forming groups to share in the learning, expenses, and work of home energy savings projects. Unless someone in your group is a home energy expert, you'll have to start by gathering information. Get a book about home energy saving, such as *The Home Energy Diet: How to Save Money by Making your House Energy Smart,* by Paul Scheckel (New Society Publishers), or download some do-it-yourself resources off the Internet. For example, AARP has an online Group Organizer's Toolkit for people forming energy saving groups. If you need more information, you can divide your group into teams to research topics like water heating, insulating, appliances, heating and cooling systems, and so on. You can also look into pricing, discounts, rebates, and tax credits for various improvements.

Gather your findings and inspect each home, looking for places where you can save energy. Figure out what improvements you can make to each house and what they'll cost. Typically, each house pays its own costs, but you can probably save some money by purchasing supplies together.

Once you've made your list of improvements, buy supplies and schedule some work days. The group can go from house to house, making repairs and changes. When January rolls around, you can have a party to celebrate your lower heating bills!

> **TIP**
>
> **Kick the energy savings up a notch.** If your group wants to get ambitious, there are all kinds of energy- and water-saving projects you can do—such as rainwater barrels, grey water systems, and solar panels. In New Hampshire, for example, one organization holds "energy raisers," similar to an old fashioned barn raising, except that the volunteers build and install solar water heaters, not barns. For more information about this group's work, see www.plymouthenergy.org.

Better Recycling Through Sharing

The world is full of creative people who could fix, reuse, recycle, or make art out of most of the things we throw away. The average American sends nearly a ton of garbage to landfills each year—that's a ton of potential. We can cooperate with others to ensure that our trash becomes someone else's treasure.

1. Form a group of friends or neighbors and brainstorm a list of things you can't recycle at curbside, such as batteries, CD jewel cases, medications, packaging materials, used envelopes, Styrofoam, toner cartridges, plastic yogurt cups, scrap metal, electronics, aerosol cans, paint, scrap wood, appliances, building materials, wires, cell phones, broken furniture, clothing, and broken ceramics.

2. Brainstorm ways to keep these things out of landfills. Start with people in your group. There may be a mosaic artist that will take everyone's broken ceramics and plastic bits. There may be a preschool teacher who will take everyone's toilet paper rolls and yogurt cups. Someone with a home mail order business could take everyone's packing materials and used envelopes. Start a compost group for food scraps and yard waste (see Chapter 8).

3. Do some research to deal with what's left. Start with your local recycling agency, and then talk to local businesses, schools, second-hand stores, and recycling or reuse centers. Come up with a list of places to take different kinds of trash/treasure.

4. Assign each group member a type of waste to collect from other members and deliver to the appropriate place. One person could handle all electronic waste. Someone with a truck could take all the scrap metal and wood. Someone else could volunteer to make regular runs to the local Goodwill store.

If you will be collecting toxic materials, such as paint or cleaning chemicals, and driving them to a disposal or recycling site, you may need a toxics hauling permit. An alternative is to schedule a neighborhood toxics pick-up by a properly licensed agency.

Liability Issues

Whether you're starting a home improvement group or making homes more energy efficient, you might be concerned that projects combining ladders, power tools, insulation, furnaces, and unskilled labor sounds like a liability nightmare. Certainly, it's important to be extra careful when you're working with a group under fairly uncontrolled conditions. Safety should be your group's top priority. Group members who know how to use equipment or perform tasks should convey safety instructions to the rest of the group, and you should review safety rules at the start of each work day.

Beyond that, you will probably want to rely on each member's homeowners' insurance to cover any accidents. In the event of an injury, most people want their homeowner's insurance to apply, in case the injured person doesn't have health insurance. If homeowners are worried about liability beyond what their homeowners' insurance will cover, they could ask people to sign an indemnification agreement like the one below.

Sample Work Share Indemnification Agreement

I am taking part in this home repair group as a fun way to learn about home repair, get help with my household projects, and spend time with neighbors. I recognize that there are significant injury risks involved in performing home repair tasks. If I am injured on someone else's property, I agree to indemnify and hold harmless the homeowner for all injury-related costs that are not covered by his or her homeowner's liability insurance. I am not waiving my right to make a claim against his or her homeowner's liability insurance. I am, however, agreeing not to hold the homeowner responsible for any additional costs beyond those paid by the homeowner's insurance.

> ⓘ **CAUTION**
>
> **These agreements may not provide surefire protection against liability.** Agreements that release people from liability and responsibility aren't always enforced by courts, especially if the homeowner's gross negligence caused the injury. It's still a good idea for members to think about and agree in advance to release one another from responsibility after the homeowner's insurance policy has paid out, but keep in mind that your agreement may not stand up if it's challenged in court.

Solution 5: Share a Yard

For many people, outside is a great place to be. People spend a lot of money and time making their yards, decks, terraces, gardens, and gazebos appealing. And you can double your outdoor space simply by taking down the fence between your yard and your neighbor's.

Take Down the Fence Between You and Your Neighbor

If you have a good relationship with your neighbor and you both own your homes (or have the blessing of your landlords), you can expand your yard space by taking down the fence between your yard and your neighbor's. The benefits include:

- more yard space for both households
- space that's large enough for sports or parties
- a shared garden (and more gardeners)
- better views
- shortcuts
- easy access to shared tools, furniture, and other resources that are owned by each household, and
- a feeling of greater spaciousness in the backyard.

Some neighbors make a conscious decision to get rid of a fence and share space. Other times, fences come down naturally, and neighbors decide not to replace them. For example, one of the authors has a back-fence neighbor who remodeled a garage, which required the removal of a small fence and gate between the two properties. When the project was finished, both households decided that they would rather leave the fence down. Now the young boys who live in one house wander into the other yard to pick lemons off the tree, locate their cat in her favorite spot on a lounge chair, or simply have more safe places to play.

Legal Issues Applicable to Fence Removal

If you take down a fence, especially a major one, it's a good idea to have a written agreement with your neighbors, to clarify if, when, and how the fence will be rebuilt; how much it will cost; and who will pay for it. To avoid boundary disputes that could occur later, it's also a good idea to leave a few posts or something else to demarcate the boundary if the removal of the fence makes that less clear.

Also, be aware that removing a fence could affect a boundary dispute later, primarily because it could destroy an adverse possession claim. According to the law of adverse possession, if someone openly possesses someone else's land for the length of time specified in the state adverse possession law (usually five to 20 years), that person could claim title to the land. So, for example, if your fence is actually on your neighbor's property, it could eventually "redraw" the property line.

> EXAMPLE: The Fennig family and the Bodhi family removed a fence between their homes. Nine years earlier, before the Fennigs house was built, the Bodhis put up a fence that was six feet over the property line. This meant that the Bodhis were possessing a significant portion of what was to become the Fennig's yard. Two years after removing the fence, the Fennigs moved and sold their house to the Kirui family. The Kiruis requested a survey and discovered that they owned that portion of property six feet beyond where the fence had been. Had they not removed the fence, the Bodhis may have been able to keep the land, because their state law of adverse possession would have allowed them to get title after possessing it for ten years.

If you have no doubt that the fence correctly demarks the boundary line, this will not likely be a concern for you. If not, however, it's something to consider before removing a fence.

Finally, if you are going to share your yard, make sure there's nothing on your property that could be what's called an "attractive nuisance" for children. This means anything that is dangerous but that children would naturally be interested in exploring, like an old refrigerator, tools or building supplies, or an unfenced well, pool, or other body of water.

RESOURCE

Learn more about neighbors and fences. *Neighbor Law: Fences, Trees, Boundaries & Noise,* by Cora Jordan and Emily Doskow (Nolo), explains the relevant legal rules about shared fences, as well as rules about attractive nuisances and easements and other permissions to use someone else's property.

Neighborhood Garage Sales

One way to get lots of people to come to a garage sale is to coordinate with neighbors to have multiple garage sales on one day, advertise them in advance, and draw in the real garage sale connoisseurs. You can join forces to post flyers and make maps showing where all the sales will be. Encourage shoppers to stay longer by designating restrooms for their use, either in a couple of homes or in a neighborhood coffee shop or store that might get some business out of the arrangement.

Multifamily sales are also a fun idea, because they bring together everyone in a single location. At the same time, they can be less convenient because they require participants to bring all goods to one person's house. Those actually dealing with customers have to know what the sellers are willing to accept for each item, and everyone has to keep track of who owns what and how much it sold for. No matter what type of sale you have, check with your city government to find out if you have to get a permit or meet other requirements.

Sample Yard Sharing Agreement

This agreement is between VICKI and BOB ROBLES, owners of 124 Monte Vista Avenue, and DONNA and PHILLIP LEUNG, owners of 128 Monte Vista Avenue.

1. We have decided to remove the fence between our homes to create more space for our children and pets to play, and to create a pleasant shared garden environment.

2. By removing the fence between our houses, we do not intend to redraw property lines or create an easement.

3. Either of us may decide at any time to terminate this arrangement, at which time we will reconstruct the fence. If one of us moves or sells their house, we may decide to reconstruct the fence then.

4. We will reconstruct the fence in the same location, which is marked by a few remaining posts. If and when we reconstruct a fence, the fence will be constructed in the following manner: (*Describe fencing materials, height, and so on*). We will split the cost equally.

5. Both parties carry homeowner's liability insurance.

6. If one of us is injured on the other's property, we agree to indemnify and hold harmless that property owner for all injury-related costs that are not covered by that property owner's homeowner's liability insurance. We are not waiving our rights to make claims against that property owner's homeowner's liability insurance. We are, however, agreeing to not hold that property owner responsible for any additional costs beyond those paid by the homeowner's insurance.

7. This agreement is only between the current owners of the homes and does not attach to the properties or bind any future owners of the homes. We will not record this document.

Sharing Your Yard for Recreation

Even if you don't take down your fence, sharing your yard is a great idea, especially if there are children in the neighborhood. Everyone could have access to swing sets, swimming pools, trampolines, basketball hoops, tetherballs, gardens, hot tubs, exercise equipment, or large lawns for sports.

The primary concerns that arise when you allow other people to use your yard and equipment for recreation are safety and liability. In many ways, neighborhoods where people share yards are safer than most, primarily because everyone knows and looks out for everyone else. At the same time, it's good to set clear limits about who has access to your yard, when, what they may do there, and whether they should notify you before coming over.

As for liability concerns, many, but not all, homeowners will be protected from liability by laws made for the purpose of encouraging recreation. Every state has a recreational use statute, to encourage private property owners to allow others to use land for recreational purposes. These statutes typically exempt the property owner from liability for injuries that take place as a result of the types of recreational use listed in the statute. Take a look at your state's statute and find out what it covers; you can find a list of state statutes at http://asci.uvm.edu/equine/law/recreate/recreate.htm.

Homeowner's liability is a complicated area of law, and it's difficult to completely protect against liability. There are always exceptions to recreational use laws and ways to get around liability waivers. You should still make sure that you are adequately protected by your homeowner's insurance. If you have a swimming pool or hot tub, check with your homeowner's insurance company to find out whether you are covered for pool-related injuries and deaths. Some pool owners obtain special insurance policies that apply just to swimming pools. And of course, anyone with a pool or other potentially dangerous equipment, such as a trampoline, should take extra precautions. These may include keeping lifesaving equipment nearby, never allowing children without a parent, and prohibiting anyone from swimming alone, for example.

**The Bigger Picture: Sharing Household
Goods, Purchases, Tasks, and Space**

Here are some ways that businesses, nonprofits, community leaders, lawmakers, and others can help encourage household sharing:

- Expand public library systems to include tool and goods lending libraries.
- Owners of multiunit housing: Provide a way for residents to share household goods, by designating an accessible space for shared goods, or by making certain goods available to all residents, such as vacuum cleaners, tools, and sports equipment.
- City governments: Provide free emergency preparedness kits and training to neighborhood groups who cooperate to plan for disasters.
- Lawmakers: Change energy regulation to allow for and encourage medium-scale community renewable energy projects.

The Triple Bottom Line:
The Benefits of Sharing Household
Goods, Purchases, Tasks and Space

Social and Personal Benefits

- Get help and have fun getting your home improvement projects done.
- Gain access to all kinds of useful and/or fun items, by forming a goods-sharing group.
- Make your neighborhood safer by cooperating to prepare for emergencies and by creating a community where everyone looks out for each other.
- Save time on shopping or household chores, by cooperating with others to buy goods and services.

Environmental Benefits

- Reduce extraction of natural resources and the manufacture of disposable consumer goods by sharing high quality goods with others.
- Cooperate with your neighbors to recycle and reduce waste.
- Reduce your home's carbon footprint by taking part in a home energy saving group.
- Cooperate on projects to save, purify, and recycle water.
- Save product packaging by buying in bulk with others.

Financial Benefits

- Save thousands of dollars by sharing ownership or use of household goods, equipment, tools, or clothing.
- Reduce monthly expenditures by forming groups to buy household supplies and staples.
- Bargain collectively for expensive goods and services, and save a lot of money on things like solar power.
- Save labor costs for home repair, by forming a home improvement group with friends or neighbors.

Sharing Food

In our busy lives, it's possible to have a diet made up mostly of fast food, packaged snacks, frozen dinners, energy drinks, and "just-add-water" meals. In fact, this type of fully processed meal plan is the cheapest and most convenient option dished up to us.

But the alternatives sound wonderful: fresh, local, organic, humanely raised, unprocessed, artisan, nutrient-dense, home-cooked, and even home-grown food! To find the time and the money for such epicurean delights, you need to add the missing ingredient: sharing.

Sharing makes it easier and more affordable to enjoy a diet that's healthier for us and for our planet. In fact, sharing can change not only the way we consume food, but also the way that we grow, process, and distribute it. There are many reasons to share food, not the least of which is the pleasure involved in cooking with and for others, and sharing a table with friends, neighbors, and loved ones. But even before food gets to our table, it has taken a long journey—from seed to plant, through harvest, transport, processing, packaging, distribution, stores, preparation, and finally to our plates. Sharing can come into play at every stage of this journey.

The benefits of sharing food include:

- **Better nutrition and variety in our diets.** Mass-produced food is often cheap, but it has lost a lot of its natural taste and nutritional value, a fact that is masked by artificial flavors and preservatives. When we collectively support a local farm, we get food that is fresher and higher in nutrients. Group purchasing can help us afford foods that are grown without pesticides and chemical fertilizers. And when we share meals and cook for others, we are more likely to eat full meals, spanning all food groups, and to have a more diverse diet (not to mention tasty dinners).

- **More sustainable food sources.** Our cheap and abundant food supply is due largely to mass production and government subsidies. But our society and planet pay the real cost of our food in other ways. Beyond the enormous carbon footprint of food transport—most of us eat food that comes from many miles away every day—industrial agriculture is responsible for lots of air and water pollution, especially due to chemical pesticides, fertilizers, machinery, and silt runoff. This food system is vulnerable to crisis from climate change, depletion of cheap energy sources, loss of plant diversity caused by genetic engineering, and disease. Through the sharing arrangements described in this chapter, we can create smaller-scale, localized, and more diverse food supplies—our best defense against threats to our food system.

- **Support for small farms and food producers.** A century ago, one-third of the U.S. population lived on farms; today, that number has fallen to less than 2%. Most farms are no longer owned and operated by independent farmers; instead, most people who work in the food or farming industry are employed by large companies, often at low wages and in poor working conditions. Farmland itself is also being rapidly depleted and replaced by commercial or housing developments. Sharing gives us many opportunities to reverse these trends. When we buy collectively from small farmers and responsible food producers, the food is more affordable for consumers, and the small farmers and food producers receive the support they need. As communities, we can also work together to preserve agricultural land (see "Agricultural Land Trusts," below).

- **Benefits to food-insecure communities.** More than a tenth of the U.S. population is food insecure, meaning they have limited or uncertain access to nutritionally adequate or safe foods. Community food gardens and food recovery programs help ensure that everyone gets enough to eat.

- **Greater personal satisfaction and appreciation.** Food is a source of life. It can also be a source of great pleasure, an expression of caring for others, and a way to slow down the sometimes frenetic pace of our lives. Sharing food—whether by sharing meals, gardening, or harvesting—is a tangible way to express our desire for community and our willingness to nurture others and be nurtured in turn. Because food is closely connected to our cultural heritage, sharing also allows us to celebrate and experience diverse culinary traditions.

Sharing Food

Localizes our
food system

Supports small farms
and food enterprises

Reduces waste and
energy consumption

Builds community
and infuses joy into
cooking/eating

Diversifies our
diets and enhances
nutrition

Promotes stability
in our food system

Helps meet everyone's
food needs

Cultivation
- Community gardens
- Community supported
  agriculture
- Farmer cooperatives

Seed
- Seed exchange
  libraries

Food Waste
- Neighborhood
  compost rotation

Harvest
- Community backyard fruit harvesting

Distribution
- Grocery cooperatives
- Food buying clubs
- "Cowpooling"

Preparing/Processing
- Community supported kitchens and restaurants
- Cooking and food preservation groups
- Meal exchanges at home, work, and for school lunches

Food Surplus
- Community food recovery projects
- Leftover sharing

Eating
- Mealsharing
- Potlucks
- Food tastings
- Safari suppers

Solution 1: Share Meals

Mealsharing can mean either sitting down and actually eating with others, or sharing meal preparation by trading meals with others in any of a variety of ways. Sharing meals allows us to eat better, save preparation time, and save the cost of eating out or buying prepared meals. It also allows us to try new cuisines, diversify our diets, and get creative with our cooking.

Mealsharing also builds relationships. People who share meals tend to form bonds and trust, from which other kinds of sharing relationships arise. When you sit down to a shared meal at the end of day, you share more than food—you also share time, conversation, community, and support.

The Power of a Shared Meal

Mealsharing was practiced formally in South Africa during the 1980s and 90s to create bonds between polarized racial groups and to counter the mistrust and misunderstanding fostered by apartheid. Tens of thousands of South Africans took part in the practice of "Koinonia," which often involved two white families and two black families who would take turns having dinner at each other's homes. In the United States, Jewish and Palestinian Americans have formed similar mealsharing groups to promote dialog and understanding between groups. As these sharers discovered, the act of going into someone else's home and sharing dinner creates a powerful sense of connection and trust. To learn more, see: http://traubman.igc.org/mealshar.htm.

Sharing Meals in Your Neighborhood or Home

Most of the time, it's easiest to share meals with people who live close by—in a neighborhood, apartment complex, retirement community, or shared housing.

Group Meals

Group meals are very common in shared housing, especially in cohousing, which often has a common house with a large kitchen and dining space. People who live in group houses share meals regularly. Mealsharing is also great for retirement communities or any neighborhood where people want to enjoy each other's company and share great food.

> **TIP**
>
> **Talk about other ways to share over dinner.** People who share meals are well positioned to share a variety of other things. For example, mealsharers make good partners for collective buying, doing a food recovery project, or participating in community-supported agriculture. Of course, you can also go beyond food sharing to share tools, household goods, childcare, yards, and much more. Some night over dinner, suggest that the group brainstorm other ways of sharing.

EXAMPLE: A group of ten neighboring households shares meals on Sundays, Tuesdays, and Thursdays. Each adult and teenager—27 people—shares in the cooking, with a team of three people assigned to plan, shop, cook, and clean up after each meal. Each person helps prepare a meal once every three weeks and enjoys eight other meals without lifting a finger or spending a dime.

Cooking and eating rotates among three different households, each with a large dining room with adjoining living room, a spacious kitchen, and, most importantly, a dishwasher. When they began the mealshare, everyone chipped in to buy a set of plates and bowls, silverware, and cloth napkins. The dining set is kept in two large crates and travels from house to house. Families bring empty food containers to dinner, so all leftovers find good homes.

Each cooking team emails the group two days before its assigned meal to announce the menu. Meal attendance is optional. Sometimes, people come to dinner, fill up a plate, and return home to eat or save the food for later. Most of the time, however, everyone attends and enjoys the time they spend with their neighbors. There are also guests at most meals. From time to time, the group has theme dinners or special discussion topics. Every Sunday during dessert, the group has "Updates and Announcements." Those with information to share or interesting updates about their lives raise their hands and talk for a minute or two each. Every three months, the group has a meeting dinner to plan the schedule for the next three months and discuss other housekeeping matters.

Cooking for Large Groups

It's one thing to whip up dinner for you and your family, and another to feed a crowd. If you are ready for the challenge, there's plenty of advice and help out there. Here are some basic tips on cooking for groups:

- Do as much preparation in advance as possible. This is easier if you serve cold items, such as sandwiches and salads.
- Serve things that you can make in a large pot, such as soups, stews, or curries; or serve large noodle dishes, such as spaghetti, casseroles, and lasagna.
- Use a slow-cooker—they're great for creating large and simple meals in advance.
- Make something that will taste good as leftovers, in case you make too much.

Appendix A includes a list of cookbooks with recipes for large groups.

TIP

Plan a tasting party. How often do you get to compare different brands or varieties of a food? Have you ever wanted to taste every type of salami or try different coffees to learn about their subtleties of flavor, or try varieties of locally grown apples? While it's not practical to buy 20 apples or make ten pots of coffee for yourself, a group of people could share this fun endeavor. You could plan a gathering where each attendee brings a thermos of coffee or a different kind of cheddar cheese, for example.

Meal Exchanges

Another way to share meals is through meal exchanges, where one household doubles or triples a recipe and delivers the extra food to others. This can be done on a flexible schedule, with meals that can be reheated later. To assist with meal planning, however, a fixed schedule, with each household cooking on a particular night of the week, works best.

> **EXAMPLE:** Joline and Paulo live across the street from Maxine and Dave. Once or twice a week, each couple prepares a dish to share. The couples don't have a fixed schedule for sharing food. One week their food-sharing looked like this:
>
> On Sunday afternoon, Maxine and Dave roasted a large pan of winter vegetables and delivered half to Joline and Paulo. On Monday evening, Paulo knocked on Maxine and Dave's door with a pot of soup and some home-baked bread. On Wednesday evening, Maxine made a large chef's salad to share with Joline and Paulo. On Friday, Joline and Paulo delivered a casserole dish full of pasta, ready to be baked. The two couples have a shared vegetable garden in Paulo and Joline's yard, and most meals contain some of its bounty.

Potlucks

Potlucks combine the social aspect of a group meal with the ease and flexibility of cooking a single dish at home. Traditionally, everyone brings a dish to a potluck, but all kinds of variations are possible. For example, a large mealsharing group could assign five people to bring dishes for each meal.

A good potluck takes a little planning. Left to their own devices, for example, potluck attendees could end up with a dinner composed of a big bowl of salad, another big bowl of salad, a fruit salad, and another big bowl of salad (true story). One way to plan a potluck is to give one person, often the host, the assignment of making the "anchor dish," which is a large item such as lasagna or a ham, while others are assigned peripheral dishes such as salad, sides, soup, or dessert. A much more coherent meal is likely to result.

These days, the Internet has made potluck planning much simpler. Tools such as Evite (www.evite.com) allow potluck planners to have attendees sign up to bring certain dishes. There are also websites with special potluck planning features, such as www.centerd.com and www. luckypotluck.com.

When the potluck is over, you can either bring home the dish you brought or everyone can bring food containers to divide up the leftovers. There are a few ways to share the cleanup. Everyone can bring their own dishes and take them home afterwards, either washing them at the host's house or at home later. Or, a rotating team, "The Clean Plates Club," can be assigned cleanup duty.

TIP

Have a safari supper. For a fun variation on potlucks, try holding a "safari supper," where guests have three courses (appetizer, entrée, and dessert) at three different houses and with a different group at each house. This works best if you have at least nine participating households. For example, for the first course, the Aguilars could host the Browns and the Chens, the Davidsons host the Ellisons and the Frieres; and the Greens host the Huangs and the Isaacsons. For the second course, the hosts get to be guests at another house, and some guests become hosts, and everyone is matched up with new people. By the end of the night, everyone has had the opportunity to share food with at least six other families.

Accommodating Diverse Diets in Mealsharing

The more people you have in a mealsharing group, the harder it becomes to accommodate diverse dietary requirements and preferences. People may avoid foods for different reasons—for health reasons, religious reasons, allergies or sensitivities, ethical or political reasons, plain old dislike, and so on. It helps to keep in mind the most common food allergies—nuts, sesame, shellfish, milk, eggs, wheat, and soy— and alert people when your dish contains them. To make sure everyone can eat the meals you share, have each member of your group fill out the "Diet Preferences for Mealsharing" chart, below (you'll find a blank copy in Appendix B).

Increasingly, people are turning to vegetarian diets. Between 3% and 4% percent of people in the United States are vegetarians, and many more limit the amount of meat they eat, eat only organic or free-range meat, or try to buy meat that has been produced without unnecessary cruelty. Some people are "vege-aquarians," meaning they'll eat seafood, but not meat; others are vegans and avoid animal products altogether. This calls for some creativity when you cook for large groups, perhaps to come up with a vegetarian version of your main dish.

Diet Preferences for Mealsharing				
Types of Food	Food I Don't Eat	Food I Prefer Not to Eat (but I Can Be Flexible)	Food That Is Fine If I Can Pick Out	Food That Is Fine in Small Amounts
Milk/cheese				✓ (I'm lactose intolerant, but I can take a lactase enzyme with dairy foods.)
Mushrooms			✓	
Spicy food		✓ (I am wimpy about spicy foods sometimes.)		
Lamb	✓ (Baaa-a-a-a-ad!)			
Foods high in cholesterol		✓ (My doctor says I should avoid.)		

Share Your Food Scraps:
Start a Neighborhood Compost Rotation

Converting food waste into compost is a wonderful way to send less trash to the landfills. Some cities collect food scraps and yard clippings in curbside bins, and then truck them to a compost facility. But composting in your own neighborhood is a much greener alternative—and it's fun!

Collaborating with neighbors can be much more efficient than doing your own compost. Food scraps and yard clippings take four to ten months to decompose, depending on conditions. Doing a compost rotation allows you to have multiple compost bins, each at a different stage of composition. As each compost pile matures, you will have a regular supply of free organic fertilizer, which your gardens will love.

Here's how to start a compost rotation:

1. Go door to door and invite your neighbors to a compost meeting and class. Rent a how-to video about composting or find an experienced composter to teach the class.

2. Build compost piles or bins in three or more neighbors' yards. Designate a trash can to collect food scraps.

3. Start the first compost pile by inviting neighbors to bring their vegetable food scraps, grass clippings, and dry leaves to the home of the first composter and dump them in the compost can one day per week. When that neighbor's compost bin is full, begin the process at a second neighbor's house, and so on.

4. When the first neighbor's compost bin has matured, invite neighbors to come collect the bounty. If you have too much, your local community garden will happily accept it.

A compost rotation is just one of many ways to set up a neighborhood compost project. Some people are surprisingly passionate about composting and relish watching rotting food magically transform into organic fertilizer. If you are one of them, you could set up the bins in your own yard, and invite your neighbors to bring their food scraps over.

> TIP
>
> **Create a mealsharing cookbook.** Your mealsharing group could compile a binder full of recipes and a list of what people have cooked—and enjoyed eating—in the past. You may also want to keep track of dishes that didn't work (or go over) as well, to make sure you don't repeat these mistakes. Some dishes are easier than others to make in large quantities, and it helps to have a ready list of ideas.

Sharing Meals at Work

In some workplaces, coworkers share lunch during the week. It makes for a fun social break, saves everyone lunch money, and offers a change of pace from the office vending machines, local lunch spots, or even your own leftovers.

Coworkers can share meals in many ways:

- **Prepare lunch in the office kitchen.** Each day, designate two people to make the meal and two to clean up. This works especially well if there's an office dishwasher (talk that idea up to your boss).
- **Take turns bringing lunch.** Each day, designate one or two people to bring lunch for others.
- **Hold regular pot lucks.** Each day, assign each person a part of the meal to bring. For example, one person brings a main dish, one person brings fruit, one brings a vegetable dish, one brings a starch, and one brings dessert.
- **Keep basics on hand.** A group of employees could take turns making bulk purchases to keep certain staples on hand, such as fresh fruit, nuts, chips, salsa, sandwich bread, lettuce, tomato, sandwich meat, cheese, mayonnaise, and mustard. That way, everyone could go into the kitchen each day, make themselves a sandwich, have healthy snacks, and grab some cookies!

Many of us use our lunch break for more than just eating. Perhaps you occasionally use your lunch hour to relax and get in some quiet time, you sometimes need to work through lunch, or you spend that time doing errands or getting some exercise. An office mealsharing group will be most successful if it accommodates these needs by making food available to those who won't be sitting down to eat with the group.

Sharing School Lunches

Parents of school-age children are all too familiar with the morning rush to get out the door. There never seems to be enough time to dress and feed everyone, find everyone's bookbags and homework, and prepare everyone's lunch. Here's an idea: Propose a school lunch-sharing arrangement with some other families at your child's school. Agree with other parents to make meals for the kids on a rotating schedule. If the kids are all in the same class, you can just drop off the lunches in the classroom in the morning. Sharing school lunches can also dovetail well with a carpooling group.

Every parent should complete the "Diet Preferences for Meal Sharing" chart, above, for their kids; Appendix B includes a blank copy. You may want to agree to be honest with each other about what your kids like—and don't like—about particular meals. It won't save money or the planet if you make meals that the kids throw away in favor of snacks from the vending machine.

Solution 2: Buy Food Together

Another way to share food is to purchase it together as a grocery cooperative or buying club. By pooling your purchasing power, you can pay much less for food, which makes it easier to afford sustainable, local, organic, responsibly produced, or hard-to-find items. It also saves packaging, transportation, and waste. And, it's a fun way to get to know people.

Grocery Cooperatives

Grocery cooperatives (co-ops) are stores that are owned and run by the consumers. Some grocery co-ops look like typical grocery stores, at least on the surface. But a closer look reveals many differences in how things operate:

- **Co-ops are owned by their patrons.** Any profit is either refunded to members, reinvested in the co-op to lower food prices, or invested in the community as members see fit.

- **Co-ops often have a mission that goes beyond providing food.** Some co-ops provide health education to the community, hire people with special needs, pay a living wage to employees, support small businesses and food producers, and buy fair trade, organic, and other environmentally and socially responsible products.
- **Because the co-ops are operated for and by their members, food is kept cheap.** While many grocery stores sell food for about 70% more than wholesale, some cooperatives can reduce prices to about 20% more than wholesale. Using volunteer hours helps keep costs low. According to the Cooperative Grocery of Berkeley, CA, typically grocery stores use 70% of their income to pay employees. Co-ops often require members to work a few hours a month at the register, stocking shelves, or doing whatever needs to be done.

RESOURCE

Looking for a local grocery co-op? You may not have to start your own co-op; with at least 300 grocery co-ops in the United States, chances are good that you'll be able to find one to join near you, especially if you live in a metropolitan area. Appendix A includes co-op websites and directories.

While every co-op operates differently, many have these things in common:

- New members typically make a one-time payment to become shareholders in the co-op. Typically, this payment is $100 to $200, refundable if you leave. You may also be asked to pay a non-refundable fee, usually about $50. And, you'll probably be asked to attend an orientation to learn how the co-op works.
- You'll probably be asked to come in once a month or so for a work shift of two to four hours. Most co-op members report that they enjoy this, because they can get to know other members and learn how to run a grocery store.
- The co-op may be open only to members, or may allow non-members to shop, too.

- Once a year, you may get a refund check for your share of the store profits, based on how much you spent at the co-op. This is often called a "patronage refund."
- The co-op may go beyond simply buying and selling food. Some co-ops host fun events, such as cooking and nutrition classes.

Co-op Profile: Park Slope Food Coop

Established in 1972, Brooklyn, New York's Park Slope Food Coop is one of the oldest and most successful cooperative grocery stores in the country. Founded by Brooklyn residents whose goal was to bring affordable, nutritious food to their own neighborhood, the co-op now has more than 13,000 members. Only members can shop at the co-op, and membership is open to anyone who pays a one-time joining fee, makes an investment of $100 (which the member can get back on leaving the co-op), and work a few hours per month. Fees can be reduced for low-income members. The co-op has monthly general meetings and every member has a vote. Many other cooperative groceries all over the country are modeled on the Park Slope Food Coop. Learn more at www.foodcoop.com.

Buying Clubs

Buying clubs come in many sizes and forms, but the basic concept is the same: A group of people get together to purchase items in bulk at a lower cost than they would have to pay for smaller quantities. A buying club may be a simple, informal arrangement or it may be a large, well-oiled machine.

There are thousands of buying clubs throughout the United States, and there may be one in your area that you can join. One way to find a buying club is to contact food distributors who specialize in selling to buying clubs, such as United Buying Clubs (www.unitedbuyingclubs.com) or United Natural Foods (www.unfi.com).

Chapter 7 explains how to start a buying club for household goods and supplies. The steps to start a food buying club are largely the same. The two biggest challenges in operating a food buying club are (1) finding sources and distributors, and (2) timing orders to avoid wasting food.

Many buying clubs order everything from a single large distributor or warehouse, such as United Buying Clubs or United Natural Foods. You may also want to enter into a direct buying relationship with a handful of smaller food producers, like a local bakery or farm. Distributors have different policies about how they sell; some require very large minimum orders or frequent ordering. You'll need to call around to find out how each works. Also, talk to other buying clubs to find out what food distributors work well for them.

Large buying clubs have a fixed location where food is delivered, stored, divided, and distributed to members. Smaller clubs often have food delivered to members' homes or offices—either to one or two designated spots or rotating among the members—or distribute food as soon as it arrives.

Food buying clubs make more frequent orders than clubs that buy nonperishables, because food needs to be replenished regularly. This requires careful coordination and planning by members. But for many, the benefits of receiving fresh, healthy, and affordable foods make it worth the effort.

TIP

Are you interested in starting a small food business? Perhaps you want to sell your amazing sauces or cookies at a market, or start an occasional catering business. Consider sharing resources with other small food enterprises. For more information about sharing commercial kitchens, equipment, and purchasing with other food businesses, see Chapter 11.

Solution 3: Community Fruit Tree Harvests

Anyone with a mature fruit tree is familiar with the annual quandaries: How do you get all that fruit out of the tree and what do you do with 500 plums? If you've ever tried to preserve, freeze, and eat it all yourself, you probably got plum tired! Most fruit trees produce a lot of fruit—300 peaches, 400 apples, and more lemons than most people know what to do with.

This is where sharing saves the day. Cooperating with others to harvest, preserve, distribute, and eat the fruit can be a fun and fruitful activity. And, it saves you from trying to use up all that fruit through "creative" recipes, fruit-only diets, and strong-arming neighbors and friends to take some off your hands, which brings to mind Garrison Keillor's joke: "Why do the inhabitants of Lake Wobegon lock their cars in the month of August? So their neighbors won't leave bags of zucchini on the back seat."

There's Enough to Go Around: Recovering and Sharing Surplus Food

According to the U.S. Department of Agriculture (USDA), about a fifth of edible food in the United States goes to waste, while at least 11% of our population struggles to meet basic food and nutrition needs. With proper organization, it's possible to close this gap. The USDA promotes "food recovery," by which organizations collect and redistribute surplus food that would otherwise be headed for the landfill. Policy makers in every state have taken steps to encourage this by adopting Good Samaritan Food Donation laws, which provide liability protection to people who donate food to charities.

Consider starting a food recovery project in your community. There is plenty of food to be collected—including excess fruit and vegetables harvested from your very own yard—and plenty of resources to help you get started. The USDA has produced a helpful online guide to surplus food collection, "A Citizen's Guide to Food Recovery," available at www.usda.gov/news/pubs/gleaning/content.htm.

One model organization, Food Not Bombs, is a network of volunteer groups in hundreds of cities throughout the world. With a message of promoting peace and ending hunger, these volunteers collect surplus food from farmers, distributors, stores, and restaurants, and cook large meals for the hungry in public places. Food Not Bombs has created a handbook to help you get started, including tips on collecting food, recipes, and more; you can find it at their website, www.foodnotbombs.net.

Community Harvest Programs

Some organizations plan community harvesting efforts, often targeting the homes of elderly people or those with disabilities, who might be unable to pick their own fruit. The volunteers deliver some fruit to the homeowner and donate or sell the rest.

If you are thinking of starting a program like this, there are many organizations you can use as a model. One excellent example is Village Harvest, based in suburban Silicon Valley, California. Village Harvest organizes volunteers to harvest fruit from backyards, distribute fruit to food banks and shelters, and educate the community about fruit growing and preservation.

Village Harvest has a full calendar of harvesting events when fruit is in season. They invite anyone to show up at a designated meeting place, and then disperse to area homes for harvesting. They also encourage tree owners to pick their own fruit, providing a list of numerous drop-off locations for donation. The Village Harvest also has a volunteer "Jammin' Team," which meets monthly at a church kitchen to make preserves, later selling them to raise funds. Find out more at the Village Harvest website, www.villageharvest.org, which provides many helpful resources on fruit growing and preservation, as well as links to similar organizations.

Starting a Neighborhood Harvest

Here are the steps you'll need to take to start a neighborhood fruit tree harvest:

- Go door-to-door to find volunteers and do an inventory of neighborhood trees and berry bushes.
- If tree owners want help harvesting, have them sign a harvest agreement (see below). Find out when their fruit is in season.
- Schedule some fruit picking days. For example, you might plan to have volunteers meet at a designated spot every other Saturday (or even weekly), then begin the neighborhood rounds. Be sure tree owners know when you'll be visiting their house.

- Get some extension fruit pickers (long poles with hooks and baskets at the end) or borrow a sturdy ladder or two. A tarp is also useful for catching fruit shaken off a tree.
- Decide what to do with the fruit. You should give some to the neighbors who own the tree, if they want it. The rest can be delivered to other neighbors, donated to charity, preserved, frozen, or used for a pie-baking party.
- During the off-season, organize a neighborhood fruit tree pruning project. The tree will show its appreciation by giving healthy and plentiful fruit. If everyone takes part, it'll be quick, easy, and fun.

Liability Concerns

Homeowners may be concerned about the risk they could be taking in letting someone harvest their fruit. What if a fruit harvester is injured or someone gets sick from eating the fruit? There isn't a simple answer to the question of who will be liable for injuries like these. In part, it depends on how the person is injured.

One way to significantly reduce the risk is to use extension fruit pickers rather than ladders. Homeowners should also take care to eliminate all hazards in the yard, such as holes, sharp objects, biting dogs, and so on. And, if there are any unavoidable risks, like a rickety fence or a sharply sloping hillside, the owner should let the harvesters know up front.

Homeowners who donate all of their fruit to nonprofits are probably protected from liability from injuries that befall fruit pickers on their property, and for illness stemming from eating the fruit. Every state has a Good Samaritan Food Donation law protecting people from liability for donating apparently wholesome food to a nonprofit, unless the injury involved gross negligence on the part of the donor. A "nonprofit organization," for the purpose of this law, is a group that operates for religious, charitable, or educational purposes, and does not provide net earnings to, or operate in any other manner that inures to the benefit of, any officer, employee, or shareholder of the organization. The nonprofit doesn't have to be a registered corporation. It could be an unincorporated group, as long as the group is picking the fruit for charitable purposes, not to provide significant benefit to themselves. In other words, it could be your group.

Whether or not you believe that your group meets the above definition of a nonprofit organization, a liability waiver is always a good idea. The waiver won't always guarantee that the homeowner will avoid legal responsibility for injuries arising from the harvest, but it will likely provide the homeowner with some level of protection.

Fruit Harvest Agreement

It's a good idea to use a written agreement to harvest fruit from someone's property. The agreement should set some ground rules, specify dates and times for harvesting, and address liability concerns. An agreement that could be used for a fruit harvest is shown below.

Sharing in All Kinds of Food Processes

A lot happens to food between the time it's harvested and the time you eat it. Many of these food processing activities take skill, time, or special equipment, and are best accomplished through cooperation with others. Some processes should be done under carefully monitored and controlled conditions. Some require large machines, such as hulling a tree's worth of walnuts.

If you are harvesting 1,000 apricots with your neighbors, you might want to have a neighborhood "jam session." Or if you buy a whole pig or a large quantity of grain with friends, you have to figure out what to do with it. Here are some of the food processes you can share with others:

Fermenting	Canning	Curing
Smoking	Bottling	Making Cheese
Hulling	Aging	Making Yogurt
Grinding	Candying	Making Pasta
Pasteurizing	Cleaning	Baking Bread
Drying	Butchering	Roasting Coffee
Milling	Juicing	Making Ice-cream
Pickling	Extracting	Churning Butter
Conserving	Freezing	

Fruit Harvest Agreement

This agreement is between the ___Neighborhood Fruit Harvest Group___
("Harvesters") and _____ ("Owner").
We enter into this agreement to allow Harvesters to pick fruit from Owner's
fruit tree(s) and bushes.

1. On the following dates and times, Harvesters will pick the following fruit:

   _____[Date]_____ : Harvesters will pick _____ .

   _____[Date]_____ : Harvesters will pick _____ .

   _____[Date]_____ : Harvesters will pick _____ .

2. Check one of the following:

   ☐ It is ok for Harvesters to enter the yard when Owner is not home. If
   owner is not home, Harvesters should [*describe procedures, such as
   "close the gate behind them."*]

   ☐ Harvesters should enter the yard only when Owner is at home.

3. Harvesters will follow these rules when in Owner's yard: _____
   [*describe rules, such as "Harvesters will not smoke;" "Harvesters will not
   make unnecessary noise while in the yard;" "Harvesters will take care to
   not damage flower beds or break any branches of the fruit trees."*]

4. Harvesters will pick all fruit that appears ready to be picked and leave
   less mature fruit on the tree.

5. Harvesters will take care to avoid damaging the tree or breaking
   branches.

6. Harvesters will give [*amount*] of fruit to Owner.

7. Harvesters may do the following with the remainder of the fruit. (Check
   all that apply.)

   ☐ Give fruit to other neighbors

   ☐ Donate fruit to a food bank or other charity

   ☐ Consume the fruit

   ☐ Preserve or prepare the fruit, to eat or share

8. Harvesters will take reasonable steps to ensure that the fruit is not
   wasted.

9. Harvesters will use all proper care and safety precautions when climbing trees and ladders. (*Or:* Harvesters will not climb the trees or use ladders. Harvesters will use extension fruit pickers, which they will provide.)

10. Owner does not ask for any compensation.

11. Harvesters, as consideration for the right to harvest fruit from Owner's tree(s), agree not to make a claim against or sue Owner for injury, loss, or damage that occurs during fruit harvest and/or consumption of Owner's fruit, including injury, loss, or damage arising from the negligence of Owner. Harvesters agree to indemnify, hold harmless, and defend Owner from all claims, liability, or demands that Harvesters or any third party may have or in the future make against Owner for injury, loss, or damage arising from harvesting and/or consuming fruit from Owner's trees, including from food-borne illness.

HARVESTERS:

Name: _____

on behalf of __Neighborhood Fruit Harvest Group__

Signature: _____

Date: _____

OWNER(S):

Name: _____

Signature: _____

Date: _____

Name: _____

Signature: _____

Date: _____

Solution 4: Shared and Community Gardens

With half of the world's population living in cities, growing food locally requires us to find space between buildings, parking lots, and streets. Available land exists in many places—vacant lots, undeveloped regions, and private yards. Together, these spaces constitute a large amount of land and could feed significant portions of urban populations, if shared and cultivated.

Urban gardens are a proven solution to food crises elsewhere in the world. Following trade and oil embargos in the early 1990s, for example, Cuba's large-scale industrial agriculture system experienced a meltdown. As a result, people began to plant food gardens in every plot of available land in urban areas. Cuba was able to avert a crisis by taking advantage of land resources, quite literally, in its backyard. Mexico, Kenya, Ghana, Argentina, and the Philippines have all made extensive use of urban gardens.

Victory Gardens

During World Wars I and II, more than a third of our vegetables were produced in "victory gardens"—small gardens planted in yards and vacant lots. The government encouraged people to cultivate every unused plot of land as a way to reduce the burden on railroads and other means of transportation, reduce demand for material used in food processing and canning, make more food available to armed forces, and maintain the morale of American civilians. Today, there is a growing movement to revive victory gardens. San Francisco, for example, has funded projects to convert yards and unused lands into organic food production, and even installed a victory garden in front of city hall. For more information, see www.sfvictorygardens.org.

In addition to meeting our need for food, urban gardens bring a variety of benefits to our communities by:
- creating habitats for birds, insects, and native plants
- cleaning polluted city air

- providing local job opportunities
- creating a beautiful setting where people can socialize and build community
- providing a positive and healthy activity for everyone, and
- raising property values.

Back and Front Yard Gardens

When people with yards get together with people who love to garden, many sharing arrangements are possible:

- Several neighbors might get together to plant and tend a vegetable garden in one neighbor's yard.
- A group of neighbors could agree to help each other garden and share their harvests. One neighbor grows a lot of tomatoes, another has three fruit trees, and a third has a large herb garden.
- A garden matchmaking website or organization can connect garden enthusiasts and people with yard space to share.

EXAMPLE: A group of volunteers in Berkeley, California recently collected names and addresses of 300 city residents, each of whom had either a yard to share or an interest in gardening in someone else's yard. They held meetings and divided attendees into groups based on neighborhood. From those meetings, many informal garden-sharing relationships formed. Similar organizations in Portland, Oregon and Canada have created websites to help link people interested in sharing a garden. For an example of such a match-making website, see www.yardsharing.org.

- A neighbor might invite everyone on her block to four Saturday gardening parties, with a promise to share the harvest with everyone involved.
- A homeowner could invite a local nonprofit garden organization to use his front lawn to grow vegetables and create a community demonstration garden.

Sharing and gardening go well together. When groups of people garden together, each brings different skills, tools, and knowledge. More people keep an eye on the garden, making sure it's watered and watching out for pests. And everyone can help eat all of those green beans.

> **EXAMPLE:** Mel and Cara bought a house with a large front lawn. During a block party, they met many of their new neighbors, including residents of a large apartment building down the street. One family from the apartment building, the Postles, talked about their interest in growing vegetables, but lamented the fact that they had no yard. Mel and Cara invited them to help install a vegetable garden in their yard. They all agreed that the Postles would cultivate and tend half the yard, and Mel and Cara would take care of the other half. While they did not create a written agreement, they had a thorough discussion about the arrangement. They discussed issues such as what would be planted, whether any nonorganic gardening methods would be used, how they would share costs, how they would share the vegetables, what they would do if a conflict arose between them, and so on.

RESOURCE

Want to know more about planting a food garden? Take a look at *Food Not Lawns: How to Turn Your Yard into a Garden and Your Neighborhood into a Community,* by Heather Coburn Flores (Chelsea Green). Also, check out the resources listed in Appendix A.

Community Gardens

A community garden is a place where people can come together to help grow food. The gardens educate, provide food, and create a pleasant space for people to be together.

There are many different ways to set up community gardens. Some community gardens are overseen by nonprofits and have volunteers help in all aspects of gardening. Other gardens are divided into individually assigned plots (see "Garden Allotments," below).

Seed Exchange Libraries

Collecting and growing heirloom plant varieties is becoming increasingly popular—it's fun, it yields interesting strains of fruits and vegetables, and it helps us preserve and appreciate the diversity of edible plants that have developed throughout history. It's also an important part of food security. Large-scale commercial agriculture has led to a loss of about 75% of the genetic diversity in crop varieties. Preserving and sharing the remaining varieties will help us re-establish diversity.

A great way to do this is through a seed library, which collects, catalogs, and shares seeds. For example, the Bay Area Seed Interchange Library (BASIL) allows members to "check out" seeds, grow them into plants, and then harvest some of the seeds to replenish and grow the library.

What do you need to start a seed library? Lots of envelopes, some enthusiastic gardeners, and a good lesson on seed saving. One helpful resource is *Seed Sowing and Saving: Step-by-Step Techniques for Collecting and Growing More Than 100 Vegetables, Flowers, and Herbs,* by Carole B. Turner (Storey's Gardening Skills Illustrated).

Creating Community Gardens

Organized efforts by community members could transform a city landscape into a garden paradise. Even in the most populated cities, there are vacant lots everywhere, many owned by the city itself. For example, New York City owns about 14,000 vacant lots, on which there are hundreds of community gardens. The remaining lots are privately owned. San Francisco, a mere seven by seven-mile peninsula, has at least 5,000 empty lots, of which more than half are privately owned. The potential is huge.

If community members and organizations want to use a vacant lot for gardening, it's a good idea to enter into a written agreement or lease with the landowner. An agreement between a small group of individuals and a landowner is shown below.

Sample Garden Sharing Agreement

This garden sharing agreement is made between Marcel Paez ("Marcel") and Leticia Houston, Reyanna Carabay, and Robert Mayhem, (collectively referred to as "Gardeners"). Marcel owns a vacant lot located at 12461 Ethel Avenue in Van Nuys, CA. Marcel thinks that a garden would be a nice addition to the neighborhood. Gardeners are a loose affiliation of friends with an interest in farming and a desire to plant a vegetable garden on Marcel's lot.

1. Marcel agrees to allow Gardeners daytime access to the lot for the purpose of installing and maintaining a small vegetable garden beginning on the date this agreement is signed.

2. Gardeners will plant and tend vegetables, fruit, and herbs on the lot year round.

3. Gardeners have made separate arrangements with a neighbor to use that neighbor's water and store hoses, gardening tools, and supplies in that neighbor's shed.

4. Marcel agrees that Gardeners may invite guests onto the lot to visit the garden or to help with the garden, as long as at least one of the Gardeners is with the guests at the garden. If Gardeners wish to give anyone else regular and unsupervised access to the garden, they must first receive Marcel's permission. Marcel encourages Gardeners to invite and include neighbors in the garden project. Gardeners may invite neighbors to periodic "garden parties."

5. Gardeners may construct raised beds on the lot. Construction of a shed or greenhouse must first be approved by Marcel and by the local building department (if necessary).

6. Gardeners are responsible for all costs related to the garden, including but not limited to, soil, tools, water, seeds, seedlings, and fertilizer.

7. All fruits, vegetables, and herbs grown on the lot will be consumed by the Gardeners, shared with Marcel, given to neighbors or friends, or donated to charity. Gardeners will not sell the produce and do not intend to profit from the arrangement.

8. Gardeners agree to tend the land responsibly and use organic farming methods if possible. Gardeners will take care to ensure that water run-off, dust, or noise do not bother neighbors. Gardeners will maintain a

tidy appearance on the lot. Gardeners will take care to remove hazards from the lot, including but not limited to holes, sharp objects, or items that could cause people to trip and fall.

9. Gardeners, as consideration for the right to garden on Marcel's land, agree not to make a claim against or sue Marcel for injury, loss, or damage that occur on Marcel's land, including for injury, loss, or damage arising from the negligence of Marcel. Harvesters agree to indemnify, hold harmless, and defend Marcel from all claims, liability, or demands that Harvesters or any third party may have or in the future make against Marcel for injury, loss, or damage arising from gardening on Marcel's land or consuming food grown on the land.

10. Marcel or the Gardeners may terminate this agreement at any time, with or without cause. Gardeners understand that at some point in the future, Marcel may want to sell or build on the lot.

11. At the termination of the agreement, Gardeners will remove all possessions from the property. Marcel will not require removal of the plants, but Gardeners may remove plants in order to plant them elsewhere.

12. If a conflict arises between us that we are not able to resolve through discussion, we agree to attend at least one mediation session with a mediator we all agree on, and to share the cost of the mediation.

Marcel Paez	_2/9/xx_
Signature	Date
Leticia Houston	_2/9/xx_
Signature	Date
Reyanna Carabay	_2/9/xx_
Signature	Date
Robert Mayhem	_2/9/xx_
Signature	Date

Garden Allotments

Garden allotments are a type of community garden that usually involves dividing land into small plots, sometimes as small as 25 to 100 square feet, and allowing people or groups to rent them or use them free to grow vegetables for their own consumption. It's a great way to transform a vacant lot into a wonderful community space.

The city of Seattle, Washington sponsors a "P-Patch" program, whereby citizens can sign up to garden in one of more than 2,500 plots in 70 neighborhood gardens throughout the city. Garden allotments are very common in England and derive from a tradition that is centuries old. Garden allotments are also used in poverty-stricken countries and urban areas to battle hunger and poverty.

> **TIP**
>
> **Want to find a garden plot?** If you are interested in finding a garden plot near you, call around to local community garden organizations and find out whether there are plots available. If not, let your local city government know about Seattle's P-Patch program, an excellent example of a city-sponsored garden allotment program.

Selling What You Grow

If you plan to sell your produce, be sure to find out what regulations will apply. For example, if you plan to set up a small weekly farm stand, check your state's laws governing farm stands and local zoning laws. Laws governing farm stands generally encourage people to sell what they grow themselves, and may restrict sale of packaged or processed foods or produce that isn't grown by the farmer. Zoning laws may also prohibit or require a permit for roadside stands in residential areas.

> **RESOURCE**
>
> **Want more information about selling what you grow?** Take a look at *Backyard Market Gardening,* by Andy W. Lee and Patricia L. Foreman (Good Earth Publications) and *Micro Eco-Farming: Prospering from Backyard to Small Acreage in Partnership With the Earth,* by Barbara Berst Adams (New World Publishing).

Farmer Cooperatives

In the United States, there are at least 3,000 farmer cooperatives, also called agricultural cooperatives. Farmer cooperatives provide services, supplies, and marketing to independent farmers who collectively own and govern them, which allows independent farmers to compete with large industrial agriculture operations. Cooperatives can purchase supplies in bulk or purchase equipment and machinery for farmers to share. Some cooperatives also provide services, such as hulling, storage, processing, packing, marketing, and distributing food.

Solution 5: Community-Supported Agriculture

The Community Supported Agriculture (CSA) movement grew out of a desire to see small farms thrive and create a market for local, healthy, and organic produce. A CSA creates a direct partnership between farmers and consumers, based on a mutual commitment: Consumers support the farm financially, usually through advance payments or a subscription, and farmers provide the consumers with a share of the produce.

The "members" or "subscribers" to a CSA share the farmers' risk. When a member makes an advance payment on a season's produce, that member shares the risk that the crop will be damaged by disease, frost, pests, or floods.

Benefits of CSAs

Members of a CSA benefit by receiving fresh produce and herbs (sometimes for less than they would pay in a store); having an opportunity to participate in farming; learning about growing food; helping the local economy; building community with other sharers; helping preserve farmland and open spaces; budgeting food costs in advance; and learning about food growing and cooking.

CSAs benefit farmers by linking a farm with people who are personally and financially invested in the farm's success. The CSA model is a great way to provide startup funding to a farm and foster stable operations, because it provides an advance cash flow. A CSA is a form of direct marketing, which is also a benefit to farmers. It takes out the middleman (the distributors) and gives the farmer a better return on produce. The farmer receives direct support and payments from consumers, and doesn't need to worry about market-related concerns. Farmers can develop a personal relationship with consumers, teach about farming, and take pride in what they do. CSAs can also grow the market for small farms and create jobs in organic agriculture.

CSAs benefit the earth by helping to preserve farmland, promote sustainable farming practice, and reduce long-distance transport of food. CSAs can reduce the risk of crop disease, because members usually encourage farmers to produce highly diversified crops and grow a little of everything—fruits, grains, vegetables, and herbs.

Agricultural Land Trusts

Agricultural land trusts are a way for communities to invest in the protection of farmland. Farmland in the United States is being rapidly depleted, as farms are sold and developed for housing and commercial buildings. According to the American Farmland Trust, between 1997 and 2003, the United States lost farmland equal to the combined area of Vermont and Connecticut. As farmland dwindles, we lose a significant source of U.S. jobs and must rely on imports to feed us.

Agricultural land trusts typically preserve land by purchasing something called a conservation easement from the farm owners. The farm owners maintain title to the property and continue to farm the land, while the land trust owns all development rights to the property. The farmer and all future owners of the land are thereby prohibited from developing the land.

To learn about a successful agricultural land trust, visit the website for the Marin Agricultural Land Trust, www.malt.org.

Different Kinds of CSAs

There are different CSA models. In some, farmers do all the farming and deliver a weekly box or bag of produce to members. In other CSAs, members do some work as part of their payment—either on the farm or in distribution. Some farms invite members to come to the farm and pick their own food.

Some CSAs dedicate all of their produce to members, who decide what to do with any excess. In this type of CSA, members can take as much produce as they need and donate the surplus to a charity or shelter, for example. In some CSA programs, the farmer creates a relationship of complete transparency with members, showing them the annual farm budget—including salaries, land lease, equipment, and so on—and a summary of the annual farm produce. From these numbers, the CSA can determine the approximate cost of a share of the produce. Often, a single share entitles a member to the approximate amount of vegetables required to feed a family of four.

Most CSA farms practice organic and sustainable farming. Being organic is not part of the definition of a CSA, but most are. CSAs don't just provide vegetables; a CSA can arrange for bulk purchasing of other farm products—wine, cheese, bread, eggs, meat, syrup, honey, and so on.

Join a CSA

There are more than 2,000 CSAs in the United States. To find one near you, ask around at the local farmers market or check online; one good place to start is www.localharvest.org/csa.

Starting a Simple CSA

You can start a CSA by gathering a few people and "adopting a farm." Survey neighboring families to find some who would like to collaborate with you. Find a small local farm that you want to support. Offer to buy produce in advance in exchange for regular vegetable deliveries, or come up with another plan based on other models of CSAs.

Cowpooling and Lobster Accounts

When you take the CSA model and apply it to meat and poultry farms, what do you get? Cowpooling! Farms such as Stillman's Turkey Farm in Hardwick, Massachusetts, offer meat CSA programs, whereby subscribers make an advance payment and receive a share of meat once per month—frozen and vacuum-packed. Restaurants and other food businesses also sometimes practice "cowpooling"—for example, by jointly purchasing a whole cow or pig to share on a weekly basis.

For everyday consumers, sustainably and conscientiously raised meats are not available in many grocery stores, and can be pricey. Consumers can help grow the market for conscientiously raised meat not only by buying it, but also by helping support the farms that have made the choice to raise animals humanely and free of hormones and antibiotics. If there isn't a "cowpooling" program in your area, gather some friends, and talk to a local meat farm about starting one.

Community supported fisheries (CSF) are also a growing trend. With the fishing industry in crisis, taking part in a CSF supports local and small-scale fishing operations. One lobstering CSF, Catch a Piece of Maine, works like this: "Your lobster trap will be set the day after purchasing and fished for one year. During each fishing trip, your lobsterman will record everything caught from your trap. This data [...] will be recorded in [your] personal lobster account (accessible 24-7) where you can view your trap's performance [...], manage your catch and schedule shipments with the click of a mouse."

If the farm doesn't grow certain items that you want, ask them to. If your group agrees in advance to buy 50 bunches of kale, then you've given the farm a good incentive to grow kale.

If CSA members will be helping out on the farm, it's a good idea for the farmer to purchase "pick your own" insurance, in case anyone gets hurt.

Community Supported Restaurants and Kitchens

The Community Supported Agriculture model is easily transferable to other types of businesses, including restaurants and food service businesses. The Bee's Knees, in Morrisville, Vermont, is one such restaurant. When the restaurant needed to undergo a renovation and expansion, the owner asked community members for loans of $1,000. In return, each lender would receive a $90 meal coupon four times per year, for three years. In other words, they got a small return on the loan, paid for in food. The Bee's Knees raised the necessary $70,000 in capital and is assured a constant stream of customers with friendly faces. While the lenders share in the risk that the restaurant could go out of business, they also share in the joy of helping to enhance a much-loved community gathering place. Since it opened in 2003, the Bee's Knees has become a popular hangout, serving locally grown foods and hosting live music.

Community supported kitchens are also appearing on the scene. In Berkeley, California, the Three Stone Hearth operates a subscription-based prepared food service. Members make advance orders, selecting from a variety of unique foods—sauerkraut, soups, coconut sweets, cereals, hamburgers—and pick up their food boxes each week. In the spirit of sharing and being green, Three Stone Hearth helps members organize carpools, so that neighbors can pick up each other's food.

The Bigger Picture: Sharing Food

Here are some ways that businesses, nonprofits, community leaders, lawmakers, and others can help everyone share food production and consumption:

- Provide property tax incentives for urban food production, to encourage owners of empty lots to allow community members to garden on their properties.
- Make government-owned vacant lots available for community gardens.
- Create and fund seed exchange libraries.
- Municipal waste agencies: Provide free compost bins to neighborhood compost groups.
- Create and fund community-wide food recovery and distribution projects, to reduce food waste and feed the hungry.
- Provide public assistance and marketing support to community supported agriculture (CSA) programs.

Create space for and support local farmers markets and farmers stands; allow community members to sell produce grown and/or prepared at home and in community gardens.

The Triple Bottom Line: The Benefits of Sharing Food

Social and Personal Benefits

- Enjoy better nutrition and a more diversified diet through mealsharing.
- Save up to 30 minutes of cooking time per day through mealsharing.
- Get fresher, tastier, and more nutritious food through community supported agriculture or a community garden.
- Support small and local farmers and food producers.
- Build community by cooperating to grow, prepare, and eat food.

Environmental Benefits

- Reduce cross-country and inter-continental food transport by cooperating to get locally grown food.
- Reduce packaging waste through bulk buying.
- Reduce the large amount of edible food that goes to landfills.
- Support organic and sustainable farmers through community supported agriculture.
- Create "green collar" jobs by collectively supporting small-scale and sustainable food producers.
- Preserve farmland through involvement in agricultural land trusts.

Financial Benefits

- Eat healthy, artisan, and organic foods at affordable prices.
- Save between 20% and 50% on groceries by taking part in a cooperative or buying club.
- Save up to $30 per week by doing a lunch-share with your coworkers.
- Eat out less and save money by sharing meals with your neighbors.

Sharing Care for Children, Family, and Pets

T he baby boomer generation is full of "sandwich" people: adults who are caring for growing children and aging parents at the same time. Whether you're caring for parents, children, or both, taking care of others is a lot of responsibility. Sharing childcare or elder care with others is a great way to lighten the load. It can ease your financial burden, free up your time, and help you—and your parent or child—build relationships with others.

Elders and adults with disabilities can also benefit from sharing their own care, whether by joining together to hire an assistant or helping each other with chores and errands. Other sharing arrangements can be tailored for adults with disabilities or elders who can't participate in some of the group's activities. For example, an elder who needs help with home maintenance and repairs could join a home improvement group and, instead of providing hard labor, could offer to pay some of the cost of materials, provide food for all of the work days, or provide other services to group members.

Of course, trusting others to provide care for a loved one—or for yourself—is very different from sharing tools or a car. You'll probably spend much more time choosing your sharing partner(s) and coming up with the terms of your agreement. You'll have plenty of details to work through, from schedules to diets to television rules, and more. You may spend more time meeting or discussing ongoing concerns once your group is up and running, too. But the payoffs for the time and effort you put into planning and maintaining your arrangement are enormous.

This chapter covers some ways to share childcare. It also discusses care of elders and adults with disabilities, whether that care is arranged by a family member or by the person receiving care. And, we explain some options for sharing the responsibility of caring for that other important member of your family: your pet.

Issues to Consider When Sharing Care

Sharing care is different from the other sharing arrangements we cover in this book, because it involves sharing responsibility for another person. As such, it raises some unique concerns.

Why Share Care

When you share care, you are trusting others with your own care or the care of the people you love the most. This is clearly quite different from sharing possessions or space, and perhaps more anxiety-provoking. But many common forms of child and elder care actually involve sharing, even though they aren't necessarily viewed that way. In day care centers, camps, schools, and after-school programs, for example, children from many families come together for care and education. Elder care facilities, senior centers, and government and community services for elders also gather people together for care and companionship.

The sharing arrangements we cover in this chapter add another benefit to the cost savings, companionship, and efficiency of these familiar models: control over, and participation in, the caregiving process. For example, in a babysitting cooperative (see Solution 1, below), each family participates in running the program by helping with administration and providing the actual care for the kids. Similarly, if you hire someone to provide care to a parent and a neighbor's parent, you and your parents get to decide whom to hire, how much time the care receivers will spend together, what the caregiver will help with, and much more.

This opportunity to shape and participate in the caregiving process goes a long way toward making it possible to get help with our caregiving responsibilities. For some parents, the thought of sending a child to full-time day care raises concerns—or even guilt—over questions like: Will my child be safe? Will my child develop properly? Will my child be happy? Will my child miss me? Will I miss watching my child grow up? Similarly, some who have considered seeking care for an aging parent have had to wrestle with these issues: Will my parent be well cared for? Will my parent suffer neglect or abuse? Will my parent resent me? Am I treating my parent like a child? When we know the caregiver, participate in providing care, and manage the process, many of these concerns are alleviated. Knowing that we and our chosen caregivers are doing a good job makes it possible to share the sometimes tremendous stress and burden of providing care on our own.

For those who need care, opportunities to make choices and act independently can be too few and far between. Paid care can be costly, but it may not be possible for elders and adults with disabilities to live on their own without some assistance. Sharing can close the gap: Partnering with another adult who needs care can make it less expensive to hire paid help. If you can find someone whose skills and needs complement yours, all the better: Your share can be free. For example, perhaps one friend no longer drives but is otherwise physically active, while the other has physical disabilities but drives. A rides-for-chores exchange could meet everyone's needs.

Involving the Person Receiving Care

Unlike the other arrangements we cover in this book, some of the solutions in this chapter require you to consider not only your own needs and those of your sharing partner(s), but also the needs of the person receiving care. In some cases, the person receiving care can't make decisions or offer detailed feedback. A very young child, an elder with advanced dementia, or an adult with certain disabilities won't participate much in care decisions. However, older children and many elders will want to have a say in—or be in charge of—decisions like who will provide care, other children or adults with whom they might share care, and what the care will include.

- **Talking with your kids.** Let your children know that their opinions about how they're taken care of matter. And take the time to find out what those opinions are: Kids often don't communicate as clearly and quickly as adults, so let the conversation be as long (and perhaps, as scattered) as it needs to be. Try not to interrupt or to use up all of the airtime with that well-meaning parental tendency to explain everything at great length.
- **Talking with adults who need care.** A sense of independence is enormously important to most elders and people with disabilities. Having a say in their own care can go a long way towards preserving independence and control. Sit down with the adults whose care you're helping with and find out what's important

to them in a care situation, what they might not want, and how they want their day-to-day routines structured. It's fine to suggest a plan you've developed, but try to offer genuine opportunities for input rather than presenting it as a done deal.

Solution 1: Form a Community Babysitting Cooperative

A community babysitting cooperative is a grassroots type of arrangement in which families share child care without any money changing hands. Instead, the care itself is the currency of exchange. For example, in many babysitting cooperatives, families earn points for providing care and spend points on care for their own kids. Points are typically assigned to each half hour or hour of care. This type of cooperative usually doesn't have an educational component—it's basically shared babysitting.

Not everyone wants to devote the time and energy required to actually provide care in a cooperative child care arrangement. Another way to share care at home is to share a paid care provider with another family or two, thereby spreading the cost and responsibility. See Solution 2, below, for more on this type of sharing.

CAUTION

Are you a child care facility? You may think that providing occasional care for a few neighborhood children doesn't make you a child care provider, but your state could see things differently. Many states provide that someone who provides care for more than a minimum number of children, or more than two or three unrelated children, must be licensed and meet other requirements. If you'll be providing child care in an informal setting with other families, make sure that your group either complies with the state's requirements—for example, by getting licenses—or that your group is small enough or otherwise structured to fit within an exception to the state's law. You can find out your state's rules at the website of the National Resource Center for Health and Safety in Childcare and Early Education, http://nrckids.org/STATES/states.htm.

Group Size and Members

Many babysitting cooperatives are started by a few families who know each other because they are friends, live in the same neighborhood, or have children that play together. A small group has the benefit that parents and children will all grow to know and trust each other. At the same time, with just a few families, you may not be sure that you'll get child care when you need it; a larger group makes it more likely that someone will be available when your child needs care. That's why most groups will need to consider how many members to have and how to choose new members.

A babysitting cooperative can have as few as two or three families, although groups that small will probably need to agree in advance on how often members will generally ask for (and provide) care. The maximum number of families in the group will depend on how much record keeping, scheduling, and other administrative tasks you're willing to take on. The more families you have, the more "back office" work you'll have to do. Most groups find that 25 families or so is a manageable high end.

Because you may need more families to get your group off the ground—and because children grow up, families move away, and the membership of your group will otherwise change—you'll also have to decide how to choose and admit new members. Often, new members will appear organically as children change schools, join new activities, or make new friends. You can also put an advertisement on your neighborhood or school listserv or in a school newsletter. It's a good idea to agree in advance about how new members will be admitted—does everyone in the group have to agree, or will there be a voting system? And what about the uncomfortable situation in which someone is denied membership? You'll need to have a party line for these circumstances—for example, "our group requires unanimity to admit a new member, and we didn't get complete agreement on having you join."

Scheduling and Record Keeping

The group can either have one person take care of record keeping and other duties or share these responsibilities. If you choose to have one person in charge, that person can also be responsible for matching child care needs with available caregivers and keeping track of each family's points. (This person is sometimes called the secretary, administrator, or leader, though the term "leader" is used in a limited sense, as the person has no authority to make decisions for the group.) The administrator schedules who goes where at what time and keeps track of how many points each family has earned and spent.

Often, the administrator is compensated with points, which can be earned on a flat-rate basis—ten points for each month worked, for example—or an hourly basis for time spent on administrative duties. The administrator can serve for as long or as short a period as you want. Some groups rotate leaders every month, some every six months, and others even less frequently.

Another option is to have a leaderless system in which participants schedule care directly with each other, "paying" for their time by exchanging tickets or scrip with assigned time values. Each family receives a certain amount of time upon joining the co-op, and may then exchange care with other families, using the tickets or scrip to keep track of hours spent and earned.

> EXAMPLE: Jessie and Sara want to see the thirteenth "Rambo" movie, so they ask Eva, another member of their babysitting co-op, to care for their son, Sylvester. Eva agrees to watch Sylvester from about 5 to 9 p.m. on Friday evening. Jessie and Sara drop Sly off at 5. When they pick him up at 8:30, they hand Eva seven tickets worth 30 minutes of child care each, for the three and a half hours he actually stayed with Eva. The next week, Eva wants to go to a poetry reading at her local book store. Jessie and Sara aren't available to watch her son, Wadsworth, so she takes him to Barb and Marty's house instead and passes along four tickets for the two hours he's there. And so on.

Without an administrator or leader, it can be more difficult to track which parents need care or are available to provide it. Some solutions include using an online calendaring system, regularly exchanging information (for example, in a weekly or biweekly email) on each family's needs and availability, or creating a listserv where group members can post this information.

Other Ways to Organize the Cooperative

Although the point or ticket system works well for larger groups of parents who want occasional help, there are many other ways to organize a babysitting share. If you need regular babysitting, for example, you could come up with a set weekly schedule for child care. For example, you could take care of the kids after school on Mondays and Wednesdays, while your neighbor takes care of them on Tuesdays and Thursdays.

One group of six families we heard about does it this way: Every Saturday night, two families pair up to make dinner together and care for all of the kids, while the other four sets of parents go out on "dates." That way, each parent gets two dates and has one dinner party every three weeks, and the kids have a ball. (The same families have been sharing babysitting for so long that other sharing arrangements have arisen from it; for example, they all share a large emergency preparedness kit.)

Other Issues and Rules to Consider

There are quite a few other issues you'll want to consider if you're arranging a community child care co-op, including some or all of the following:

- whether parents should request or provide babysitting when their kids are sick
- how members may join and leave the co-op
- how much notice is required when seeking child care
- rules about snacks, television, bedtimes, and discipline
- how you'll resolve disputes

- whether parents can borrow against time they haven't earned yet, and whether earned time is transferable to another family when someone leaves the group
- whether holiday and weekend care earn (and cost) extra points, and
- how often co-op members will meet.

The sample agreement below shows how one group decided to handle many of these concerns.

Sample Babysitting Co-Op Agreement

Your co-op should have written policies and a standard agreement that each new member must sign before requesting or providing care. A sample agreement, including the co-op's policies, is below. Try to keep your policies and agreement as simple as possible to start with. You can always add more rules later when you see how things are going and what's actually happening in your group.

> CAUTION
>
> **What's a cooperative?** Some states have specific legal definitions of what makes a cooperative business. For example, in California you're not supposed to call yourself a cooperative if you're "doing business" and you haven't organized your business under the California Corporations Code rules for cooperatives (which require the establishment of a corporation with bylaws and a board of directors, and control the structure of the business). If you're setting up a babysitting cooperative in which no money changes hands, you don't need to worry about the Corporations Code—you're not doing business and you can call yourself a cooperative if you wish. But if you're planning on developing a cooperative school (see Solution 2, below) you'll need to make sure your business complies with the applicable rules to use the word in your name.

Sample Babysitting Cooperative Agreement

This agreement is between all members of the Montclair Babysitting Cooperative. By signing this agreement, each member agrees as follows:

1. Our purpose is to help each other by providing occasional child care for one another's children.

2. We're starting with seven families. The maximum number of families who can participate is ten. The minimum is four, and if we have fewer than that and can't engage new members within a month of dropping to that level, we'll disband.

3. Each member family begins with 20 points, which can be exchanged with other member families for child care. Each point is worth 30 minutes of child care and each 30 minutes of child care is worth one point, with two exceptions:

4. On legal holidays, the points are doubled—that is, each half-hour of care is worth two points.

5. For overnight care—care provided between 9 p.m. and 8 a.m.—each half-hour of care is worth half a point.

6. No extra points are given for meals prepared for someone else's child in our home. Children with special food needs will bring their own food unless the families agree otherwise. We all agree to be mindful of any special food needs, especially allergies, that we're notified of.

7. We'll have an administrator who will keep track of each family's points and arrange for care when a family requests it. Each family will provide the administrator with emergency information, including contact numbers, the name and number of the family's doctor, and important medical information about their child(ren) (such as information about medicine the child is taking or allergies). The administrator will compile this information and distribute a copy to each family. Each time a new member family joins or any family's contact information changes, the administrator will distribute a new information list.

8. The first administrator will be Sharon Rule. She'll serve starting on September 1, 2009, until the next person, Frank Putter, takes over on March 1, 2010. At our regular meeting in June, 2010, we'll decide who will take over from Frank in September of 2010. If either Sharon or Frank isn't able to do the job, we'll meet and choose another person.

9. The administrator will earn points for time spent on administrative duties at the same rate as the rate for child care—for each 30 minutes spent, the administrator earns one point. The administrator won't get any other compensation.

10. The administrator's duties are to maintain and distribute membership records, including contact information; to take requests for care and match the requesting family with a family able to provide care; to keep records of each family's points earned and spent; and to report to the group each month on each family's point total and any changes to contact information. The administrator agrees to act on all requests for care within 24 hours of receiving them. If that doesn't happen, the participant who needs care can contact another family directly, but should later report their transaction to the administrator.

11. We'll meet on the second Tuesday of every January and June to review the records, consider new members, and discuss how things are going. Meetings will be held at the Montclair Community Center in the evening, and the administrator is responsible for reserving the room.

12. We all agree that if anyone in our family is sick, we won't ask for or offer child care in our home without fully explaining the circumstances. Each family should feel comfortable declining to provide care for a sick child. We will take every precaution to avoid spreading the sickness.

13. If any family has concerns about the care being provided by another family or thinks another family shouldn't be in the co-op, or if any conflicts arise between any of us that we can't work out privately, we agree that we'll all get together to discuss it. If we need to, we'll hire someone from the community mediation center to help us with that discussion. If our dues aren't enough to cover the cost, we'll all chip in.

14. Each family will pay dues of $20 per year, in cash, to cover the cost of the room for our meetings, a mediator (if we need one), and any supplies involved in the administrator's work. The administrator will keep track of the money and pass it along to the next administrator, with an accounting of money collected and paid out during the administrator's term.

15. To bring in a new member family, we must all agree. To join, the family must live within the city limits of Montclair and must agree to these policies.

16. Each family agrees to maintain homeowners' or renters' insurance on their residence that covers accidents and injuries occurring there.

17. Anyone can leave the group at any time by notifying the administrator. However, a family that owes time to the group must make themselves available for child care until the time owed is used up.

Each person's signature below indicates consent to all terms of this agreement.

Signature: _____ Date: _____

Signature: _____ Date: _____

Signature: _____ Date: _____

Signature: _____ Date: _____

Signature: _____ Date: _____

Signature: _____ Date: _____

Signature: _____ Date: _____

Signature: _____ Date: _____

Signature: _____ Date: _____

Signature: _____ Date: _____

Signature: _____ Date: _____

Solution 2: Join a Cooperative Nursery or School

If you want to take your sharing to a higher level, you can join or even create a cooperative school with other parents. Many communities have cooperative schools, which often look a lot like small private schools. But cooperative schools are different: In fact, they're the ultimate public schools, because they are owned by the people who use them—the parents of the students.

Generally, parents buy into ownership in a cooperative school by paying tuition. By definition, ownership turns over as children grow up and leave the school and new students and their parents join. In addition to the tuition, parents must contribute a certain amount of time, whether in the classroom, kitchen, playground, or office. Often, parents also agree to do some fundraising to bring additional money into the school.

Shared Tutoring

Rather than sharing a whole school, you can join together with other families to provide small group tutoring. Perhaps all the kids could use a little help with math, study skills, or even preparation for the SAT or other standardized tests. Maybe you'd like for the kids to learn Spanish, take piano lessons, or get some woodworking instruction. No matter what your kids need help with, you can make it less expensive by hiring a tutor to work with all of the kids at the same time in one of your homes. You can use the same type of agreement provided in Solution 3, below.

By definition, a cooperative is democratically controlled by its members, but that control can be exercised in a number of ways. Many cooperative schools incorporate in order to create a governing structure that allows a large number of families to participate (and exists separately from its members, which is important with a constantly changing student body), shield the participating families from liability, and take advantage of favorable tax treatment.

Cooperative corporations must establish a board of directors made up of stakeholders in the cooperative. In the case of a cooperative school, the board is usually comprised of parents with kids in the school, and sometimes parents of former students. The board sets policy, does long-range planning, and supervises the school's director. The cooperative employs caregivers, teachers, and administrators who bring the necessary skills, training, and certifications, and ensure the school is in compliance with state educational and child care services requirements. Parents take shifts, either assisting the professionals or working in other ways that benefit the school.

A Co-Op Nursery School

The Sunset Co-op Nursery School in San Francisco is one of the longest-running co-op schools in the country—in operation since 1940! Most parents feel lucky to take part in the Sunset Co-op—it's one of the best deals on childcare around, plus it's a great place for parents and kids.

About 50 or 60 families take part in the co-op, and a parent from each family helps out at the school for one morning or afternoon each week. With the addition of three full-time childcare staff, there are around eight or nine adults present at any given time. Each parent brings a unique contribution to the school. One creative mom taught "circus classes" during her shifts at the nursery. The children loved it when she arrived with circus props to teach them juggling, tumbling, and hula-hooping. In addition to helping with care a few hours per week, parents also take part in preparing snacks for the children, doing maintenance chores, and fundraising for the school. The Co-op also provides almost daily parenting classes or discussion groups for parents.

The relationships that form at the Sunset Co-op last beyond the nursery school years—both parents and children have come away with lifelong friendships. For more information about the Sunset Co-op Nursery School, see www.sunsetcoop.org.

The parents' time at school is probably the most noticeable difference between cooperative schools and other private and public schools (where parent involvement may occur, but is almost always voluntary and not as frequent as is required by a cooperative). In most other respects, you wouldn't be able to tell a cooperative school from any other school. Depending on the parental involvement and other factors, the cost of a cooperative school can be similar to that of other private schools. However, some co-op schools manage to keep tuition rates low, primarily through fundraising and high levels of parental participation.

Cooperative schools are much more common at the preschool and elementary level than in the higher grades.

Child Care Co-Ops as a Benefit of Employment

Some employers, recognizing that lack of reliable child care is a common reason for employee absences, are stepping up to create child care options for employees. One such option is a child care cooperative, either on-site or near the workplace, for which the employer pays the setup costs and provides some level of continuing financial support, then leaves the ongoing ownership and operation to participating employees. As in any cooperative, the board of directors is made up of participating parents, possibly with the addition of an employer representative. In most ways, this type of cooperative is very much like any other child care co-op. Because it's underwritten by the employer, however, it may cost less than an independent co-op. And the employer's support makes it easier for employees to take the time they need to participate in the activities of the cooperative.

RESOURCE

Want more information on cooperative schools? Check out the website of Parent Cooperative Preschools International, at www.preschools. coop. The National Cooperative Business Association has information about cooperatives generally, and a page about child care and preschools, at www. ncba.coop.

Solution 3: Share an In-Home Nanny

Some families keep child care in the home—or a few homes—rather than taking their children to a child care program. To spread the cost, they hire a shared private nanny to take care of more than one family's children at the same time.

Ground Rules and Issues to Consider

Sharing in-home care can be a nice way to go if you can afford it and can find a compatible family to share with. But before making any kind of commitment to this type of arrangement, make sure you and your proposed sharers have the same expectations about how the arrangement will work.

Some issues will be easy to decide. For example, you won't have to think much about how large the group should be or how to admit new members: The size of your group will necessarily be small if you plan to rely on one paid care provider. Most nanny shares involve only two families, though sometimes three or more can work.

Other issues will require more discussion. Many a shared child care arrangement has foundered because of disagreements over day-to-day issues, from whether children can play with toy weapons to whether television is allowed, which parks the children may play at, and what types of snacks are appropriate. And, of course, you'll need to discuss how much you're willing to pay, what the caregiver's schedule will be, and so forth. Some of the issues you should resolve ahead of time include:

- how to find and choose a caregiver, and the qualifications the caregiver must have (for example, a driver's license or CPR training)
- where care will be provided—you can either choose one home or agree to alternate in any way that works for everyone
- how often care will be provided, including hours and days of the week
- expectations about timing, activities, food, and discipline

- financial issues, including how much you will pay the caregiver and whether to enter into a formal employment relationship, and
- how to resolve conflicts if they arise.

Advance planning will help ensure that all of you will be comfortable about the care your children receive. It can also help you avoid serious conflicts in the setup process and down the road. Once you've agreed on all of these issues, prepare a simple written agreement memorializing them. (We provide a sample below.)

Public Toy Sharing

The idea of leaving toys in public parks to be shared by many kids is one of those things that people just started doing. One family would leave a toy car, another a basketball, and other children would come and use the toys, then leave them for the next kid.

Sounds simple and kind of sweet, right? Proponents say that the practice teaches sharing, creates community, and fosters and improves communication between kids as well as adult neighbors. But in some communities neighbors have complained, arguing that the toys look messy, attract miscreants, and lead to dumping.

There may be liability issues for the city, as well. If the city knows there are toys in the park and those toys somehow become hazardous, an injured child's parents could sue the city for negligence. However, as far as we know, most complaints about toys left in parks have come from local neighbors, not from the cities themselves.

Dividing Costs

Many sharing arrangements involve little or no ongoing costs, but sharing a paid caregiver isn't one of them. You'll want a fairly detailed agreement on how much each family will pay, how often payments will be required, how payments will be adjusted, if at all (for example, if a family goes on vacation and their child doesn't need care for a week, or a child "ages out" of the care arrangement), and what happens if a family doesn't pay on time.

If you're paying a nanny by the hour and you and the other family use exactly the same hours and have the same number of children, there's no issue about how you'll divde the cost—each family will pay half. But if one family uses the nanny more, one family has more children, or the nanny lives with one family and the other brings their child over for day care, you'll have to negotiate who pays what part of the salary and other expenses. Make sure your written agreement spells this out clearly.

> **RESOURCE**
>
> **You also need a written agreement with your child care worker.** For sample agreements that you can tear out or use on CD-ROM, see *101 Law Forms for Personal Use*, by Ralph Warner and Robin Leonard (Nolo).

> **CAUTION**
>
> **Avoid having your own Nannygate.** Quite a few politicians have been brought low by "nannygate" scandals when it was revealed that they did what so many people do: pay their child care provider under the table, in cash, instead of complying with state and federal employment laws. If you choose to go this route, you'll deprive your caregiver of Social Security credits. You'll also expose yourself to several possible consequences, including financial penalties and liability for your caregiver's medical costs as a result of the failure to obtain workers' compensation insurance. You also won't be able to take the child care tax credit on your federal income taxes. And you can forget about becoming a Supreme Court Justice or cabinet-level Secretary.

Agreement to Share Child Care

Sarah Graham and Barbara Marks agree that they will together hire a child care worker to care for their children. Sarah has two children, Jonathan and Eva, who are 2 and 3, respectively. Barbara has one child, Sophie, who is 3. We agree as follows:

1. We will hire a caregiver for our three children, with child care beginning on June 1, 20xx. We'll find the caregiver together by asking friends and posting an advertisement on Craigslist. Barbara will draft the advertisement and Sarah will review it and take care of posting it. She'll also arrange for interviews with prospective caregivers on dates that we both agree on.

2. The caregiver will provide care for all three children five days per week from 8 a.m. to 2 p.m.. On Mondays, Wednesdays, and Fridays, care will be in Sarah's home and on Tuesdays and Thursdays, in Barbara's home. Each of us will drop our child(ren) off for care at the other one's home on the appropriate days. The caregiver's responsibilities will be to play with the children, take them to the park at least three times per week, weather permitting, make sure they are fed and changed as appropriate, and make sure they have naps according to their schedules at any given time.

3. We'll pay the caregiver $13 per hour. We'll pay every week at the end of the day on Friday for that week's hours. We'll deduct (and pay our share of) payroll taxes, and we'll pay for workers' compensation insurance. Sarah will research how to do all of this, set up our account with the Workers' Compensation Board, and research what forms we need for paying other taxes. We won't pay any other benefits, but we will give the caregiver a week (30 hours) off with pay every six months, which can be taken all together or by the day, as long as the caregiver gives us at least a week's notice of planned time off.

4. We have set up a joint account at the Bank of America for the purpose of paying our caregiver. Each of us deposited $250 to start the account. Starting on June 1, 20xx, we each agree to deposit $1,000 per month on

the first day of the month, to cover that month's expenses. We think this is more than what we'll actually need, but until we learn the cost of taxes and insurance, we'll continue to put in this amount. After six months, we'll decide whether we want to change the monthly contribution.

5. If one person doesn't put in her contribution for one month, the other can put in the contribution for her and it will be considered a loan to the one who didn't pay. If the person who paid doesn't want to make the loan, then the person who didn't pay can't use the services of the caregiver until she pays her share. In that case, the person who paid has the right to decide whether or not she wants to terminate the caregiver's services.

6. Each of us will make sure that snacks and lunch food are available at her house on the days the caregiver will be there. We'll get together and agree on a list of foods that both of us think are nutritious and okay for the kids to eat. We acknowledge that Sarah will be paying more for food because care is provided at her house three days per week; we've agreed that this balances out the fact that she has two children in care while Barbara only has one, so no adjustment will be made for the extra expense.

7. We won't make any adjustments for days a child doesn't use the child care services.

8. We agree to meet once a month over lunch to discuss how the child care system is working out.

9. Our preference is that if disagreements arise between us that we can't work out ourselves, we'll try mediation (at our local community mediation center) before terminating this agreement. Each of us has the right to terminate this agreement at any time, but must provide at least two week's notice or pay for two weeks after ending her participation in the agreement.

10. Each of us will maintain liability insurance on our residential property. We each are comfortable with the level of child-proofing in the other person's home, and feel both of our homes are safe environments for the children.

11. We'll have a separate written agreement with the child care worker, which we'll prepare using sample forms available on the Internet or in books. Sarah agrees to research this and draft the agreement.

Signature: _____ Date: _____

Signature: _____ Date: _____

Solution 4: Start a Carpool

For as long as there have been kids who need to get places and parents with cars, there have been carpools. Although carpools are relatively simple arrangements, they should nonetheless be put in writing, both because safety is at stake and because there's a surprising amount of room for confusion—and possible conflict—over issues like lateness and whose turn it is to drive.

We recommend a simple written agreement to lay down the rules of the road—things like what will happen in the event of a late pickup, whether snacks are permitted in the car, and of course, that all drivers will carry adequate insurance.

Carpool Agreement

This agreement is between the families listed on the attached information sheets, all of whom agree as follows:

1. The purpose of the carpool is to transport children between their school (Edison School, located on Redwood Road) and each of their respective homes.

2. The carpool will begin on September 4, 2009 and end on May 24, 2010, unless we end it sooner by agreement, and will transport the kids every day that school is in session.

3. In the morning, the carpool will pick up the children in the order that makes the most sense given who is driving; the order will be established by each parent before the first week of school. The first child will be picked up at 7:45 a.m. The plan is to get them to school by 8:20 in time for classes at 8:30.

4. In the afternoon, all the kids will be waiting outside the school, near the stop sign at the corner of Skyline Boulevard and Redwood Road, within sight of the school personnel assigned to watch the kids after school.

5. The carpool will meet the kids at 2:55, and will drop them off in reverse order from the morning trip.

6. We'll rotate driving duties by week. [*name of parent*] will be the first driver, followed by [*list other drivers in order*]. Parents are free to trade weeks, or individual days, with other parents, but we'll try to make sure the driving chores stay even.

7. We all agree to maintain current insurance coverage on our vehicles as required by law.

8. Any of us can leave the carpool at any time, but we agree to try to give as much notice as possible before ending our participation.

Signature: _____ Date: _____

Signature: _____ Date: _____

Signature: _____ Date: _____

Signature: _____ Date: _____

Signature: _____ Date: _____

Information Sheet for Children's Carpool

Child's Name: _____

Address for Pickup: _____

Parent/Guardian Names: _____

Parent 1: _____

Phone (please put a checkmark by the best number to reach you)

☐ Home: _____ ☐ Work: _____

☐ Cell: _____ ☐ Other: _____

Email: _____

Parent 2: _____

Phone (please put a checkmark by the best number to reach you)

☐ Home: _____ ☐ Work: _____

☐ Cell: _____ ☐ Other: _____

Email: _____

Name of Parent Who Will Drive Carpool: _____

Drivers' license no.: _____

Car make/model: _____ License plate: _____

Insurance co.: _____ Policy number: _____

Emergency Contact

Name: _____

Relationship to child: _____

Best number to reach: _____

Child's Physician

Name: _____

Best number to reach: _____

Homeschooling and Sharing

Between 2% and 3% of children in the United States are homeschooled, and there are thousands of homeschooling support groups and networks throughout the country. While the word "homeschooling" may conjure up a picture of kids attending school at *home*, homeschooling parents will tell you that it feels like anything but.

When homeschooling families come together, they may organize countless group activities for students, tapping into the unique skills and resources offered by diverse parents and the community as a whole. In any given week, one homeschooled teenager (an author of this book) may have attended a ceramics class, a sign language class, band practice, drama practice, and a tour of a marine reserve—all taught or led by homeschooling parents or other homeschooled youth. One homeschooling mom felt that she was on the go with her sons so much that she wrote a whole book called *Carschooling*.

Most parents choose to homeschool so that they can tailor a quality educational program to meet their child's interests, learning styles, and other needs. While families are often creative in doing this on their own, collaborating with other homeschooling families can create a wealth of resources. Here are some ways that homeschooling families share and collaborate:

- **Support groups.** Through support groups, homeschooling families join together for mutual support, networking, sharing information, and creating social opportunities for their children.
- **Cooperative classes.** Co-op classes teach children together in larger groups, especially for projects or events that are more difficult in a home environment or simply more efficient if resources are shared, like sports, languages, science experiments, or crafts. Co-op classes also give parents a chance to share their special knowledge and expertise. A parent who is a mechanic could teach a class on auto repair; in exchange, a parent with especially good math skills could do math tutoring, and so on.
- **Group activities.** Homeschooling groups may organize play groups, sports or debate teams, foreign language conversation

Homeschooling and Sharing (continued)

groups, theater outings, field trips and tours, group campouts, musical groups, and countless other activities.

- **Sharing curriculum and books.** School books and materials can be expensive, but less so if you share. Textbooks and curricula can be passed on to other homeschooling families like regular hand-me-downs.
- **Umbrella schools.** In most states, the law requires homeschooling families to form an independent private school, hire a certified teacher for tutoring, or take part in a public or private school's independent study program. Some families share the administrative task of forming an independent school—often called an umbrella school—which is essentially a registered private school, under which each family homeschools its child.

Homeschoolers are subject to many legal rules, which you can learn about at www.homeschooling.about.com, along with lots of other information about homeschooling.

Solution 5: Share an In-Home Care Provider With Another Elder or Adult With Disabilities

Elders and adults with disabilities may need many different types of care. Some may need only occasional assistance with chores and errands, or even just a daily visit or call to check in and make sure everything's okay. Others may need more extensive daily help with walking, hygiene, meal preparation, or skilled nursing care. At every point on this spectrum, sharing provides a number of solutions.

This section covers sharing an in-home care provider. Below, we also cover sharing care with another family (Solution 6).

Getting Light Assistance

An in-home assistant can provide occasional or light help, with tasks such as:

- preparing meals
- shopping for groceries and other necessities
- caring for pets
- doing housework
- keeping track of medication
- managing finances, and
- driving.

Adults (or their families) can pool their resources to employ someone who will come regularly to help, possibly spending an hour or two at each person's house per day. The assistant could also save time (and the care receiver's money) by running errands for several people at once. For example, several seniors could hire an assistant to make a weekly trip to the grocery store and pharmacy, picking up food and medicine for everyone, based on shopping lists they prepare, at the same time.

Getting Help for More Extensive Needs

For adults who need more help, such as with walking, eating, and other fundamental needs, more than occasional assistance is needed.

If two people (or their families) want to share an in-home caregiver, one option is to have the caregiver split time between households. Alternatively, an elder or other person who needs care and has sufficient mobility could travel to another's home— usually a friend's or family member's—during the day, to share the help of the caregiver. Even if you don't have another family member or friend in mind, you could use the Internet to find another family seeking adult care in your area. In addition to the cost savings, this type of care sharing provides an opportunity to socialize.

If you're going to make an arrangement with a friend, family member, or neighbor to share a caregiver, make sure you decide on these important issues (and put them in a written agreement):

- how to find and choose the caregiver
- where care will be provided—you can choose one home, agree to alternate homes, or have the caregiver split time between homes
- expectations about timing, activities, and food
- issues relating to medication schedules and other special needs
- financial issues, including how much to pay the caregiver; whether to enter into a formal employment relationship; how to divide payments if you're not using the same number of hours or the caregiver lives at one home; whether families have to pay for time they don't use (if one of the elders stays home one day, for example); and what to do if the level of care each person needs is different, and
- how to resolve conflicts if they arise.

The Role of Elders and Adults With Disabilities in Other Sharing Arrangements

Many of the needs of elders and those with disabilities could be met through participation in other neighborhood sharing arrangements we cover in this book. For example:

- **Home improvement groups:** While some elders or adults with disabilities may not be able to replace drywall or clean gutters, they could provide other services in exchange, such as sewing, cooking, or car repair. (For more information about these groups, see Chapter 7.)
- **Mealsharing groups:** Someone who cannot shop and cook for a large group could participate by making smaller dishes, helping with food preparation, or chipping in to pay for beverages. (For more information about mealsharing, see Chapter 8.)
- **Neighborhood fruit harvests and gardens:** Someone who can't fully care for a yard could let neighbors pick fruit or plant a vegetable garden, in exchange for some of the bounty. (For more information about yard sharing and neighborhood harvests, see Chapters 7 and 8.)
- **Helping with child or pet care:** Elders or adults with disabilities could take part in a childcare or pet care cooperatives—even if they have no children or pets—by providing occasional supervision for children or keeping a cat while the owner is away. This provides companionship for everyone, and the favor could be returned in many ways—grocery runs, meals, or driving.
- **Carsharing:** Many seniors drive less as they age, but aren't ready to give up the independence of owning a car. Carsharing is a great option here. For example, an elderly woman, Yolanda, shares her car with a neighboring graduate student who uses the car to travel to an internship three times a week. The graduate student runs occasional errands for Yolanda, handles routine maintenance, and fills the gas tank; Yolanda pays for all other expenses (insurance, registration, and so on). (For more information about carsharing, see Chapter 10.)

Sample Caregiver Sharing Agreement

Fran Sampson, Josh Laurence, and Betty Serpa (Fran's mom) agree with Joan and Mark Morgan and Alice Phillips (Mark's mom) to share an in-home caregiver. The caregiver will be providing care for Betty and Alice. Betty lives with Fran and Josh in their home on Roberts Avenue, and Alice lives on her own at the Piedmont Garden apartments on Pleasant Valley Road.

The parties all agree as follows:

1. The caregiver will work at Fran and Josh's home on Roberts Avenue on the following schedule: Monday through Friday, 8 a.m. to 5 p.m.

2. The caregiver will assist Betty in the following activities as needed: bathing, dressing, grooming, transferring from chair to walker, doing exercises, managing medications, driving to medical appointments, and preparing food and snacks.

3. On Mondays, Wednesdays, and Fridays, Mark will bring Alice to the house at 8:30 a.m. and pick her up at 4:30 p.m.

4. On the days that Alice is present, the caregiver will assist Alice in the following activities as needed: managing medications, preparing food and snacks, doing exercises.

5. Fran, Josh, and Betty will be the caregiver's employers, and they agree to pay the caregiver $15 per hour. It's up to them to work out a contract with the caregiver stating when and how the caregiver will be paid, and arranging all the other terms of employment. Fran, Josh, and Betty agree that they'll deduct taxes and Social Security and pay their share of taxes, as well as pay for workers' compensation insurance. Mark won't pay any share of the taxes or workers' compensation insurance.

6. Mark will reimburse Fran and Josh for the care that Alice receives at an hourly rate of $10. The parties agree that it's fair for Mark to pay more than half of the hourly rate, to account for Fran, Josh, and Betty's added expense in paying taxes and insurance expenses.

7. Mark will reimburse Fran and Josh monthly for Alice's care, based on the hours that Alice actually used the caregiver's services that month. Mark

is free to notify Fran, Josh, and Betty that Alice won't be coming to their home on any given day, but he will pay for at least two days of care per week even if Alice uses less care.

8. Any party may end this agreement by giving one week's notice.

9. If disagreements arise between us that we can't work out ourselves, we'll try mediation (at our local community mediation center) before terminating this agreement.

10. Fran and Josh agree that they will maintain liability insurance on their home.

11. Fran, Josh, and Betty can seek Medicare reimbursement for the care expenses for Betty, and so can Mark. Fran, Josh, and Betty will provide documentation of Mark's payments, and will deduct his contributions from the amounts they claim.

Fran Sampson	*10/11/xx*
Fran Sampson	Date
Josh Laurence	*10/11/xx*
Josh Laurence	Date
Betty Serpa	*10/11/xx*
Betty Serpa	Date
Mark Morgan	*10/11/xx*
Mark Morgan	Date
Alice Phillips	*10/11/xx*
Alice Phillips	Date

Sharing in Residential Facilities

Adults in residential facilities can enhance their lives through sharing in a myriad of ways—they're in the ideal sharing situation, with easy access to fellow sharers and a high likelihood of finding people with similar interests.

Adults in residential care and assisted living facilities can share:

- books and movies
- hobby supplies , like sewing machines, art supplies, or tools
- computers or other electronics
- grocery shopping, buying in bulk for those who cook
- cooking for special occasions—even though meals are often provided in assisted living facilities, residents may want to arrange to share special treats with one another on a regular basis, and
- skills, such as teaching others to draw, knit, write stories, build models, scrapbook, cook, and so on.

Residents may even be able to share caregiving responsibilities by providing care for each other. By pooling their resources, they may be able to meet many of their own needs. For example, someone who drives could run errands, another could help with cooking, another could provide light housekeeping assistance, and so on.

Solution 6: Share Caregiving Responsibilities With Another Family

Caring for an elderly or disabled adult can be exhausting and sometimes lonely. By sharing, you can get some help and companionship from others in the same situation. There are many tasks you can share to ease burdens for the caretaker and those receiving care.

To do this type of sharing, you'll need to find another family or person who needs care, lives relatively nearby, and has needs that are at least somewhat similar to yours. That way, you will be better able to share the caregiving responsibilities equally.

Finding others to share or cooperate with is easy to do in retirement communities and senior cohousing, but elsewhere it requires a more concerted search effort. You may want to post an Internet advertisement or contact your local senior services agency or senior center to find out whether it has a message board or other means of communicating with other families. And ask around among your friends, neighbors, and co-workers—perhaps one of them knows someone who would be a fit.

Here are some of the tasks you could share:

- **Cooking and meal delivery.** You can work with other families to cook for each other's relatives on a rotating schedule.

- **Transportation and carpooling.** You can share driving to medical appointments, activities, or simple errands that require transportation. If your family members have shared activities, such as day care, physical therapy, exercise classes, or events and lectures at the local senior center, you can even set up a carpool.

- **Errands.** You can trade off buying groceries and doing other errands for your family members.

- **Household chores.** Basic cleaning and other chores can be challenging for an elder or person with disabilities who is otherwise able to live alone. Instead of doing all the chores for your family member each week, you can agree to a rotating schedule of chores with your fellow sharers. You'll end up doing double the work on the day that you're responsible for the chores—but the next week, you'll get the day off. Of course, you could also share the cost of hiring someone to do chores at both homes.

- **Companionship.** Many elders who live alone wish that they had more contact with other people from day to day. Volunteers may be available to visit people in their homes. Often, however, the problem isn't a lack of potential companions, but an inability to physically get together. If the person you care for has friends or other family nearby, you could help set up an ongoing social event, rotated among your homes. For example, each family might host a bridge night or an afternoon get together, with arrangements to share transportation to and from the gathering.

- **Respite care.** Perhaps you don't want to enter into a full sharing arrangement that covers the majority of your caregiving time, but you need an occasional break from your responsibilities. You can trade with another caregiver on a rotating basis, taking your charge to the other person's house to give you a day off, and then returning the favor when asked. You could do this ad hoc, or according to a set schedule.

RESOURCE

Want more information on elder care? Check out Elder Care Link, www.eldercarelink.com, which has information, articles, and links to elder care providers.

Sharing Care With Siblings

If you have an aging parent who needs care, you and your siblings may share that responsibility. If you live in the same community, you may be able to share the day-to-day routines, like driving your parent to medical appointments, to run errands, or to socialize with friends. Or, you could hire a paid care provider and share the cost.

Even though you're cooperating with your siblings, it's not a bad idea to write down your agreement about how you'll share responsibility, so that things are clear and real conflict is avoided. In the simplest situations, you might make do with a calendar you keep online or at your parent's home. If you're sharing costs in any way other than an even split, it's definitely a good idea to write down the arrangement to avoid later arguments. If you're hiring paid help, decide among yourselves who will deal with the person you hire. This will help you make sure your parent's needs are being met; it will also help you avoid a situation in which the care provider is receiving different information and instructions from different people.

Solution 7: Share Dog Walking

So far, we've covered the human members of your family. But what about Fido, Fluffy, and Butch? They need care too—and there are lots of ways to share the responsibilities. Sharing pet care is a great way not only to help you meet your pet's needs, but also to enhance your pet's life—bringing them more love, more attention, and more long walks in the park. Busy pet owners often lament that they can't spend more time with their pet, playing or getting out for a good romp. And often, when people can't take care of their own pets temporarily, they look for a paid solution: hiring a dog walker, kenneling the animal, hiring someone to stop by the house and care for the pets at home, or paying someone to take the pets into their own home.

But it's also possible to make sharing arrangements that don't cost anything. The chores that pet owners need help with most often are dog walking (covered here), and care either for the day or for out-of-town trips (see Solution 8, below).

If you walk your dog regularly, you probably know many of your neighbors who also have dogs. You may not know their names, but you know where they live, what their dog's name is, and their dog walking schedule. If you have a dog who's friendly and relatively well-behaved, you could approach the neighbor and ask about sharing the dog walking chores, in one of a few ways.

Dog walk exchange. Perhaps your neighbor can take both dogs on the morning walk, while you walk them both in the evening. This is a nice even trade that doesn't require much setup or maintenance. You just need to be sure that you and the neighbor have similar ideas about how long the walk should be, leashing and controlling the dogs, and cleaning up after them. You could also take each other's dogs to the dog park or to another open space where the dogs are free to run. Chances are your dogs will think your dog walk exchange was an excellent idea.

Dog walk cooperative. If you have a number of neighbors or friends with dogs, you could get together and set up a community dog walking cooperative, similar to the community babysitting cooperative discussed above. Dog walking would be the currency earned and spent, with points assigned by time or per walk, perhaps with a minimum time also set for each walk.

You could use tickets, scrip, or a point system, just as described above. You'd have the same choices to make about how to keep track of what each participant has earned and spent, and about the parameters of your agreements. One additional issue is how participants get into each other's yards and houses—you would have to decide whether you were willing to share keys or combinations with your neighbors. If not, you'll have to come up with a way the dog walker of the day can get your dog.

Pet Sharing

Some people go beyond sharing responsibilities and share a whole pet! This can happen any number of ways; here are some we've heard of:

- **Sharing with an elder or person with disabilities.** For those who aren't able to take full responsibility for pet ownership, the companionship of a cat or dog can nevertheless provide strength and joy—and benefit the pet, too. Our friend Violet has a very gentle Dalmatian, "Dottie," whom she "shares" with her retired neighbor, Roberto, during the day. Roberto loves Dottie and enjoys the daytime companionship. For Violet, it's the perfect arrangement, because she knows Dottie is safe and happy while she's at work.

- **Sharing with another family.** Families that share a lot or a yard can easily share a pet—and this is an especially great solution if someone in one of the households is allergic. The pet can live in the other house, but receive care and attention from the (nonallergic) neighbors.

- **Sharing pets by accident.** Pets that adopt families often can't stop at just one: That stray cat you feed every night may well be making the neighborhood rounds. In fact, we know of one formerly stray rabbit who adopted two neighboring households and lived in both back yards. In this situation, you can chip in for food and veterinary bills, for example.

Hire a shared dog walker. Before you picked up this book, you might have hired someone—perhaps a neighborhood teenager—to walk your dog while you're at work or otherwise busy. To turn this into a sharing arrangement, you could arrange to have the same person walk a number of dogs at once, then split the cost. Of course, you couldn't have too many animals in the group, and you'd have to make sure the person you hired could handle them. But this can be a great sharing solution for people who aren't home enough (or at the right times) to walk the dogs themselves.

Solution 8: Share Pet Care

Spending a week at a kennel or even a day alone while you're at work is not most dogs' or cats' cup of tea. Luckily, sharing can help.

Care for Extended Periods

Sharing care for your pet while you're out of town can work on the same principles discussed under Solution 7. You could do a basic exchange with a neighbor, regularly caring for each other pets when one of you goes away. Or, you could build a larger pet care network or cooperative, which is an effective way of ensuring that you'll have pet care when you need it. As with the dog walking cooperative, participants can collect or spend points for pet care.

In a cooperative arrangement, you'll probably want to assign points differently depending on the pets and the type of care. Some pets are more self-sufficient than others. A turtle with an automatic feeder could get by on a twice-per-week visit, a cat might be happy with a daily visit, and many dogs require walks and food twice per day. You might decide, for example, to make each home visit worth one point and each walk worth one point. In other situations, you might just drop your cat off at someone else's house for the week, at a cost of one point per day. Your group can iron out many of the details in advance, or people can decide on points on a case-by-case basis.

Pet Day Care

Some pet owners need more than just a walk for Fido. If you're at work all day and your cat or dog can't spend the entire day alone (due to health problems, separation anxiety, or simple high energy), a pet day care program is an option, albeit an expensive one. A cheaper or free option is to leave your pet with a friend or neighbor during the day. For example, if you have a neighbor who telecommutes from home, your dogs could keep each other company during the day while your neighbor keeps an eye on them. You'll have to figure out something you can do in return, like taking over most of the responsibility for walking both dogs when you are at home in the mornings and evenings, paying for all the kibble and treats, or perhaps caring for the neighbor's dog when the neighbor is out of town.

You could also team up with someone else in need of pet day care and share the cost of a day care provider. The care provider could be anyone who works from home or a retired person who wouldn't mind some extra money and some animal companionship during the day.

The Bigger Picture: Sharing Care

Here are some ways that businesses, nonprofits, community leaders, lawmakers, and others can help encourage shared care:

- Publicly fund and charter parent-run cooperative schools.
- Employers: Create workplace childcare cooperative centers and give employees time off to work in the center.
- Lawmakers: Create licensing exemption programs for certain kinds of parent-run childcare and babysitting cooperatives.
- Residential facilities for the elderly and adults with disabilities: Create programs that facilitate sharing among residents, such as staffed offices where residents can borrow a variety of household goods, resident buying clubs, skillsharing classes, or book and music libraries.
- Provide increased public and private funding and programs for in-home adult care, including incentives for shared and cooperative care.

Your Triple Bottom Line: The Benefits of Sharing Family Care

Social and Personal Benefits

- A shared child care environment can help your child learn to socialize with other children, to share, and to be flexible. Kids who spend time with a variety of other kids and adults tend to be more well-rounded people.
- Often, both you and your children will make lifelong friends of the other kids and adults with whom you share.
- Elders and adults with disabilities can benefit from the company of others.
- People caring for adult family members can benefit from a supportive community of others in the same situation.
- Sharing pet care is fun for the dogs, makes them better behaved, and provides a great opportunity to be neighborly.

Environmental Benefits

- If you're at home alone with your child, you're using utilities and other resources; if you share with even one other family you'll be halving the resources used. And when multiple households share child care, even more resources are saved.
- Combining shopping and errands for a number of elders or people with disabilities reduces driving.

Financial Benefits

- A live-in nanny can cost $600 per week, plus health insurance benefits and taxes. If you invite even one other child into your home to share day care, you can reduce the cost significantly.
- If you share an hourly child care worker with one other family, you'll cut your costs—including health benefits and taxes—in half, and you can do the math on what it will mean to share with more than one other family. (But watch out for state and local

laws limiting how many children can be cared for together before child care regulations kick in.) The same is true if you hire a caregiver for an adult family member.

Sharing Transportation

Many of us share transportation by taking the bus, train, or subway, but these systems rarely satisfy all of our transportation needs. As a result, the rate of car ownership in the United States is enormous. In fact, we have more cars than licensed drivers. Here are some reasons to find alternatives:

- **Money.** Most studies show that between 10% and 19% of our household budgets are spent on transportation. According to the American Automobile Association (AAA), in 2008, the average annual cost to own and operate a mid-sized sedan driven about 15,000 miles was $8,273.

- **Time and stress.** It's not easy getting from here to there, especially when *there* is so far from *here*. According to an ABC News poll, people who drive to work average almost an hour a day in commute. Getting places can be stressful; it even sends some people into fits of road rage.

- **Efficiency.** The way most of us use our cars is inefficient. Most cars spend most of their lives sitting in a parking space. When they are on the road, cars have only one person inside 85% of the time.

- **Our neighborhoods.** Because we own so many cars, much of the architecture of our society has been built to accommodate them: roads, parking lots, gas stations, and so on. Parking lots and spots are valuable real estate—in urban areas, the value of the land you park on could be $5,000 to $8,000. Imagine what our communities would look like if even a fraction of the parking spaces were converted into park land (or community gardens), or some of our streets were closed to through traffic. One study showed that the more cars that drive down a street, the less likely people are to know their neighbors. Heavy traffic also deters people from walking or riding their bikes.

- **Our planet.** Driving cars puts toxins into our oceans, waterways, and the air we breathe, and it releases carbon into our atmosphere. The manufacture of cars requires us to continually mine our planet's natural resources. Our need for fuel leads to drilling for oil, which has caused many ecological disasters.

This chapter explains some solutions to the high cost—to our wallets, our communities, and our planet—of car ownership. How much can you save by sharing the cost of a car or a ride? The worksheet below will help you figure out your annual car expenses and how much you could save by sharing your car or carpooling. You may be surprised at how the numbers add up!

Start by calculating your current car expenses. You may wonder why we didn't include the cost of your car itself on the table below. This cost will appear on the table in the form of depreciation, which is the value your car loses as it gets older and you put more miles on it. (See "Calculating Depreciation," below, for tips on calculating the year-by-year depreciation of your vehicle). The interest you pay on your car loan is a separate expense—it represents the cost of your car loan, not the car itself.

To figure out how much money you would save if you shared a car or carpooled, you'll need to consider three kinds of costs related to cars. First, there are expenses that don't depend on how much you drive, such as registration costs. Second, there are costs that increase somewhat with mileage or additional drivers, such as insurance premiums. Third, there are costs that are closely tied to how much you drive your car, such as fuel expenses, depreciation, and maintenance.

If you are calculating how much you'll save if you share your car with one neighbor, you will be able to cut the first kind of cost—fixed costs—in half. For costs that vary somewhat, you will likely pay a little more than half. And for costs that rise in direct proportion to your driving, you will pay approximately the same amount as you do now, unless you change how much you drive as well.

To calculate how much you'll save if you leave your car at home and carpool with others to work five days a week, first figure out how much of your driving is spent on your work commute. If driving to work makes up 80% of your total driving, you will be able to cut most of the variable expenses—like gas and maintenance—by up to 80% (depending on whether you share costs with your fellow carpoolers). You may be able to eliminate other major costs, such as parking and bridge tolls. And once you tell your insurance company that you've cut your driving significantly, it may reduce your rates.

If you give up your car entirely and join a carsharing program, you can erase most of the expenses below and start fresh with a new number based on the carsharing program's rates, which are usually based on how many hours and miles you drive the shared cars. Chances are you'll save thousands of dollars.

Worksheet: Annual Car Expenses			
Type of Expense	Annual Costs	Costs to Share a Car	Costs to Carpool
Annual registration cost			
License fees			
Smog check (where applicable)			
Insurance (average is $850 per year)			
Depreciation			
Interest on car loan (finance charges)			
Roadside assistance program membership			
Fuel			
Parking			
Maintenance (regular replacements, tires, fluids, filters, tune-ups, windshield wipers, cleaning)			
Major repairs			
Tolls			
Title fee and transfer tax (usually applies only when car changes ownership)			
Total			

Solution 1: Share a Car With One or Two People

People may decide to share a car with a friend or neighbor for many reasons. Here are a couple of examples:

- Marlene and Jory are a couple and own two cars; they live down the street from another couple, Kristen and Colin, who own one car. When Marlene and Jory heard that Kristen and Colin were contemplating getting a second car, they proposed sharing their second car instead. Marlene and Jory felt that it was convenient to have a second car, but they didn't use it on a daily basis. Likewise, Kristen and Colin just wanted an extra car around for those occasional times when they both needed a car. Marlene and Jory put Kristen and Colin on their insurance as secondary drivers, and they started splitting all expenses related to the car.

- Diana lives in a popular neighborhood in Chicago and owns a car. She drives her car a few times a week for errands, appointments, and outings, but commutes to work on the bus. She sometimes spends ten minutes or more searching for a parking space in her neighborhood, and often has to park blocks away from her home. She meets Eileen, who lives two blocks down and does not own a car, but has an empty driveway. They strike up a deal: Diana starts parking at Eileen's house; in exchange, Eileen uses the car on Thursday nights to travel to her ukulele group practice, one weekend per month, and on other occasions that the two arrange.

A Famous Carsharer

"In 1950, when the Giants signed me, they gave me $15,000. I bought a 1950 Mercury. I couldn't drive, but I had it in the parking lot there, and everybody that could drive would drive the car. So it was like a community thing."

—Baseball Hall of Famer, Willie Mays

Ownership

Who actually owns the car is important and may affect insurance rates, how you split costs, and who is ultimately responsible for the vehicle when issues come up, such as an accident or impoundment. If you share your car with your neighbor, your options are simple: Either one or both of you can own the car.

One Owner

Keeping the car in one owner's name is a simple approach, leaving no question about who will get the car if you ever end the arrangement. You also won't have to deal with transferring partial title, paying transfer taxes, and so on. The downside is that some insurance companies will not add a second driver who is not an owner or a family member of the owner.

Two or More Owners

Another option is for both of you to own the car. You could buy a car together or, if you already own a car, you can sell a share to your neighbor. You'll have to come up with an appropriate price and keep a written record of your transaction, and your neighbor may have to pay a sales or use tax to buy half of the car. In some states, transferring partial title may trigger other requirements, such as a smog check or transfer fee.

If you are buying a share of someone else's car, find out whether there are any liens on the car. Usually, the loan company that financed the car has a lien on the car until the loan is paid off. This isn't necessarily a bad thing; most cars are financed this way. But make sure the owner is current on the car payments and plans to keep it that way when you become a partial owner—otherwise, the car could be repossessed.

> CAUTION
> **Watch out for certain kinds of liens.** Liens can also be placed on a car if the owner takes out a loan, often called a "car title loan," which uses the car as collateral. Be wary of sharing a car with this type of lien. These loans are often predatory and difficult to pay off, and may indicate that the car owner is in a tough financial situation.

To get both of your names on the title, also known as the "pink slip," you will need to follow the procedures required by your state's motor vehicle department. These requirements are often spelled out on the department's website.

You should specify on the title whether you are holding the car in joint tenancy, tenancy in common, or some other form. Joint tenancy means your half of the car automatically goes to the other owner if you die. Tenancy in common means you can leave your half to whomever you'd like, as part of your estate. If you want to leave your share of the car to your co-owner, it makes sense to own the car in joint tenancy.

Share Your Car When You Don't Need It

Sometime soon, a service may be available to "convert" your car to a shared car when you aren't using it. If your car sits in the driveway all day, you could allow a carsharing company to use it between 7 a.m. and 6 p.m., for example, and you could even make enough money to pay for the car. A British company called Wombat Convert Your Car has already started doing this. Wombat advertises cars, provides insurance, installs a numeric key system, and takes care of booking and billing. Members reserve and use the car during the day and return it by the evening. Find out more at www.wombatconvertyourcar.co.uk.

Rules for Using the Car

It's important to work out the details of your car sharing arrangement ahead of time, to make sure sharing will meet everyone's needs and to help prevent confusion or conflicts. Here are some of the questions you may need to consider:

- What's our schedule for using the car? Will we use it equally or will one of us use it more often than the other?
- Will we have any rules for longer trips? For example, will we have to get permission from the other to take the car out of town, or will there be an annual mileage limit on our car use?

- Who may ride in the car and who may drive it?
- Who owns certain accessories inside of the car?
- Are there any rules about pets or smoking in the car?
- Are there any rules about fueling, such as requiring sharers to refill the gas tank or to leave at least a quarter of a tank at all times?

Share a Station Car

Here's a sharing idea for commuters who take trains to work but need a car on one or both ends of their trip: station cars. To share a station car, you need to find someone whose commute is the opposite of yours. One of you leaves a car at the station where you board the train; the other takes the car after getting off the train, uses it during the day, and returns it to the station in time for you to drive it back home.

EXAMPLE: Jenny lives in Baltimore and commutes to Washington DC; Yoki lives in DC and commutes to Baltimore. Jenny drives her car to the train station in the morning, parks, and takes the train to DC; Yoki arrives at the same station later, uses Jenny's car for the day, and returns it in time for Jenny to drive back home.

Yoki could pay Jenny to use her car or leave a car for Jenny in DC to make it an even exchange. In a more organized network with many people or locations, Jenny could use a car left by Rob, who commutes from DC to Arlington. Rob could, in turn, use a car left in Arlington by Carl, and so on.

Station cars make it easier to take public transit and use cars more efficiently by taking advantage of the time they would otherwise sit idle in a parking lot. Try setting up a station car exchange by posting an ad online, or, better yet, form an organization to facilitate station car sharing in your area.

> **TIP**
>
> **Even commuters can share a car.** If you commute by car, carsharing is not out of the question. For example, you could use your car to commute and share it with someone who needs to use it only on evenings and weekends. You could also consider combining carsharing with ridesharing, which frees you from daily dependence on your car.

Sharing Expenses

Many car expenses are easy to determine using standardized calculations —such as the Blue Book value, standard mileage costs, and depreciation tables.

If There Is Only One Owner

If you own a car that you share with your neighbor, your main benefit is the money you save by sharing the car's expenses (plus the bonus goodwill it creates with your neighbor). There are different ways to calculate the costs: Your neighbor could pay a fee based on mileage or a flat monthly fee based on estimated use, you can reckon car expenses at the end of each month, or you could use a combination of these methods.

> **CAUTION**
>
> **Turning a profit could lead to trouble.** If your neighbor pays expenses in a way that clearly profits you, you could run into trouble with your insurance company (which might refuse to pay an insurance claim because you didn't disclose this "business" arrangement) or with the IRS (which could require you to pay taxes on what you earned). To avoid these problems, make sure the expenses you charge are "reasonably calculated so as not to exceed" the actual expenses of owning and driving the car. You should write down your method of calculating expenses and keep good records, in case the IRS ever questions you.

Charging for Mileage

The benefit of charging based on mileage is that it's easy to keep track of and add up. The hard part is figuring out how much to charge per mile.

If you decide to use a straightforward mileage method, you can adopt either the standard mileage rate set each year by the IRS or a different per-mile cost tailored to your particular vehicle.

The IRS sets standard mileage rates based on its calculation of the actual costs of owning and operating a car, including fuel. For the beginning of 2009, the rate was 55 cents per mile. However, using the annual IRS mileage rate may not accurately reflect the cost of driving. It usually costs less to own and drive an older car than a new one. The IRS rate factors in depreciation and insurance based on newer cars, and both these costs are lower for older cars. Thus, depending on gas price fluctuations during the year and your car's age, you may want to charge less than 55 cents.

To come up with an accurate mileage rate, you could use the worksheet above to find out your annual car expenses, estimating fuel, maintenance, and other variable costs based on how many combined miles you and your neighbor expect to drive. Divide your annual total by that number of miles for an approximate per mile cost.

No matter how you calculate mileage, if the rate factors in the cost of fuel, then the owner of the car should be responsible for paying all fuel costs. The non-owner driver can buy gas, keep receipts, and subtract the gas costs from the total mileage costs.

Sharing Expenses Without Using Mileage

Another way to share expenses when someone else uses your car is to split overhead costs and then divide variable expenses based on how much you each use the car. The overhead costs include insurance and registration; these costs will be relatively static, or vary only slightly based on how much you drive your car. You could even calculate in the cost of three oil changes and one tune-up per year, and an annual roadside assistance membership. It may also be appropriate to ask your cosharer to pay part of the monthly interest charges on your loan—the loan is one of the expenses of owning a new car, after all. And rather than asking the cosharer to help you pay off the principal, you can share the cost of the vehicle by asking for a contribution to the cost of the depreciation, which represents the gradual loss of value of the car (see "Calculating Depreciation" below). The biggest variable cost is fuel, which you can each pay for based on how much you drive.

Calculating Depreciation

Depreciation is a measure of how much value your car loses every year. The best way to calculate how much your car has depreciated is to figure out how much less you would get for it if you sold it this year than if you had sold it last year. You can get a good rough figure using Kelley Blue Book (www.kbb.com), a generally accepted measure of a car's resale value. Plug in your car's year, make, model, features, and mileage and find a value for it. Then, look up the value of the same make and model, but one year older and with the additional mileage you expect to put on the car in one year of your sharing arrangement.

For example, let's say your car's current value is $11,000, and the value of the same car from the previous year and with 15,000 more miles is $9,800. You can use those figures to estimate that your car will depreciate $1,200 this year, or $100 per month. You can ask your sharing partner to split this cost with you by paying you $50 each month. At the end of each year, you should reconcile your figures by using the mileage you actually put on the car to come up with its current value, then subtract that from the car's actual value at the start of the year. If this actual depreciation figure is significantly different from the estimate you used, one of you might owe the other some money. You can also use your actual mileage to come up with a new depreciation figure for the coming year.

The cost of "wear and tear" on the car is partially covered by depreciation, but not entirely. This is because wear and tear is partially remedied each time you do maintenance or make repairs. If you are the owner of the car, it may not be fair to ask for your sharing partner to split the cost of expensive replacements, such as brakes, the transmission, or the timing belt. After all, you could end the sharing arrangement any time, and it's difficult to calculate how much your cosharer will have benefited from such a repair. One way to deal with this is to discuss the costs and find out whether there is an amount your cosharer could contribute which you will both feel is fair.

If You Share Ownership of the Car

Sharing expenses is more straightforward if you both own the car. Either of you could pay for gas, maintenance, insurance, registration, and so on, and each keep your receipts in a separate file. Periodically, you could get together, add up each set of receipts, split the total down the middle (or some other division if one of you drives more than the other), and reconcile it with the amount each of you paid. Alternatively, you could do a 50/50 split on all costs except for fuel, which you could divide based on how much you each drive.

If you want to be even more precise, you could each keep track of the number of miles you drive the car and pay in proportion to use. However, keeping a mileage log can be a hassle. Rather than calculate precise mileage, you could simply guess at the difference in the amount each of you drives the car.

Really, you could probably come up with all kinds of ways to calculate expenses. However, most experienced sharers would advise you to keep it simple, even if it means you might pay a little more than your share. When you try to make everything even out perfectly, it gets tedious and dampens the spirit of generosity that leads people to share in the first place.

Financing a Shared Purchase

If you and your neighbor purchase a new or used car together, you will need to decide how to finance the car. There are different ways to share the purchase cost, depending on your financial needs. For example, if you and your neighbor buy a used car for $9,000, your neighbor may just want to pay a lump sum, rather than take out a loan, while you need to get financing. In that situation, your neighbor could make a $4,500 down payment on the car, and you could take out a loan in your name only for the remaining $4,500. Your neighbor could even choose to pay the full $9,000 and you could arrange to pay her $4,500 (plus interest) in monthly installments.

If you both sign a loan, both of you will be liable for the full monthly payments. If one of you doesn't pay, the lender is entitled to seek full payment from the other. If you default on the loan, both of your credit reports will suffer, even if you made your share of the payments faithfully, on time. The car could also be repossessed.

Buying Insurance

Insurance companies respond in different ways to carsharing arrangements. Our best advice is to call different insurance companies, tell them how you are planning to share the car, and get some quotes. Some companies will tell you that sharing won't raise your rates at all. At the other end of the spectrum, other companies will refuse to write a policy for a shared car.

If You Both Own the Car

If you and your neighbor share ownership of a car and are both listed on the title, your insurance company shouldn't have too many qualms about insuring you both. Co-ownership gives each of you an "insurable interest" in the car, which means each of you would suffer a financial loss if the car were damaged.

If you both own the car and take out a joint policy, both of you could be liable for the vehicle and any accidents. Still, your insurance company will probably want you to designate a primary and secondary driver. Usually, the primary driver is the person who drives the car the most. If you and your neighbor use the car equally, you might want to designate as primary whoever has the best insurance rating (the best ratings typically go to women who are older than 25 and have clean driving records). Some insurance companies will list two primary drivers, but may require that the owners be spouses or legal partners under a domestic partnership or civil union law.

If One of You Owns the Car

If you own the car and allow your neighbor to use it, you must tell your insurance company and add your neighbor to the policy. You should not try to pass your neighbor off as an "occasional" driver, meaning someone who does not have regular access to your vehicle but is driving it with your permission. If your neighbor has an accident and the insurance company concludes that he or she is actually a regular driver, the company may deny the claim and even rescind your policy.

Some insurance companies will add another driver to your policy as a "secondary" driver. They may not even raise your rates unless your neighbor has a bad driving record or your sharing arrangement will put a lot more miles on the car every year. Some companies won't allow you to add a secondary driver who doesn't live with you. If you run into this problem, just call another insurance company.

The owner of the car is the primary person liable for accidents. If your insurance is not enough to cover the damage and injury from an accident, accident victims could seek additional compensation from you or from your neighbor, if the neighbor was at fault in the accident. The best way to avoid this scenario is to carry a high limit of liability, such as $500,000 to $1,000,000. This will make your insurance somewhat more expensive, but at least you will be splitting the monthly premiums.

Another option is to have your sharing partner get non-owner's auto insurance. Non-owner's insurance is for people who drive someone else's car on a regular basis. It only kicks in if the car owner's policy is not sufficient to cover the cost of an accident. Non-owner policies do not cover damage to the vehicle, but they'll provide extra liability coverage in case your neighbor is at fault, and may include additional personal injury coverage. These policies usually cost between $200 and $300 per year, but may cost more if your neighbor has a poor driving record. Even if your neighbor's record is clean, however, it's usually cheaper to simply have one policy (your policy) with a high limit of liability.

If There's an Accident

You and your neighbor can make additional agreements to compensate each other for accidents; lawyers refer to this as indemnification. You may want to make different agreements depending on whether you both own the car or only one of you owns the car. You will also want to think about what happens if one driver is in an accident that isn't that person's fault. Should both drivers bear the cost of that misfortune or should the driver bear it alone? One option is to have both owners share the cost of the insurance deductible and car repair, and have each driver pay individual medical costs that aren't covered by the insurance of the person who was at fault. You should also decide who is going to pay if the monthly insurance premiums go up as a result of the accident. If you both own the car and carry joint insurance, here's an example of language you could add to your carsharing agreement:

> *"If one owner is involved in an accident for which that owner is partially or completely at fault, that owner will pay any insurance deductibles, and will indemnify and compensate the other owner for any expenses related to the accident that are not covered by insurance. That owner will also pay for any increases in the insurance premium rates.*
>
> *If one owner is involved in an accident for which that owner is not at fault, owners will each pay half of the insurance deductible (if applicable), any costs related to fixing the car, and any increase in insurance premiums. Any other costs related to the accident, such as medical bills, will be paid by the owner involved in the accident."*

If only one of you owns the car, you'll need to use different language, as in the example below:

> **EXAMPLE:** Nancy owns a car and shares it with Silvio. They add this to the agreement:
>
> *"If Silvio is involved in a car accident, he agrees to indemnify Nancy for any accident-related costs not covered by Nancy's insurance policy. If Silvio is partially or completely at fault in the accident, he will pay the insurance deductible and any increase in insurance premiums. If Silvio is not at fault in the accident, Nancy and Silvio will split the deductible and any increase in insurance premiums.*
>
> *If Nancy is involved in a car accident, she will pay for all accident-related expenses, except, if Nancy is not at fault in the accident, Silvio will pay for half the deductible and any increase in insurance premiums."*

Sample Carsharing Agreement for Two Owners

This agreement is between Catherine Love and Theo Dancer, who agree as follows:

We agree to share ownership and use of a 2007 Toyota Camry, VIN#: 97233lksfd9f7f, ("the car").

Transferring title: Within one (1) week of signing this agreement, Catherine will transfer title of the car from her name to both of our names, "Catherine Love and Theo Dancer, as tenants in common." Theo will pay all taxes and title fees related to the transfer.

Ownership of the car: In consideration for 50% ownership of the car, Theo will pay Catherine $4,150, which we agree is half of the current Blue Book value of the car.

Accessories: We agree that the following accessories in the car will remain Catherine's separate property: the roadside emergency kit and the steering wheel locking device.

Parking: We will keep the car at Theo's apartment on Sluggage Street.

Use of the car: Catherine can use the car on Sundays, Mondays, and Tuesdays, and Theo can use the car on Wednesdays, Thursdays, and Fridays. We will take turns using the car every other Saturday. We may from time to time negotiate a new schedule. If either of us needs to use the car on a day when the other person is designated to use the car, that person may ask the other for permission to use the car. The person to whom the car is designated may refuse without giving a reason.

Long trips: Unless we agree otherwise, if one of us wants to use the car for a trip longer than three days, that person will rent a car for the other to use on the days the other normally would have had the car.

Decisions: We will both take part equally in decisions related to the car. Neither of us will agree to sell, encumber, or make expensive repairs or improvements to the car without the other's permission. If we cannot reach an agreement about any matter pertaining to the car, we agree to discuss the issue with the help of a mediator.

Responsibilities: We will each be equally responsible for filling the gas tank and keeping the car clean. Catherine agrees to take the car for regular maintenance.

Rules: Each of us agrees not to lend the car to anyone without first discussing it with and getting permission from the other. We will never lend the car to an unlicensed driver. Smoking is not allowed in the car.

Costs: We will divide all insurance, registration, maintenance, and repair costs equally. We will each keep our receipts in separate envelopes in the glove compartment. Every three months, we will add up our costs and reimburse each another for any differences in expenses. Each of us will pay for the gas we use. Rather than keep strict records of our mileage and gas expenses, we will try to buy gas in rough proportion to the number of miles we drive. The car gets about 30 miles per gallon.

Insurance: We will carry an auto insurance policy with the following company: _____ . Our policy will cover up to $500,000 per victim, $1,000,000 per accident, and $50,000 for property damage. Catherine will be listed as the primary driver and Theo as a secondary driver. We will each pay half of the insurance premiums. If one of us receives a speeding ticket or does anything to mar his or her driving record, that person will be responsible for any increase in insurance premiums that result. If the insurance company deems that the car is "totaled" and pays us to replace it, we will split those proceeds.

Indemnification: If one owner is involved in an accident for which that owner is partially or completely at fault, that owner will pay any insurance deductibles, and will indemnify and compensate the other owner for any expenses related to the accident that are not covered by insurance. That owner will also pay for any increases in the insurance premium rates.

If one owner is involved in an accident for which that owner is *not* at fault, owners will each pay half of the insurance deductible (if applicable), any costs related to fixing the car, and any increase in insurance premiums. Any other costs related to the accident, such as medical bills, will be paid by the owner involved in the accident.

Dispute resolution: If a conflict or dispute arises that we are unable to solve through discussion, we agree to attempt to resolve the dispute through mediation. We will seek to mediate through Los Alamos Community Mediation.

Termination: If one of us wants to stop sharing the car, we will consider these options in the following order: (1) the other owner will keep the car and pay the departing owner half of the Blue Book value of the car at that time; (2) the departing owner will keep the car and pay the remaining owner half of the Blue Book value of the car at that time; or (3) we will sell the car and split the proceeds.

Name: _____

Address: _____

_____

Date: _____

Name: _____

Address: _____

_____

Date: _____

Sharing a Truck

Most of the time, it's possible to get by with a small vehicle, but there are times when you just need a truck—to bring home some soil and large plants or to pick up a great recliner you saw on the sidewalk. Or maybe you run a small business and occasionally need to make large deliveries. A van is also great for camping, hauling seven kids to the beach for the day, and all kinds of fun outings.

We know one group of families who went in together to buy a $2,000 truck, and each family got regular access to the truck for far less than what they'd pay to rent one occasionally. Because nobody invested a significant amount of money in the truck, they decided to put just one person's name on the title. This kept things simpler for everyone, except that the person whose name was on title had to bear the extra risk of being sued or stuck with higher rates if the truck was in a wreck.

There are ways to avoid these risks, including entering into a written agreement specifying how liability will be distributed and clearly agreeing—on the vehicle title or other written document—how much of the truck each person owns. As with sharing a car, you could choose to put everyone on title, have one person own it, or create a separate entity such as a carsharing club, described in Solution 2 below. No matter how you arrange your share, you should tell your insurance company that you are sharing the truck.

Ending the Arrangement

The questions in Chapter 3 give some general guidelines about planning to terminate a carsharing arrangement. When you end your carshare, make sure that you transfer title to the remaining owner. If you leave both names on the title, you may have to track down your former co-owner in order to sell the car later. Best to get all of the paperwork done at once.

Solution 2: Start a Small Carsharing Club or Program

While sharing a car with your neighbor can be a wonderfully convenient and cost-saving arrangement, there are plenty of reasons to grow your carsharing arrangement or start a carsharing group instead:

- **Save money.** Bringing in more sharers reduces your costs even more.
- **Increased availability of cars.** Bringing in more cars and more sharers can increase the likelihood that a car will be available when needed.
- **Access to fuel efficient vehicles.** Even if you own a car, you could still use a shared electric vehicle for your around-town errands.
- **Spread affordable and green transportation alternatives.** If carsharing were more widely available, many people who have been thinking of giving up their cars could take that plunge.

Large carsharing programs have already spread to 40 major cities in North America, but have yet to break onto the scene in many smaller towns and cities. If you live in a city that already has an established carsharing program, your best option may be to join that program. (See "Join an Existing Carsharing Program," below.) The larger car sharing programs—such as City CarShare and Zipcar—benefit from economies of scale. They have hundreds or thousands of members, centralized administration, automated reservation and billing systems, and other technologies that make the system efficient and keep costs low.

Small carsharing clubs (of five to 30 members) can benefit from their size, too. A small group can keep things simple, do without the fancy automated systems, and let members do the administrative work.

There's a lot to think about when you start a carsharing group. We can't give you all the information you'll need, but we'll summarize the steps and the decisions you have to make. Fortunately, in smaller towns and cities, grassroots organizations are already paving the way for carsharing by developing the necessary organizational models, car access technologies, and so on. You won't have to reinvent the wheel if you start a carsharing club; you'll be able to draw on the experience and knowledge of existing carsharing organizations, large and small. You can also check out the resources available from City CarShare, which offers guidance to start-up carsharing programs, including a manual on starting carsharing in your community: www.citycarshare.org.

Sharing Neighborhood Electric Vehicles

Small electric vehicles are slowly appearing on our streets, but because of their small size and limited travel distance, they've yet to replace typical cars. At the same time, probably all of us could imagine short trips and errands for which we could easily use an electric car and leave our gas guzzlers at home—a run to the post office, grocery shopping, or a nighttime outing to the local theater.

Here's an idea: Place neighborhood electric vehicles ("NEVs") in neighborhoods or apartment complexes for residents to use for around-town errands. Residents who don't own cars will have wheels when they need them, and residents who do own cars could "spare the air" and take the NEV for quick trips. In crowded urban areas, small electric cars are a great way to get around, especially because you can park them in tiny spots.

Shared NEVs will be easiest to establish if there's an existing entity that can purchase and manage the vehicles, such as a homeowners association, apartment owner, or property manager. Individuals could also form small groups to buy and share them. Or if you want to buy one yourself, offer to share it with your neighbors, especially if they are willing to plug it in at their house to charge it.

Forming an Ownership Organization

The major difference between sharing with a neighbor and forming a carsharing club is in how you own the cars and distribute liability. If you plan to share a car with more than a few people, liability becomes a concern, and nobody should be expected to bear the risk for the whole group. In addition, without an intermediate entity, title to the car would have to change every time a member joined or left.

As discussed in Chapter 3, forming an intermediate entity, such as an LLC or nonprofit organization, solves many concerns about liability and ownership. The entity owns and insures the vehicles and administers the sharing program. If one member gets in an accident, the entity's insurance is the main source of compensation; other members of the carshare generally won't be liable. As members come and go, title to the car remains in the name of the entity.

The intermediate entity may take a variety of forms, including a nonprofit organization, for-profit business, or cooperative. There are benefits and disadvantages to each. Forming a nonprofit and obtaining tax-exempt status is a lengthy process, yet it can help you get grants, donations, and even free parking. At the same time, forming a for-profit company, such as an LLC, can encourage people to invest money. Creating a cooperative allows you to raise capital by selling shares to members.

Another option is to find an existing organization to sponsor your carsharing program, which spares you the trouble of forming a new entity. Suitable sponsors might include your local transit agency, an urban development organization, or an environmental organization. For example, the Center for Neighborhood Technologies, a nonprofit that promotes sustainable communities, sponsors I-GO (www.igocars.org), a large carsharing program with more than 200 cars in Chicago.

Starting the carsharing club under the umbrella of an existing nonprofit or government agency can save you a great deal of administrative legwork.

Membership Requirements

Most carsharing organizations require only that members have a driver's license and a decent driving history. Your insurance company will likely require you to check driving histories because a member with a poor driving record could raise insurance premiums for everyone. You could either check the driving history of prospective members or require them to submit a copy of their record with their application.

Join an Established Carsharing Program

If you want to share a car occasionally but don't want to start a group from scratch, consider joining an established carshare. Many larger cities already have these programs. Typically, these programs keep cars in designated spots throughout the city. Almost anyone can sign up for a membership, which allows them to reserve (often using a cell phone or the Internet) and use cars. Most programs use an automated system to give members access to the car and track and bill usage.

In contrast to renting a car, carsharing is typically for short-term use of a vehicle, such as to run errands. If you plan to use a car for more than ten hours, it's likely cheaper to rent a car. Another difference between carsharing and car renting is that most carshares are set up so you can reserve and access the car yourself, without going to a central office and getting checked in by staff. This makes carsharing more convenient and easier to use.

Carsharing programs are already having an impact on our environment and attitudes about car usage. According to a 2008 survey by Innovative Mobility Research, 279,000 people share nearly 6,000 vehicles in these programs across the United States, and these numbers are growing rapidly. Research has shown that for every car in a sharing program, eight cars are taken off the road. As carsharing programs grow, this could significantly change our landscape and free up a large amount of space currently dedicated to parking.

To find out whether there's a carsharing program near you, ask your local transit agency or search the Internet. A good place to start is www.carsharing.net, which keeps track of cities that have carsharing programs and posts news stories about carsharing.

Obtaining Tax-Exempt Status for a Carsharing Program

If your carsharing program would like to solicit tax-deductible donations and grants, you will need to obtain tax-exempt status under section 501(c)(3) of the tax code. (For more information about starting a nonprofit and applying for a 501(c)(3) status, see Nolo's *How to Form a Nonprofit Corporation*, by Anthony Mancuso.) The IRS has approved tax-exempt status for some carsharing organizations, but it is prone to view some carshares as car rental businesses. The key to obtaining tax-exempt status under 501(c)(3) is to demonstrate that your organization is motivated by social and environmental goals.

For a carsharing organization, these goals might include discouraging car ownership and unnecessary driving, reducing urban congestion, providing affordable access to cars in neighborhoods with less access to transportation, and decreasing dependence on fossil fuels and high-emission vehicles. To achieve these goals, nonprofit carsharing organizations often make decisions that won't result in financial gain, but will further their social and environmental purposes. This may mean placing cars in low-income neighborhoods, using hybrid and electric vehicles, and adopting pricing structures that discourage people from driving, such as charging per mile driven.

If you plan to seek tax-exempt status under section 501(c)(3), talk to a carsharing organization that has already done so. Find out the basis on which the IRS granted their application, and maybe even ask to see a copy of the exemption application. The IRS is becoming increasingly familiar with the concept of carsharing, which makes it easier for carsharing nonprofits to qualify for tax-exempt status. Nevertheless, if you plan to go this route, your best bet is to model some of your organization's mission and practices after other successful groups.

Where to Keep the Cars

Figuring our where to put the cars can be an initial challenge. If your carsharing club is composed primarily of neighbors, you could probably just designate one person's driveway or park on the street, if available. If members are more spread out, you should park shared cars in a location served by public transportation so people can get to and from the car easily if they don't live nearby. Here are some options:

- Find a nonprofit or business that will donate a designated parking spot for you in its lot.
- Ask a local bus or train station to give you free parking.
- Ask your city to create designated on-street parking for carsharing organizations.
- Use someone's private driveway, either free or for a small monthly rent.
- Contract with an existing business to oversee use of a specific car. For example, you could work out a deal with the local video rental store to park the car in its lot, and even have its staff check the car in and out.

Procedures for Using Cars

There will be procedural issues to work out for your carshare club, including:

- **Reserving the car.** If your group is small, you could just schedule use of the car with an online calendar to which all members have access. Larger groups typically use online reservation software. Carsharing nonprofits are usually generous about sharing software they develop, so ask around.
- **Access to the car.** If your carsharing club is small, you could just give each member a key (though in newer cars, keys are expensive). For larger groups, here are some options (see www.carsharing.net for information on businesses that provide these devices and more):
  - Keep the car key in a coded lock box where the car is parked and give members the code.

- Install a numerical entry system on the car. This can cost $500 or so. You could put a lockbox in the car and keep the ignition key in that box, or install a numerical ignition system as well.
- If your shared car is kept at an apartment complex with 24-hour staffing, drivers can pick up and drop off keys with the staff.
- Keep the car parked at a store or other business with long hours. Come up with an agreement with that business to provide the key to members upon request.

- **Procedures for drivers.** Decide whether you'll ask drivers to do anything once they're in the car. Some carsharing programs keep a defects list in the car and ask drivers to inspect the car and note any new defects. You should also come up with procedures for drivers to follow if the car breaks down.

- **Fueling the car.** Most carsharing clubs require drivers to return the car with at least a quarter or half tank of gas. Here are some options for having drivers fuel the car:
  - Keep a credit card in the car to be used only for gas.
  - Create an account with a local gas station (often the station nearest to the car's parking spot).
  - Have drivers fill the tank and submit receipts for a credit to their carsharing account.
  - Have drivers fill the tank completely at the end of every trip, so they pay for the exact amount of gas that they used.

Funding Your Group

Your group will need to raise money to buy its car(s). There are many options: grants, individual donations, investments, member contributions, and so on. The type of funding available will depend on whether you start a nonprofit or for-profit group.

Many carsharing groups have gotten started by partnering with local transit agencies, city governments, or other entities that would benefit from the presence of a carsharing program. Through these partnerships, carsharing organizations have obtained grants, free parking, assistance with marketing, and other benefits.

Pricing and Cost Sharing

There are all kinds of ways to arrange for pricing or cost sharing for your carsharing club. If your group is small, you could create a group account into which everyone pays a fixed amount each month and have everyone pay for their own gas. However, if your group is larger, you'll probably want to charge members based on how much they use the car(s). Here are some considerations:

- Should you charge per mile, per hour, or some combination of the two? For example, you might charge $3 per hour and $0.30 per mile. Or you could charge $6 per hour and allow up to 10 miles for that hour, then charge for any additional miles driven.
- Will you have discounted rates for non-peak hours, such as the middle of the night?
- Should you also include monthly fees? Initial membership fees? A security deposit? Some carshares keep these fees low to make it cost-effective for infrequent users to join.
- Should you have different plans based on how often people use the cars? For example, frequent users could pay a higher monthly fee and lower mileage and hourly rates; infrequent users could pay a low monthly fee, but higher mileage and hourly rates.
- What if members need a car for a day-long trip? Should reduced rates apply?
- Will you charge penalty fees for late return of the car, late cancellation, failure to fill the gas tank, losing a key, and so on?

Insurance and Loss

You should expect to pay somewhere between $150 and $300 per month per vehicle for insurance. Your rates will vary based on the age and driving history of your members, where the car is parked, how it is used, and a variety of other factors. We strongly recommend obtaining a high limit of liability, such as $1,000,000 per accident. This will protect the whole club from folding if one member causes an accident.

You may have to shop around for insurance, and it could help to talk to other carsharing programs to find friendly insurance companies.

Some companies will be unfamiliar with carsharing groups. Others might treat you like any other nonprofit or business that insures a company car or fleet of vehicles. Your insurance company will likely require you to provide and update a list of members and their driving histories.

You should also decide what to do if a car is involved in an accident. For example, if a member is at fault in an accident, you may want to have the member pay the insurance deductible (or pay for any repairs that are less than the insurance deductible), as well as any costs that are not covered by insurance.

Other Questions to Consider

Here are some other issues your group may want to discuss:

- What kinds of cars should we have? Any stick-shifts? Hybrids? Electric vehicles? Trucks or vans?
- Can someone other than a member drive the car if a member needs a ride and is not physically able to drive for some reason?
- What are members' responsibilities with regard to checking fluids, tire pressure, and so on?
- At what point might it make sense to purchase an additional car?
- What rules do members want to have about using the cars? No food? No pets? No smoking? Keep cars locked to prevent theft? No hazardous materials?
- What if a member damages the car's interior, by spilling coffee, for example?
- What should a member do if a car breaks down? Some groups authorize members to make repairs only up to a certain cost ($200 or $300); the member must get permission from the group for more costly repairs.
- Under what circumstances will you terminate a membership?
- Will you offer membership to businesses as well?
- Will you try to grow membership? If so, how will you market the group or do outreach to the public?

Portrait of a Small Carsharing Group

The Community Car Share (CCS) of Bellingham, Washington, is a nonprofit group of 30 members who share three cars. CCS used a $10,000 grant from the regional clean air agency and a loan from private citizens to buy its first car, a hybrid vehicle. The local organic grocery store gave the group a free designated parking space, and CCS began accepting applications for membership. Later on, someone donated a bio-diesel VW Beetle; as membership grew, CCS brought in enough money to purchase a pickup truck as well.

When joining, members choose from a list of rate plans, which vary based on how much a member plans to use the cars. 20% of CCS's members don't own cars, 40% come from households with two adults and one car, and the rest are businesses and nonprofits that use the cars to replace company-owned vehicles. CCS pays about $500 per month to insure all three vehicles. To keep rates low, CCS excludes drivers with major traffic violations. For new members with a poor credit history, CCS asks for a security deposit.

Members reserve a car using an online reservation system. The cars have a numeric lock entry system, and inside the car, members enter another code to get the key out of a lockbox. For each trip, the member notes the starting and ending mileage in a notebook inside the car. Members are required to return the vehicle with at least a quarter tank of gas. When members fill the tank, they submit their receipts to CCS for reimbursement or a credit to their account.

CCS is run by a board of directors; the actual day-to-day work is done by volunteers, including a manager, mechanic, bookkeeper, and web administrator. CCS hopes to eventually have 90 members, providing a 30:1 member to car ratio. Learn more about CCS at www.communitycarshare.org.

Documents

In addition to the formal paperwork you may need to file with the government to create an intermediate entity (for example, articles of incorporation or a 501(c)(3) tax exemption application), your group may want to create some documents that you'll use over and over, such as:

- contract or agreement for new members to sign
- membership application
- member procedure handbook
- price list
- mileage log for drivers to complete at the end of each drive, and
- other documents to be kept in the car (such as instructions on what to do if there's an accident).

For help getting started, contact an existing carshare organization to find out what documents it uses and whether you can adapt them for your own group.

Solution 3: Start a Carpool

You may not be ready to share a car full time, but you can still cut your costs, stress, and carbon footprint considerably by sharing a ride to work or another regular destination. At any given time, 85% of the cars on the road hold only one person, and 77% of us commute alone. But 10% of us commute to work in a carpool. Here's why:

- Sharing a ride significantly cuts the cost of driving and parking.
- You can sit back, relax, eat, sleep, read, chat, or work while riding (unless you are the driver, please).
- Many high-traffic areas have carpool lanes, also known as high-occupancy vehicle (HOV) lanes, allowing carpoolers to sail past the congestion.
- Some areas designate special or discounted parking for ride-sharers, bridges waive tolls, and some employers offer employees valuable commuter vouchers to provide an incentive for not driving solo.
- Carpooling to and from work gives you a good excuse to leave work on time, and an extra incentive to arrive on time.

Guaranteed Ride Home Programs

What if you carpool to work but have to stay late or leave early unexpectedly? That's where Guaranteed Ride Home (GRH) comes in. In cities such as Denver, Atlanta, Albuquerque, Kansas City, and Minneapolis, local governments sponsor programs to ensure that carpoolers are not stranded without a ride home. Employers have also jumped on board to sponsor GRH programs. Typically, carpoolers register and affirm in writing that they are sharing rides on a regular basis. They then receive a certain number of free rides home in a taxi or rental car, which they may use when they unexpectedly need a ride.

Share Your Errands

Many people run errands on the way to and from work, and they fear that carpooling will take away this opportunity. But it doesn't have to: Chances are good that other members of your carpool also have errands to run. If so, you can schedule regular stops on your carpool's route home for errands. For example, some carpoolers incorporate monthly trips to the dry cleaners or a weekly stop at a grocery store or farmers market. This is just one more way to cut out more driving.

Finding Carpoolers

The majority of people in this country say they would be interested in carpooling to work, but they fear it would be inconvenient or hard to find other carpoolers. This is becoming less of an obstacle, thanks to the Internet. Carpool matchmaking websites abound (see Appendix A for a list); most major cities have them. Chances are good that people who live or work near you want to carpool—you just have to find them.

Sharing a One-Time Ride

One-time rideshares are becoming easier to set up. Sharing a ride can help everyone save travel and parking costs, and can also reduce congestion for certain events, such as ball games or holiday weekends, when traffic can be at its worst. Here are examples of common trips for which people share one-time rides:

- **Long trips or holiday weekends:** A quick browse of Craigslist reveals opportunities to share rides for anything from a cross-country trip to a weekend ski adventure. Ridesharers for long distance trips can even take turns driving and share lodging expenses. With the growth of ridesharing, it's becoming easier to count on the availability of rides or riders when you need them.

- **Sports events, concerts, or festivals:** You could save on parking and driving expenses by carpooling to events such as ball games, concerts, festivals, and so on. These sorts of rides may also be arranged using online bulletin boards.

- **Parties:** Many email users are becoming accustomed to receiving party and event invitation through an event planning website, such as Evite. You can also arrange carpools using Evite, which links potential ridesharers among party attendees.

There are websites that specialize in helping riders and drivers find each other, such as GoLoco (www.goloco.com.) Some of these websites also verify the identity of ridesharers and make sure that the driver has insurance. Websites such as GoLoco can even help you share the costs of the ride by taking payment from the rider online and depositing it in an account for the driver. (GoLoco takes a small cut of the ride cost.) The cost of the ride is usually based on mileage.

Rules for Drivers and Passengers

If you set up a regular carpool, here are some details you'll probably want to sort out with your other carpoolers:

- Will the same person drive every day or will you rotate drivers or cars? (If you rotate, you'll need a schedule.)
- What are the pickup and dropoff points?
- How long will the carpool wait for someone who is late?
- Are cell phone conversations allowed for drivers? Passengers?
- Is smoking allowed? What about strong perfumes or colognes?
- Will carpoolers listen to music, books-on-tape, talk radio, and so on? Is conversation invited at all times?
- Is there a backup plan if a driver is not available or the car has broken down? How will carpoolers notify each other? Will any of the carpoolers be available to drive on a moment's notice?

Sharing Expenses in a Carpool

There are different ways to share expenses in a carpool. If your carpool rotates drivers regularly, then you won't need to exchange money; it should all even out over time. If one or more people do most of the driving, you could come up with a reasonable fee for each trip, such as $2 a day. Or, you could use the standard mileage rate set by the IRS (currently 55 cents) or another mileage rate, and come up with a fee by multiplying round-trip miles by the mileage rate, then dividing by the number of people in the car. If you are the driver and charge a fee, make sure it's not so high that you're earning a profit; this could cause the IRS or your insurance company to see you as a taxi company.

Sometimes, riders don't pay a fee, but pay other expenses, such as road tolls or parking costs. And some carpool drivers don't ask riders to share expenses at all. The conversation, companionship, and carpool lane advantages are incentive enough.

Insurance and Carpooling

If you will be carting people around on a regular basis, you may want to increase your limit of liability. The more people in a car during an accident, the higher medical expenses and other damages could be. Carrying a high limit of liability protects you, your passengers, and anyone else injured in an accident. Although many drivers carry about $100,000 in liability coverage, you may want to consider carrying up to $1,000,000. This will increase your monthly insurance premium, but it's perfectly acceptable to ask your passengers to help pay for this.

Vanpools

Unlike carpools, vanpools are often organized by an employer or a special service with the resources to provide a van. Vanpooling services rent vans to groups and help them find riders and select a route. Because vans are so much bigger than cars, they are a very efficient way to share a commute. The van riders save time and money; the driver enjoys these benefits and gets a van to use evenings and weekends; the earth and the air quality benefit greatly as well.

Here's how one van service, Vanpool Hawaii, works: Once you find enough people, Vanpool Hawaii will rent you an appropriately sized van for $55 a month, per passenger. Passengers share fuel costs. Everything else—maintenance, registration, insurance, and roadside assistance—is covered by the company.

TIP

Employers can provide tax-free transportation benefits to employees. These benefits might include cash or vouchers for parking, carpooling, vanpooling, and public transit. Find out more at www.commuterchoice.com, and let your employer know. Some employers provide additional cash incentives for employees to carpool (because it frees up workplace parking spots). The value can quickly add up for the commuter.

Sample Carpool Agreement

Here's a sample agreement that you can use for establishing the terms of a carpooling arrangement.

Sample Carpool Agreement

This agreement is between the carpool riders ("riders") listed on the attached information sheets, all of whom agree as follows:

1. The purpose of the carpool is to transport us between our respective workplaces in downtown Boston and each of our respective homes.

2. Participation in the carpool is voluntary. Any rider may withdraw at any time, but we each agree to try to give as much notice as possible before ending our participation.

3. The carpool will begin on August 7, 20xx and will continue as long as there are riders willing to take part.

4. Any of the riders may volunteer to drive, and we will rotate drivers each week to ensure that driving responsibilities and expenses even out. Riders who do not ever drive will pay the driver $2 per day, or $10 per week, payable every Friday.

5. We will buy a quarterly parking pass for the downtown garage at Franklin and Hawley Streets. The cost is $300 per quarter. We will divide the cost evenly among riders. Since the pass may be hung on the rearview mirror, at the end of each week the driver will give the parking pass to the designated driver for the following week.

6. In the morning, we intend be on the Massachusetts Turnpike heading for Boston by 7:45 a.m. We will determine an order for pick-up based on who is driving on that day. We will select specific pick-up times for each rider, and riders will try their best to be on time. The carpool won't wait more than 5 minutes.

7. The driver will make one stop at the corner of Water and Oliver Streets, a second stop at Federal and Franklin Streets, then park the vehicle.

8. At the end of each day, the driver will retrieve the car from the parking garage at 5:40 and make the stops in reverse order. It is imperative that everyone is waiting to be picked up by 5:40, to ensure that the driver does not have to circle back to pick up late riders.

9. We will let each other know if and when we are available to be back-up drivers, in the event that a driver is sick or for any other reason not available on a day that driver is designated to drive.

We all agree to maintain current insurance coverage on our vehicles as required by law, and each carry per-accident coverage of at least $500,000.

Signature: _____ Date: _____

Signature: _____ Date: _____

Signature: _____ Date: _____

Signature: _____ Date: _____

Signature: _____ Date: _____

Information Sheet for Carpool Members

Name: _____

Address for pickup: _____

Phone numbers (please put a check mark by the best number to reach you)

☐ Home: _____

☐ Work: _____

☐ Cell: _____

☐ Other: _____

☐ Email: _____

Emergency contact

Name: _____

Relationship: _____

Best number to reach: _____

Driver information

Drivers' license number: _____

Car make and model: _____

License plate: _____

Insurance co. and policy number: _____

Solution 4: Share a Ride

The carpools described above (sometimes called "static carpools") have limited flexibility. They require you to be a certain place at a certain time, with a certain group of carpoolers. But what if you go to work early sometimes, or stay late? Or what if you just want to carpool occasionally? Casual carpooling provides this kind of flexibility, and it is growing in popularity in major U.S. cities. Following close on its heels is dynamic ridesharing, a technology-assisted concept that matches drivers and riders instantly using cellular phones.

Casual Ridesharing

Casual ridesharing could be described as an organized form of hitch-hiking, where riders gather at a specific location and wait to be picked up by drivers. The incentive for everyone is usually to gain access to a carpool lane during rush hour. Casual ridesharing is most common in large cities where many people work downtown or for a large employer, such as a factory or university. The pickup spots are usually "Park and Ride" lots or transit stations located at bottlenecks where drivers from many locations are about to merge onto a major freeway. Riders typically line up and catch rides as drivers pull up. Anyone unable to catch a ride is usually able to fall back on public transportation or their own car.

Get Casual Ridesharing Started in Your Neighborhood

Casual ridesharing has to start somewhere, and it could start with you, even if it's just on a small scale in your neighborhood. One way to do it is to create a "Park and Ride" location where participants can park in the morning and be picked up by drivers. Start by finding a parking lot in your community with plenty of open spaces during the weekdays, such as a church parking lot. If it's located near a public transit stop, that's even better—that way, anyone who can't catch a ride in a car could fall back on public transit. Get permission from the parking lot owner to use the lot as a park and ride.

Next, put the word out in and around your workplace and in your neighborhood. Get a handful of people to agree to meet in the lot starting on a particular day. You can get the system going by specifying a narrow meet-up time window, such as between 7:45 and 8:00 a.m. As the number of carpoolers grows, so could the time window. If you want to give drivers an extra incentive to pick up riders, create a standard cost sharing system, such as having each rider give the driver a dollar to help cover the cost of driving. If five riders gather in a park and ride lot, and no driver is in sight, a rider whose car is parked there could volunteer to drive. For more information and ideas on getting casual carpooling started in your community, visit www.MyCasualCarpool.com.

Casual Ridesharing Etiquette

If you are going to hop in the car with a stranger, you'll need to know the ground rules. Typically, ridesharers adhere to the following etiquette:

- The driver decides whether there will be conversation and passengers don't make conversation unless the driver initiates it.
- The driver controls the radio and temperature in the car.
- Do not take or give a ride if you are sick and contagious.
- Don't eat or drink unless the driver says you may.
- Don't wear heavy perfumes or colognes.
- Most casual ridesharing does not involve money changing hands (the incentive, for many, is to use the carpool lane). However, if you participate in ridesharing where costs are shared, pay the driver before you get on the road.
- If you are the driver, don't make extra stops unless the riders agree to them.

Safety Concerns

Fortunately, crime associated with ridesharing has been very rare. Still, safety is always a concern when you get in a car with a stranger. Some riders take precautions, such as only riding if there's another passenger. One way to implement safety precautions is to register drivers and riders, conduct background checks, verify insurance, and provide specialized

A Hybrid of the Casual and Static Carpools

Terry Lim, an employee of the University of California, Berkeley, commutes daily from Sonoma, a 40-mile ride. Terry saves a great deal of money by using a carpool group that combines casual and static carpooling.

Terry drives his first ten miles alone, then picks up a carpooler named Coda, so they can use the carpool lane through a high-traffic corridor. Ten miles later, Terry and Coda park in a lot that gives free parking to carpoolers, where they meet the Berkeley carpoolers.

This group has been around for at least 20 years, and has evolved over time. Participation has varied between ten and 25 carpoolers, and consists mostly, but not entirely, of university employees. It used to be that a coordinator stood in the parking lot with a cell phone and clipboard, matching drivers and riders. Since then, it has adapted into an almost completely self-organized system.

One thing that has simplified the process is that carpoolers show up at 7:15 in the morning and all leave at the same time. No one has to call if he or she isn't coming that day; missing the 7:15 deadline simply means you drive yourself that day. Once everyone has arrived, the carpoolers consolidate into a few cars for the remaining 20 miles of the drive. On campus, the carpoolers use designated carpool parking spots and get a discount on the monthly parking permits. At the end of the day, they gather at a specified time and place for the trip home.

Rather than paying each other for driving expenses or keeping track of how much each member has driven, one carpooler came up with a token system. He bought some cheap washers at the hardware store and had them stamped with a metal stamper. Each time carpoolers catch a ride, they give the driver a token. In this way, the group rotates drivers and the token currency keeps things even.

Taking part in the carpool saves each person a $4 bridge toll (waived for carpoolers), $3 to $6 on gas, and about $7 for parking. In other words, each person saves about $15 per day, which adds up to about $3,500 per year!

identification cards. However, because many casual ridesharing arrangements have been just that—casual—this has rarely been implemented on a large scale. This may change as dynamic ridesharing becomes more common and participants take part by registering online (see "Dynamic Ridesharing," below).

Dynamic Ridesharing

Dynamic ridesharing (also called "instant ridesharing" or "real-time ridesharing") is very likely the wave of transportation's future. Here's the basic concept: Riders and drivers are matched instantly through cellular phones equipped with a Global Positioning System (GPS). GPS, which can pinpoint a person's exact location using satellite signals, is becoming an increasingly common feature on new cellular phones. Riders and drivers register with an online ride-matching system that can determine their locations instantly by connecting with their cell phones.

> EXAMPLE: Darren needs a ride from his home into downtown Cincinnati. He inputs his destination and desired arrival time into his cell phone. Kameelah, a registered driver, signs on to the system with her cell phone before she leaves the house, indicating that she is willing to accept riders on her drive to Cincinnati. She gets in the car, and minutes later her phone beeps. A message comes through on her speaker system asking whether she would pick up a rider three freeway exits down and drop him in Cincinnati. She confirms. As she drives, the GPS system tracks her location and tells her when to exit and where to turn. Meanwhile, Darren receives a message indicating that his ride request has been accepted and his driver will arrive in approximately five minutes. He accepts and the message instructs him to walk to the end of the block and look for a red Saturn sedan. A photo of Kameelah comes up on his phone. Likewise, Kameelah's phone shows a picture of Darren, allowing the two to verify one another's identities when Kameelah arrives.

Dynamic ridesharing systems could include features that auto-matically charge riders for the mileage cost of their rides. In the preceding example, for the ten-mile drive to Cincinnati, the ridesharing system could have charged Darren's account half of the standard mileage rate of 55 cents per mile, and credited $2.75 to Kameelah's account. The systems could also allow participants to rate their experiences with riders and drivers, and allow them to prioritize certain riders or drivers for future matching. To learn more about one company that's developing dynamic ridesharing software, visit Carticipate, www.carticipate.com.

Safe Hitchhiking

Your mom may have told you never to hitchhike, but she probably didn't know about "Go Geronimo." Go Geronimo was a safe hitchhiking program in San Geronimo, California, a town of about 4,000 people, primarily served by a single road that connects the town with the city of San Rafael. Go Geronimo created a registry for drivers and riders, conducted background checks on participants through the local county Sheriff's department, and gave each registrant a large laminated card. The riders stood by the side of the road and held out their cards. When a registered driver pulled over, the rider and driver exchanged ID cards, proving their participation in the program. At the height of the program, there were 275 registered drivers, and 125 registered riders (many of whom were teenagers). Go Geronimo no longer operates this program, but they have left many helpful resources online to help other groups, at www.gogeronimo.org.

Solution 5: Share a Bicycle

Although it's less widespread than carsharing, bikesharing can really be handy, whether you're sharing a bike at work, on vacation, or just to ride around town.

Sharing Bikes at Work and on Vacation

Even if you drive your car or take public transit to work, sometimes it's useful to have a bike during the day. In places where parking is limited, it's often much easier to hop on a bike to get away for your lunch break, go to a local meeting, or run an errand. Bicycling is also a fun work break, and good exercise! Sometimes, coworkers or tenants in an office building share bicycles. (You can find a sample bikesharing agreement for tenants in a shared office building in Chapter 5.) Some employers also provide bikes for employees to share.

Another place where bikesharing can work well is shared vacation homes. It's much easier to keep bikes at the house than to rig up your bicycle rack each time you take a trip. The other owners of the vacation home probably feel the same way. Keeping a few bicycles at the vacation home will save everyone time and trouble.

Free the Bikes!

It sounds like a utopian vision: A fleet of 200 yellow bicycles are released onto the sidewalks all over a town or college campus, free for anyone to use any time. But it's actually happened, in places like Portland, Oregon, Denver, Colorado, Austin, Texas, and Olympia, Washington. Usually an organization or group of people solicits donations of old bicycles, fixes them up, and paint them all one color—often yellow. As a result, free bike programs are often called "yellow bike programs."

The free bikes usually have instructions attached, such as: "This bike is free for anyone to use, but please return it to downtown so that others may use it when you are done. If you would like to park and reserve the bike while you are in a store, turn the seat to the side so that others will know the bike is in use. Enjoy your ride!"

For tips on starting a free bike program, see these resources compiled by the International Bike Fund: www.ibike.org/encouragement/freebike/index.htm.

Citywide Bikesharing Programs

Bikesharing can transform a city's transportation system when implemented on a large scale. It's a great option for cities where streets are congested, parking is limited, and many people don't have space in their apartments to keep a bicycle.

A famous example of bikesharing comes from Paris, where more than 10,000 bikes are placed at 750 bike docking stations for rental by members. Cyclists can pick up a bike on one side of town, ride it to the other side, and leave the bike in the nearest docking station. All rentals are automated and charged with the swipe of a card.

A few cities in the United States have toyed with instituting a citywide bikesharing program, including New York City, San Francisco, and Seattle. Washington DC, has taken the lead. The bikesharing program there has about 120 bikes at ten docking stations.

Sharing Planes and Boats

If you're thinking bigger than a bike or car, rest assured that you can share larger vehicles, too. For those who want to fly but can't afford (or don't want to buy) a plane, there are several options. You could join a flying club, typically a nonprofit organization that owns small aircraft for use by members. There are hundreds of flying clubs in the United States; you can find a directory at www.flying-club.org. Or, you could own a plane cooperatively with a small group. Let's Fly, at www.letsfly.org, sets up four-member plane co-ops, for a buy-in fee as low as $12,900. Or you could go in for fractional jet ownership, which allows you to buy a share (typically one-sixteenth) of a plane.

If it's a boat you'd like to share, you can join a sailing club—similar to the flying clubs described above—for a monthly or annual fee. Or, you can find a company that arranges timeshares for boats or fractional boat ownership. Of course, you can also set up your own arrangement, whether you want to share a kayak (see Chapter 7) or a luxury yacht.

The Bigger Picture: Sharing Transportation

Here are some ways that businesses, nonprofits, community leaders, developers, and law makers can encourage shared transportation:

- Car insurance companies: Create specialized insurance policies for unrelated people who share a car.
- Create designated parking spots in lots and on streets for carpoolers and shared cars.
- Create more "Park and Ride" lots to encourage carpooling.
- Create employer- or city-sponsored vanpool programs.
- Create citywide carsharing and bikesharing programs.
- Provide transportation vouchers and pay cash back to employees who carpool to work.
- Public transit agencies or city governments: Create, sponsor, and fund rideshare match-up programs and guaranteed ride home programs.
- Ensure sufficient public transportation to all carsharing locations.
- Housing developers and owners of large apartment complexes: Provide a neighborhood shared vehicle.

Your Triple Bottom Line: The Benefits of Sharing Transportation

Social and Personal Benefits

- Get 30 to 90 extra minutes of rest or relaxation each day if you take a carpool or vanpool to work.
- Reduce traffic and urban congestion by carsharing and carpooling.
- Meet your neighbors: Studies have shown that in neighborhoods where there is less traffic people are more likely to know their neighbors.

- Help the elderly, people with disabilities, and low income households gain access to shared transportation.

Environmental Benefits

- Carpooling to work can cut your personal CO_2 emissions by a third, improve air quality, and reduce polluted runoff from roads.
- Up to eight cars will be taken off the roads for each car offered by large carsharing programs such as Zipcar and City CarShare.
- Fewer cars on the road means fewer parking lots, and more unpaved paradise.

Financial Benefits

- Save up to $3,000 per year by sharing your car with a friend or neighbor or by carpooling to work.
- Retire with an extra $660,000. That's the amount of money you will have in 40 years if you put that extra $3,000 per year into investments at a 7% rate of return.
- Earn up to $110 per month, tax free, through an employer-sponsored commuter voucher program.

Sharing at Work

There are approximately 20 million self-employed business people in America. Many of them have retail businesses, and the rest comprise a wide variety of entrepreneurs, from professionals to manufacturers to contractors to artists and everything else you can imagine. The variety of ways these business people can share is just as wide as the nature of their work, and these ways of sharing have many benefits. Sharing work space cuts costs, but also conserves resources of all kinds, including space itself and the natural resources used to heat and light it. It also allows for many other types of sharing, from sharing equipment, supplies, and subscriptions, to sharing employees. All of these solutions free up money and time that can be plugged back into the business.

What about those of us who still punch a time clock? The average American spends 45 hours a week at work, which gives us plenty of time—and lots of ways—to share with our coworkers. Through bulk buying, we can reduce our use of fossil fuels and packaging materials, and lower our costs for food and household items. Sharing meals saves us time and provides opportunities to build relationships with coworkers. Sharing a job saves time, transportation costs, and office space.

This chapter covers all of these business and workplace sharing ideas. It also provides some information about sharing a business with employees, through creating a cooperative or setting up a system of partial or complete employee ownership.

Solution 1: Share Work Space

Many, if not most, small businesses and entrepreneurs use commercial space to house their operations, and sharing these work spaces is often a smart business decision. It's best to share with others whose needs are similar to or mesh well with yours, often someone in the same or a similar profession. And, once you start sharing space with others, it will be much easier to start other types of sharing, like tools, storage space, subscriptions, or employees. Those are all discussed below.

Issues Common to All Types of Shared Spaces

Regardless of what type of business you have and what type of space you're looking to share, there are a few basic issues you'll need to sort out:

- **Responsibility for the space.** One of the first questions that will come up is who has ultimate responsibility for the work space. If you've joined with others to find a space to share, you'll probably have equal responsibility from the beginning. However, if one person owns a building, then the others could buy a share of the property to become owners, or pay rent for the space they share. If one person is already leasing the space to be shared, then the sharers need to decide whether they'll join as primary tenants or become subtenants. Note that any time there's a tenant/subtenant arrangement, it's important for the primary tenant to have the landlord's approval. You'll likely need to give your landlord the same information about your subtenant that you had to provide about yourself when you first leased the space, such as income, rental history, references, and financial condition.

- **Making decisions.** You'll need to decide how to make decisions about your shared space, on issues from appropriate use to appropriate decoration. You might defer many of those decisions to the owner or master tenant, if there is one. If you have equal ownership or responsibility, then you'll have to figure out how you want to make decisions together. Chapter 4 describes options for decision making.

- **Dividing costs.** No matter who owns the space—whether it's one of you, all of you, or a commercial landlord—you and your sharing partners will have to decide who will pay for what. Often, sharers use different amounts of space, sometimes even for different purposes. If your use isn't equal, either in terms of time or space, you'll need to come up with a payment arrangement that's fair to everyone (and flexible, in case people's needs change).

- **Use of common space.** Most work spaces have some common space, even if it's only a small entrance area at the front of a warehouse. And it could be much more than that—in many shared office suites, there's a reception area; an administrative area that includes storage space, work space, and office equipment; a separate conference room; rest rooms; and possibly even kitchen facilities. No matter how much common space you have, you'll need a clear agreement about how it will be used and paid for. You could:

- split the cost of the common space equally regardless of how much private space each sharer uses
- pro-rate the cost of the common space based on how much private space each sharer uses
- pro-rate the cost of the common space based on how much of the common space each sharer uses, or
- limit use of common space to tenants who want to pay for its use, and then split or pro-rate cost among the users.
- You'll also need to discuss how you'll keep the common space clean (be sure to get one of those signs that says "Your mother doesn't work here," so that people will remember to wash their own dishes); what standard of tidiness you want to maintain in the administrative area; how you'll calendar use of the conference room, and how you want the space to look.

Shared Offices

Sharing office space makes sense for many types of professionals, including doctors, lawyers, psychotherapists, massage therapists, acupuncturists, chiropractors, financial planners, and the like. Many of these professionals do administrative work from home and need office space only for meetings. Office sharing works particularly well for people who see clients or patients, because it can cost a lot to maintain an office with a reception area (especially if it's staffed) and private meeting or treatment rooms, and sharing the expense makes it more affordable. It's also a good value for professionals like realtors and salespeople, who spend little time in the office.

Shared office space may include any of the following:

Reception area. Professionals who see clients or patients will need a reception space where people can wait. If you're sharing space, you'll have to figure out how you want that space to look and function.

Depending on your professions, the expectations of your clients, and the other needs of your businesses, you may want to share an actual receptionist to greet people, sign for packages, answer phones, and so on. (See "Sharing Employees," below.) If you don't need (or can't afford) a receptionist, you might tell clients or patients where they can wait and how to let you know they have arrived. For example, some therapy offices use a light-switch system: When patients arrive, they flip a switch that turns on a light in the therapist's office to let the therapist know—without unduly disrupting an ongoing session—that the next patient is waiting.

Private offices. Most shared offices contain private spaces for holding confidential conversations, treating clients, or simply working without interruption. These can belong to one person alone or can be shared between two or more people if they can work out a schedule that allows each person to use the space privately or they are comfortable using the space at the same time. Anyone who needs complete flexibility in scheduling will need a private space, whereas professionals who limit their schedules to specific hours can share the private space with others, alternating days or mornings and afternoons, or even working out a schedule on an ad hoc basis.

Conference room(s). Especially for businesspeople who may need to meet with more than one person at a time, a shared conference room is a great amenity in an office suite. Some sharers, like one of the authors of this book, may use only the conference room and not even maintain a private office. And others might prefer the conference room to meeting in a private office if the latter is too small or—yes, it happens—too messy. In some office suites, there can be competition for the conference room, so it's important to have a process for scheduling its use.

If you're considering a shared office arrangement that involves sharing a conference room, talk beforehand about each person's anticipated needs for the space. If some of you plan to see clients only at certain times that the others are willing to work around, or intend to use their own private office space for meetings, you may be able to share your meeting space without any problems. But if it looks like there will be significant competition for the conference room space, you might need to reconsider either the number of people or the configuration you're planning.

You also need to work out a system for scheduling use of the room. Google calendars (or other online tools) are a great way to do this, because everyone can see the schedule in real time and access it remotely. Once you've established a scheduling system, it's also important that everyone use and respect it. Especially if you schedule meetings one right after the other, the first person needs to be sure to get out of the space in time for the next person to use it. See Chapter 4 for communication and conflict resolution tips that can help you deal with any disputes that arise about shared space.

Administrative space. In an office setting, administrative space is often used for tasks like faxing, copying, and assembling correspondence. You'll need to agree with your office mates on how this space will be used and by whom. You should talk about what type of equipment, employees, and functions the administrative space will have. Often the administrative space houses noisy equipment (such as a copier) or tends to draw a crowd (for example, if it contains the office refrigerator or microwave), so you'll want to make sure that your planned office configuration allows everyone to get their work done.

Some sharers may use more of the administrative space than others, which you'll probably want to account for in your sharing agreement. You may not know exactly how this will play out once you begin

The Coworking Phenomenon

A much less formal alternative to sharing office space is the concept of coworking: working in a space that is shared by a group of people who use it at random times, often working in one large open space at work stations that provide little more than a place to plug in a laptop computer. Coworking spaces come with different benefits, including conference space that can be reserved by the hour, espresso machines, and organized opportunities to interact with others. Freelancers, web entrepreneurs, sales reps, and others who don't need formal office space get the benefit of human contact—a difficult thing to come by if you work at home—and a more structured environment, as well as better ergonomics than they might find in their neighborhood café.

actually sharing the space, so your agreement might need to start out flexible and then become more specific as you figure out who is using how much of what.

The Authors Interview Themselves

When we talk about sharing work space, we know whereof we speak. Both authors share space in a suite of attorneys in a three-story A-frame office building in Berkeley, California. The owner of the building sublets the second floor to one master tenant, who has her own office there and subleases to the two of us and three other lawyers. Three of the subtenants have their own offices in the suite where they come to work each day; the other two just receive mail and packages there and use the conference room to meet with clients. Of the subtenants who have offices, one has his own office and two share an office; neither requires much space and they are happy to work in the space at the same time. We use a Google calendar to schedule use of the conference room, thanks to the younger lawyers who nixed the paper calendar that the old fogies were using.

Cleaning services are included in the rent, as is use of the copier and the administrative common space. We pay different amounts depending on our use; the lawyers with offices pay significantly more than those who merely use the conference room facilities and mail drop. The irregulars come and go in random ways, and often don't see each other for days or weeks on end, but we do try to get together for birthday cake periodically. In fact, the concept for this book was born of one such cake-sharing event.

Here's a sample office sharing agreement for a group of compatible professionals—a few lawyers, a financial planner, and a website developer. We chose office worker types because that type of worker tends to need many of the resources we're discussing here—as opposed to some other types of sharers who might not need certain resources, like staff—and we wanted a sample agreement that covered as many of the potential issues as possible. This agreement can be used for other types of work-related sharing as well, as discussed below.

Sample Office Sharing Agreement

This office sharing agreement is made between Benjamin Coke, Suzanne Clarkson, Tamara Lester, Marilyn Mertin, and Robyn Troxel, who intend to share the office suite located at 2525 College Avenue in Rockland. Ben is an accountant, Suzanne is a financial planner, Marilyn and Tamara are lawyers, and Robyn is a web developer.

1. We agree that we will share the use of the office suite in order to save money and resources, and have the benefit of one another's knowledge, skills, experience, and company.

2. We'll share the entire suite at 2525 College Avenue as described in this Agreement. All of us will share use of the common areas, Ben and Suzanne will each have their own private office space, Tamara and Marilyn will share a single office as described below, and Robyn will use the space more occasionally, all as described in paragraph 7, below.

3. Only the people listed above are sharing the office space.

4. None of us may sublease our individual space without the consent of each of the other people who are sharing the space.

5. Our lease on the office suite begins on July 1, 20xx and has a term of three years. We each intend to stay for the entire term of the lease. If any one of us wants to leave, that person is responsible for rent until a replacement tenant is found, and will participate in the group's decision on the best way to look for a replacement sharer. We'll agree at that time on a process for advertising the space and choosing the new tenant, and the person leaving will take the lead on doing the necessary tasks to find the new tenant.

6. Each of us is a lessor under the lease with our landlord, Janice Lubner, and we are jointly and severally responsible for the rent and any other expenses under the lease.

7. All five of us will share use of the common areas, including the reception area, kitchen, conference room, and the room we're describing as the administrative space. Ben and Suzanne will each have a private office.

Tamara and Marilyn will share the third office and they will work out their own schedule as to use. Robyn will use the conference room as meeting space and otherwise will work off-site. The administrative space will contain a desk for one staff person (discussed in paragraph 14, below), a fax machine that we will all share, a copier that we will all share, and a work table for common use.

8. Tamara has leased the copier, which is also a fax machine, and we all agreed on the model and lease terms. Each of us will pay one-fifth of the cost of the lease by reimbursing Tamara quarterly in advance, on the first of July, October, January, and April. When we first take possession of the space, we'll all contribute in equal shares to the purchase of two cartons of copy paper, and for the first six months we'll keep track of copies made and fax pages received. At the end of six months we'll tally up, and if there's a significant discrepancy in use we'll adjust the cost of paper in a way that we all agree is fair; we'll also pay for toner in proportion to our use or as otherwise agreed.

9. Each of us will have our own phone line(s) installed and will maintain our own voicemail.

10. We'll all meet together on the first Monday of each month for lunch in the kitchen, to discuss any concerns we have about our sharing arrangement. We'll try our best to reach consensus on any issues that come up; if we can't, we'll use a majority vote.

11. We agree to keep the common areas tidy and to keep our own supplies in our private offices. We'll cooperate to supply the kitchen with dishes and silverware by bringing our own extras from home, and we all agree to clean up after ourselves, including taking our old food out of the refrigerator at the end of each week. The landlord is providing cleaning service once a week.

12. We've set up a Google calendar for scheduling the conference room and we agree to use it on a first-come, first-served basis. We agree that none of us will use the conference room for more than eight hours a week, or

for any meeting longer than half a day, unless we clear it with the others first by sending out an email asking for agreement.

13. The total rent on our suite is $2,600 per month. We agree to divide the rent as follows:

Ben:	$725
Suzanne:	$725
Tamara:	$450
Marilyn:	$450
Robyn:	$250

14. Ben and Suzanne are going to hire an administrative person ("the admin"), who will also serve as receptionist for the entire suite and will greet visitors, accept packages, and sort mail for all of us. Except for those tasks, the admin will work exclusively for Ben and Suzanne unless a special arrangement is made for the admin to undertake specific tasks for another sharer. Ben and Suzanne will have a separate agreement regarding sharing the time and expenses of the admin.

15. Each of us is a sole owner of his or her business and we each will have our own stationery, telephone number, and professional liability insurance (if appropriate to our profession). None of us is responsible for any acts or omissions of any other tenant, unless we enter into a professional relationship with each other or do other types of work for or with one another.

16. If any of us has a conflict that we're not able to resolve through direct discussion, we agree to all sit down together and try to reach a resolution. If we can't, the people in conflict agree to attend at least one mediation session with a mediator they agree on, and to share the cost of the mediation. If this doesn't help to achieve resolution, we're each free to pursue whatever remedies we think are appropriate. We all agree to act in good faith and give one another the benefit of the doubt in any conflict or potential conflict.

17. We won't terminate anyone's tenancy before the lease term is up unless the person breaks the terms of the lease or of this agreement. In that case, a vote of three of the other members constitutes agreement of the group to ask the person to leave. Anyone whose tenancy is terminated involuntarily has sixty days to leave, and isn't responsible for helping to find a replacement tenant as described in paragraph 5.

Benjamin Coke   _9/30/xx_
Benjamin Coke   Date

Suzanne Clarkson   _9/30/xx_
Suzanne Clarkson   Date

Tamara Lester   _9/30/xx_
Tamara Lester   Date

Marilyn Mertin   _9/30/xx_
Marilyn Mertin   Date

Robyn Troxel   _9/30/xx_
Robyn Troxel   Date

This agreement is for a situation where all of the tenants are on the master lease. Some landlords don't allow that, however, which means that one person will have to become the master tenant and sublet the other spaces to the rest of the sharers. In that situation, your agreement should include a provision that all of you are bound by the terms of the master lease.

RESOURCE

A number of Nolo products may be helpful if you're entering into a commercial lease. *Negotiate the Best Lease for Your Business,* by Janet Portman and Fred Steingold, explains the standard clauses and provisions of a commercial lease and offers advice for reaching a fair lease agreement with your landlord. And eForms are available for download from Nolo's website, www.nolo.com, to create or amend a commercial sublease or get a landlord's written consent to a sublease.

Shared Retail Space

Although it's not as common as sharing office space, retail space can also be shared. In some sense, that's what artists do when they participate in cooperative or consignment stores where the work of different artists or craftspeople is displayed and sold in one retail space. Each artist generally manages an individualized display and pays a share of the sales proceeds toward the expenses of maintaining the space.

But it's also possible to put two full business operations together in one space. A book store and a coffee shop are an easy fit; likewise a pet store and a groomer; and then there's always the lawyer in the laundromat or bowling alley.

If you share space with another retail business, figuring out how to share costs might take some time. Even if you split the space right down the middle, one business might require more parking, employee work space, storage space, window display space, signage, electricity, water, or other resources than the other. Many businesses have some of the same type of equipment as a professional office, so retailers may also share a fax or copy machine, phone system, cash register, or other equipment.

An agreement like the sample office sharing agreement above can help you identify, consider, and make decisions about the different issues that apply to retail businesses.

> **TIP**
>
> **Think outside the box.** We heard from one book store owner who shares space with a somewhat unlikely companion: a photographer specializing in portraits of children and pets. It turned out to be a good fit. Many customers did business with both of them once they joined forces. They share not just rent and utilities, but also a fax machine and advertising costs. The bookseller gives the photographer a discount on books; the photographer takes photos for the store's website. The share allows both of the businesses to be in a more attractive location than either could afford alone.

Shared Creative Studios

It's very common for artists to share studio space. Many artists need a place where they can fire up loud machinery; use products and media that have an odor, are messy, or require certain conditions (for example, a particularly cool or warm temperature); create the best lighting for their art, whether that means lots of natural sunlight or a wall of klieg lights; work on large pieces over a long period of time; or invite the public to view their art or performances. Although artists who've hit the big time can create a separate space in their home or elsewhere for artistic pursuits, most of the starving artists we know have to rent studio space—often affordable only by sharing with other artists.

When it comes to sharing studio space, you'll do best to find a fellow sharer whose work is compatible with yours. The last thing you want if you paint in oils is to share space with a woodworker whose sawdust flies all over the place. Make sure you talk through how each of you plans to use the space: Smells, dust, noise, drips, hours, and visitors are all relevant.

One benefit of a sharing agreement for artists or craftspeople is the possibility of sharing expensive equipment like a kiln, lighting equipment, drafting or light table, or jewelry-making or woodworking tools. For new artists, this may be the only way to afford setting out on your own. A written sharing agreement is crucial here, because you need to be clear about who owns the equipment and, if you share ownership, who has the right to buy out the other if the arrangement ends.

Another benefit of sharing is bulk discounts for buying supplies in larger quantities than one person would use alone. Here you only need an agreement about who will make the initial cash outlay and whether you'll divide the items equally or in unequal shares. If you don't know how much each of you will use, you'll need to keep track of how much you use so that you can settle up later.

If your studio space is large enough for both of you to use at the same time, you'll need to decide how to share equipment when you are both there, as well as things like whether and what type of music can be played and whether visitors are allowed while you're working. If the space can only be used by one person at a time, you'll need to set up a schedule. You can choose a set schedule (for example, one of you uses the space in the morning and the other in the afternoon) that will remain the same over time, agree to come up with a schedule on a regular basis (for example, weekly or monthly), or come up with a system for signing up in advance to use the space (once again, the Google calendar can be very useful). You'll also need to agree on whether you want to share time equally and pay equal rent, pay unequal amounts based on your anticipated use, or pay based on your actual percentage of use.

Finally, you'll have to agree on acceptable uses of the space. Where will you keep works in progress or finished work waiting for transport? Do you both want to participate in open studios in your area? Do you want to open the space for selling at other times? Does the studio have to be kept clean to accommodate potential buyers?

Shared Commercial Kitchens

Cooking is another field in which equipment can be very expensive, making sharing a great idea for caterers and producers of artisan or other specialty foods. Perhaps you are a bread baker selling to local organic food stores, and your best friend from cooking school makes cookies that she sells to individual consumers on her web site. You could rent a commercial kitchen space together with the right type and size oven for your needs, agree on a schedule, and split the cost of rent and utilities.

You can also join a shared commercial kitchen—these are available in larger metropolitan areas. Many such kitchens are sponsored by "incubator" programs, which provide resources and work space to small start-up businesses. These kitchens have the advantage of being already licensed by the health department, so you don't need to worry about that regulatory hurdle. They provide all the necessary equipment, and you schedule time as needed. Most allow you to do anything there—cook, teach a cooking class, or even film a cooking video.

Solution 2: Share Business-Related Equipment and Purchases

When you share work space, you can also share some of the resources needed to run your business. Some of these possibilities have come up already: For example, office sharers can share a copier or fax machine, and art studio sharers can purchase expensive equipment together. People in every field—plumbers, sound technicians, landscapers, and contractors—can share supplies, purchases, and equipment.

Office Equipment

In addition to a copier or fax machine, there are a number of other things you can share when you are sharing office space with others:

- a shredder
- a computer printer (using a network) or high quality printing equipment (for graphic designers and desktop publishers)
- a telephone and answering system
- furniture for common spaces
- a paper cutter, three-hole punch, and binding equipment for publications
- kitchen equipment, such as a coffeemaker, teakettle, microwave, stand mixer, or refrigerator
- a fireproof safe for important documents, and
- a handcart.

Storage Space

Certain types of businesses, such as manufacturing, shipping, and retail, may need more storage space than is available at their primary business location, or they may need temporary storage when receiving large shipments of inventory. If you need extra storage and know other businesspeople in the same boat, you could share storage. Or, you could advertise for shared storage space in trade publications.

Subscriptions

Most fields, whether professional, retail, manufacturing, or artistic, have their own trade-specific publications and other resources. Often, these publications can be very expensive, and sharing might bring them within your price range. For example, many lawyers subscribe to legal research databases that allow multiple users on one account; sharing is an easy way to save money. Sharing software programs can also be cost-effective, as long as it doesn't violate the license. Trade publications like magazines and reports can also be shared among businesses. Even daily magazines and newspapers can be shared in an office or waiting room, or with nearby businesses.

Supplies and Inventory

You can save on office supplies by sharing with another business or professional. If you buy enough, you can also take advantage of bulk discounts on necessary supplies. Everything from paper, toner and ink cartridges, and binders to cleaning supplies, light bulbs, toilet paper, and candy for the bowl on the reception counter is cheaper when you buy it in large amounts.

In some fields, like retail, a business must purchase a minimum quantity of goods for inventory. Joining with another retailer to make the minimum can help you avoid spending more than you can afford on inventory you may not be able to sell. And restaurants, caterers, and cooks can make local, sustainable products more affordable by purchasing in bulk.

EXAMPLE: A book store owner purchases greeting cards from a company that requires a $150 minimum order. She's friendly with the owners of a pet store a few miles away in another business district. The pet store owners want to carry animal-related cards, but only a few designs—not enough to make a minimum order. And the bookseller wants some, but not a lot, of the same type of card. They agree to buy a number of designs, enough to make the minimum, and then split the cards. Each business spends what it can afford on the cards it needs.

Services

Businesses in close proximity can share services they need regularly, such as janitorial services, a security guard, a dedicated delivery person, even food service for their employees. You can also share occasional services, such as window washing, carpet deep cleaning, gardening or landscaping, regular maintenance of equipment, such as furnaces and air conditioning units, or even piano tuning. The service provider may charge less if one trip will result in business from several customers.

Delivery Vehicle

Many businesses have a recurring but relatively infrequent need for a truck to make deliveries, pick up inventory, or otherwise move stuff around. Chapter 10 explains how to work out a vehicle sharing arrangement.

Advertising

Businesses in the same business district can join together to purchase advertising that promotes the entire district as a shopping area and lists each establishment, or to publish a book of coupons or a list of discounts for area businesses. As the "buy local" movement grows, more small business districts are developing merchants' associations and sharing resources to get the word out about their businesses.

RESOURCE

Want more information on buying local? The Business Alliance for Local Living Economies (BALLE) is a national organization devoted to educating businesspeople and consumers about the value of producing and purchasing local goods and services. Look them up at www.livingeconomies.org. There are "buy local" organizations in many cities all over the country. Try putting "buy local" and your city's name into an Internet search engine and see what pops up.

Tools and Machinery

Business owners who work in construction and the trades can share expensive equipment and tools. Tool and machinery sharing often goes hand in hand with sharing shop space or a storage crib for tools and supplies. These businesses can also benefit from buying supplies in bulk and using fellow sharers' leftover wood, sheetrock, or other materials.

Landscaping and Gardening Tools

Professional gardeners and landscapers can often get by without heavy equipment, but they may need more expensive equipment for certain projects. For example, a particular job might call for a stump grinder, rototiller, or cement mixer. A group of landscapers could purchase items like these together. Gardeners could share soil-testing supplies and other tools and equipment.

Expense Sharing Worksheet for Businesses

If you spend a few minutes brainstorming, you may come up with quite a few work-related expenses you could share. Use this worksheet to consider the possibilities.

Worksheet: Work Expenses to Consider Sharing		
Expense	**Amount**	**Sharing Ideas**
Rent	$1,500/mo.	Could rent a larger office and share cost, probably reducing individual cost.
New York Times	$200/yr.	Yes, with attorney next door.
Janitorial services	$50/wk.	Yes, with upstairs suite.
Table saw	$400	Yes, with the contractor who uses the storage and work space across the street.

Solution 3: Sharing Employees

In the sample office sharing agreement, above, two of the professionals also planned to share an employee. Employees cost more than just the hourly wage you pay them, and spreading that cost can make a big difference for a small employer, especially a solo businessperson. Obviously, it works best when all of the employers share the same physical space and the employee has just one work area.

How Will the Employee's Time Be Divided?

When you share an employee, you must decide how much time—or how much work—the employee will do for each employer. If both (or all) employers need the same type and amount of work from the employee, the division of labor is a lot easier. For example, if you share an office suite with other professionals, and you hire a receptionist to greet visitors, answer the phones, sort the mail, and handle deliveries, you can simply schedule the employee's hours and divide the cost equally.

However, if you need different types or amounts of work from the employee, or if your needs will vary depending on your work load (as is often the case), you have a couple of options for dividing the employee's time.

The simplest way is to divide the hours as you think you will use them—for example, the employee will work 30 hours per week, and each employer will pay for 15 of those hours and have the right to use half of the employee's time. If one employer doesn't have enough work to keep the employee busy for the full 15 hours in a given week, the other can take over some of the hours and reimburse the first employer for them—but if the second employer doesn't need those hours, the first is still responsible for paying the employee for all of them.

Alternatively, the employee can keep track of hours spent working for each employer on a time sheet or computer spreadsheet. The employers can divide the costs pro rata each pay period depending on the time the employee spent on each. If the employee spends administrative time that benefits everyone (such as sorting the mail or handling issues for the shared space, like scheduling janitorial services or stocking the office refrigerator), the employers can divide that time equally. This system requires good communication, because the employers and the employee must make sure the employee's time is used efficiently and that there isn't competition for hours. It works best if there's a general idea of how much time each employer will use, and a good system for communicating needs and expectations.

No matter how you divide the employee's time, make sure you respect the agreement and the employee. Try to anticipate problems prioritizing tasks and maintaining boundaries between jobs. If the employee devotes a particular amount of time each week to each employer, you'll need rules about whether and in what circumstances you may deviate from that schedule. If the employee doesn't have set hours for each employer, the employers must decide how they will prioritize work and then communicate those priorities to the employee, so that the employee doesn't have to make difficult decisions about whose work should be done first.

> **EXAMPLE:** Two architects share work space and also split the cost of a part-time administrative assistant who answers the phone, processes mail, does filing, and takes on miscellaneous tasks as needed, including making the occasional delivery. It occasionally happens that one person has important correspondence that needs to go out the same day, while the other has a delivery that needs to be made—and it may not be possible for both things to happen in the time the assistant has. The first time it happened, she didn't stress, because her instructions were that in the event of a potential conflict, she was to inform both of her employers so that they could work it out between themselves. They did, and it also inspired them to start a simple system under which they used a white board to list "same-day projects." That way the employers could see what was going on and do the prioritizing, again without causing the employee to worry about whose work she should be doing.

How Will the Employee Be Paid?

You must also decide how to pay the employee. The easier method is to make one person responsible for payroll and issue one check, and have the other employer(s) reimburse that person for their share of the wages, taxes, and insurance. The challenge of doing it this way is that you must keep very clear records not only of the payroll checks issued, but also of the payments made by the unofficial employers, so that they can document and deduct those payments for tax purposes. If you're sharing hours in an irregular way (according to need, for example), calculating shares of taxes and other expenses can get cumbersome.

Other options are to have each employer set up a separate payroll account and pay the employee for time worked for that person, or to set up a joint account for payroll, as the employers in the agreement below do.

Agreement to Share Employee

Benjamin Coke and Suzanne Clarkson agree to hire an employee whose work time they will share, under the following terms.

1. We will hire an administrative assistant for our shared office space at 2525 College Avenue. We'll find the employee together by posting an advertisement on Craigslist and any other list-serve we agree on, and mining our own contacts. Ben will draft the advertisement and Suzanne will review it and post it. Ben will arrange interviews with prospective employees.

2. The assistant will work approximately 30 hours per week at our office (no telecommuting), from approximately 9:00 a.m. to 3:00 p.m. each day, with the exact hours to be determined in consultation with the employee when hired. The employee's duties will be to staff the reception desk and greet visitors who come to see any of the tenants in the suite, to receive packages and sort mail when it comes in, and to answer phones and do other work for each of us pursuant to our instructions. Our preference is to find someone with some experience in the financial services industry. Our intention is to split the assistant's work equally, so that we each use approximately 15 hours per week, with Suzanne's work done in the morning and Ben's in the afternoon, and we each will be responsible for half of the employee's pay. However, we don't want to be rigid about the schedule. If either of us has a need during hours that "belong" to the other, we'll discuss it and make adjustments. Likewise, if one of us has more work for the assistant to do during a given time period, the other may cede some time. If that happens a lot, we'll discuss the possibility of sharing the employee costs unequally and adjusting the amount of employee time each of us is entitled to use.

3. The employee will be responsible for keeping track of time spent for each of us. At the end of the pay period the employee will submit a time sheet that will show total hours worked and the breakdown of hours spent for Suzanne, Ben, and for the suite as a whole (receptionist and mail duties).

4. We'll pay the assistant $15 per hour, and will pay on the 15th and 30th of each month (or the business day before those dates if the pay date falls on a weekend or holiday) for hours worked during that time period. We'll deduct taxes and Social Security and pay our share of those taxes, and we'll pay for workers' compensation insurance. In addition, we'll contribute an additional $200 per month to individual insurance coverage or a Health Savings Account at the employee's election, if the employee doesn't have access to health insurance any other way. Suzanne will research how to do all of this, set up our account with the Workers' Compensation Board, and research what forms we need for paying other taxes. Other terms of employment, such as paid time off, holidays, and sick leave, will be negotiated with the employee and contained in a memorandum of understanding signed by both of us and the employee after hiring, and then attached to this agreement as an exhibit. We both agree that we'll be jointly and severally liable for all payments to the employee.

5. We have set up a joint account at the Bank of America for the purpose of paying our employee. Each of us deposited $500 to start the account. Starting on August 1, 20xx, we each agree to deposit $1,500 on the first day of each month, to cover that month's expenses. We think this is more than we'll actually need, but we'll continue to put in this amount until we learn the cost of taxes and insurance. After six months, we'll decide whether we want to change the monthly contribution.

6. If one person doesn't make the required contribution for the month, the other can make the contribution and it will be considered a loan to the one who didn't pay. The person who didn't pay must reimburse the other within fifteen days or forfeit the right to control any of the employee's time. At that point, the other person has the right to change the employment terms and make a separate agreement with the employee that doesn't include the non-paying party.

7. We agree to meet once a month for lunch specifically for the purpose of discussing how this shared arrangement is working out.

8. If disagreements arise between us that we can't work out ourselves, our preference is to try mediation (at our local community mediation center) before terminating this agreement. Each of us has the right to terminate this agreement at any time, but must provide at least three week's notice or pay for three weeks after the person's participation in the agreement ends.

Benjamin Coke   2/9/xx
Benjamin Coke   Date

Suzanne Clarkson   2/9/xx
Suzanne Clarkson   Date

Sharing for a Greener Workplace

There are countless sharing practices you could implement at work to reduce your ecological footprint.

- **Sharing office supplies and equipment.** Share staplers, three-hole punches, paper cutters and more by creating a supply station—usually a table—with all necessary supplies. You can also network computers and printers so that multiple computers print to a single printer.
- **Centralized recycling and reuse stations.** You can set aside space where everyone can bring their reusable envelopes and scrap paper, implement special recycling programs, such as battery and electronics recycling, and even encourage employees to bring recyclables from home.
- **A dishwasher and set of workplace dishes.** While many workers find it easier to use disposables, employees will be encouraged to give up their paper cups and plastic utensils if there is a set of dishes at the office, and a machine to wash them. Having good coffee at the office also encourages workers to consume coffee there, rather than buying it in a disposable cup.
- **Drinking water dispenser or filter.** About 40 million plastic water bottles are thrown away every day in the United States. If employees are buying and drinking a lot of bottled water, have drinking water delivered in five-gallon reusable jugs, or install a water filter on a workplace sink. And of course encourage employees to use washable glasses, not disposable cups.

Solution 4: Share a Job

So far, we've covered ways that employers and business owners can share. But sharing can work for employees, too. Not only can employees share *on* the job, by sharing food, a car, or other items (see Solution 5, below); they can even share the job itself. If two people who both want to work part time join forces to handle a full-time position, that's job sharing.

In a recent survey, more than a third of employers who offer flexible work approaches (such as telecommuting or part-time work) include job sharing programs.

Although it's most common in an office setting, job sharing can work for large or small employers and for all kinds of jobs. The key to making a job share work is communication. The sharers must come up with a method to keep each other updated and, just as important, to keep supervisor(s) and coworkers updated as well. If they're sharing each day—for example, one works in the morning and the other takes the afternoon—then they should try to overlap in time, so they can talk about ongoing projects and scheduling. If they don't overlap, they'll need to leave written notes or email messages for each other.

The sharing schedule should be posted where other employees can find it, whether that's on the office door or on an electronic bulletin board. Sharers should also consider whether they're willing to be contacted during off hours for questions or needs that come up in their absence. Many job sharers share one work phone number and email account so both have access to all the same information about their work.

The sharers and their supervisor also need to figure out some logistics. For example, do each of them have specific tasks, or do they simply split the time and do whatever needs to be done during their shift? How will time off and benefits work? How will they keep track of projects each has covered, for performance evaluations and accountability? It's a good idea for job sharers to plan a meeting each month, preferably with their supervisor, to discuss how the share is going.

What Job Sharing Looks Like

There are at least three types of schedules that job sharers can use:

1. Two employees each work three days a week, handling two days on their own and overlapping on one day. The result is really 1.2 employees, with each employee working 60% time.
2. Two employees each work two-and-a-half days per week, either alternating the fifth day week by week or each working half of that day. Each employee works half time.
3. Two employees share each day, either on a regular morning-afternoon schedule or according to a schedule they work out to

accommodate the needs of both sharers and management. Each employee works half time.

A job can also be shared by geography or by responsibilities. For example, two people might share a sales job that is responsible for a particular territory by each covering part of the region. Similarly, two people could share a job providing training to clients who buy the company's software by each taking half of a full client list.

Hot-Desking and Hotelling

Sharing a job usually also means sharing a work space. Even if you don't share a job, however, there are other ways to share the space you use to work. "Hot-desking," for example, is when unreserved work stations are available to employees, often in a large open work space. "Hotelling" involves reserved work spaces that are shared among several employees who work at different times and otherwise telecommute by working from remote locations.

Employers typically adopt strategies like these to save space and money, especially if they have employees who frequently work from home or on the road. Reserving a private office, or even a cubicle, for someone who's rarely there makes little sense. And, because these employees typically come to work when they need to get together with other employees, open and shared work spaces don't create the same problems as they would for employees who are always in the office and need to make phone calls or concentrate on difficult projects, or otherwise need a quiet, distraction-free work environment.

Starting a Job Share

The best way to start a job share depends on your current job situation. If you have a full-time job and want to start working part time, check within your own company for potential sharing partners. If another full-time employee is considering a switch, you can talk about whether it makes sense to try to share either of your jobs, or perhaps even create a shared job that combines features of each. Of course, you'll have to talk to your supervisor(s) to find out what's possible.

If your company offers job sharing as a flexible work option, find out whether you—and your position—are eligible for sharing. Even companies that allow job sharing don't often make it available for every job. For example, it might be quite easy to share an IT position in a large department: Each sharer works half time and keeps the other posted on shared projects. However, the company might prefer to have the director of that department work full time, to make sure someone is always there to handle emergencies and supervise ongoing work.

If you're in the job market and want to find a job share to maximize the flexibility of your work life, check out the resources in Appendix A. You can look for cosharers in the same ways you look for a job: by mining your own networks, working with a coach or headhunter, and placing and answering advertisements.

Things You'll Have to Negotiate With Your Employer

In most circumstances, you'll want to find your potential job sharer before you propose the idea to your boss. Many employers have to be persuaded that job sharing really will benefit the company. Such a proposal should lay out the many benefits to employers, such as a happier and more productive work force and the advantage of having two employees who are fully competent at important jobs. It's important that you and your job sharing partner work out the details beforehand, so that your proposal can include suggestions about these important elements of your job:

- schedule
- division of labor
- communication methods between cosharers
- communication methods with boss and coworkers
- salary and benefit requirements
- how performance and achievements will be measured, and
- any time limits on the job share (for example, if one of you wants to return to full time on a particular date in the future).

Appendix A includes a number of resources on jobsharing.

Job Rotation: Sharing Tasks and Skills in the Workplace

In a job rotation program (JRP), workers move through various jobs, rotating within the business. This may mean that each employee has one primary position and then rotates into other departments for a certain period of time per week or rotates into another department or onto another project on an as-needed basis. Employees learn more about their specialty and their business's operations, consistently find new and interesting things to do, and diversify their skills. Employers may find their employees more knowledgeable and productive, and will also have confidence that the workplace will suffer less from the loss of key employees. (With the aging of the baby boomer generation, some employers are becoming concerned about retaining institutional knowledge and planning for job succession in key positions.) There can be ergonomic advantages to workers changing jobs, too—less time spent doing repetitive tasks or working in one position means fewer work-related injuries. And in cooperative businesses, it's a great way for all owner-employees to learn every aspect of the business and create an even greater sense of ownership.

Solution 5: Sharing Things With Coworkers

As explained in Chapter 2, coworkers make ideal sharing companions for a number of reasons. First and foremost, coworkers spend a lot of time together. Most of us spend nearly as many of our waking hours at work as we do at home. Many of the things we need at work are also things that others need and can easily be shared. Because we see our coworkers nearly every day, we can share not only the things we need at work, such as lunch or a car, but also things we use when we aren't working, like groceries, household items, and recreational equipment.

Sharing Things at Work

There are many ways that sharing at work can make your work life easier, more efficient, and less expensive.

Carsharing

Often, people need a car at work to go to appointments, attend lunch meetings, or run work-related errands. But some of those people probably don't need a car to get to work, and in fact would rather not drive if they had another way to get around during the day. If your job requires occasional driving during the workday, poll your coworkers to find out whether there's enough need and interest in sharing a car.

There are a number of options for carsharing at work. You could take turns bringing a car to work, try to find a coworker who drives to work but doesn't use the car during the day, or even try to get your employer to spring for a company car. See Chapter 10 for more on sharing a car.

Bike Sharing

You could set up a workplace bicycle sharing arrangement if you could use a bike for work-related appointments, errands, and lunch breaks. Or you could replace your 15-minute coffee break with a mile or two on the bike, guaranteed to bring you far more energy and well-being than coffee, cigarettes, and donuts combined! The sample agreement in Chapter 5 shows how a bike sharing arrangement might work.

Carpooling

As explained in Chapter 10, the benefits of carpooling—both for the riders and for the planet—are tremendous. The larger your workplace, the greater your chance of finding carpool partners. Send an email to everyone at work or post a sign-up sheet on the bulletin board. Everyone who is interested should provide the neighborhood or area where they live, whether they have a car, and their phone number(s). Once everyone has submitted their information, you can sort out the geography to see whether it makes sense to put together a carpool group or two.

Your employer might be quite pleased if you carpool. It frees up valuable parking spaces for everyone, including clients and customers. Employers who provide tax-free commuter vouchers or parking vouchers could provide similar incentives for carpoolers. Employers can also create designated parking for carpoolers (many university campuses have chosen to do this).

Mealsharing

Coworkers make a great meal sharing group. Most of us have to eat lunch at work, and it's easy to get bored with nearby restaurants and our own leftovers. You can take turns bringing lunch (or preparing it at work, if your workplace has a kitchen). For more information on mealsharing with coworkers, see Chapter 8.

Work Attire

An affordable business suit is hard to come by, and both men and women often complain about the cost of building a work wardrobe for a professional job. You can cut expenses—and expand your fashion options—by buddying up with a coworker who shares your size and fashion sense. This works especially well in a workplace where employees dress down on a day-to-day basis, but throw on a formal suit for outside business meetings, calling on clients, doing press interviews, or appearing in court. You could even keep your shared outfits in a closet at work and have them dry cleaned or laundered near the office. And don't forget a nice shared briefcase for when you need to make a good impression.

Amenities and Extras

You and your coworkers could join together to purchase items you might otherwise not be able to afford in the workplace (and could never get your employer to pay for), like an exercise machine, massage chair, espresso maker, masseuse or yoga teacher, blender for smoothies, drinking water filter, dishwasher and dishes, or television. You can also use your lunch hours to share skills, like teaching someone else to knit or play poker.

For Employers: How to Create Sharing Incentive Programs

A culture of sharing can blossom in a workplace when employers not only support but also create incentives for sharing, such as:

- **Carpool, carshare, and bikeshare incentives.** There are tax benefits available to employers who give employees commuter vouchers. You could offer free or designated parking for carpoolers or provide a company car or bike for employees to use while at work, or a van for employees to form a daily vanpool.
- **Office share incentives.** Employers can save money and space if employees double up in office spaces. Some employees may not be pleased to share a space with someone, but others will find it quite workable and pleasant. Employers can offer bonuses or other perks to employees who are willing to share offices.
- **Mealshare incentives.** Buy fresh fruit and healthy snacks for employees. Install a dishwasher and provide dishes and cooking supplies.
- **On-site washer and dryer.** This may sound over the top, but at least one company we know of does this. It's a great perk: Employees without these amenities at home can avoid buying them or spending time at the laundromat. For more, see *Raising the Bar*, by Clif Bar founder Gary Erickson.
- **Arrange for picking up and dropping off dry cleaning.** This saves time for employees, and everyone can get a bulk discount. It also saves on gas and pollution: The clothes make a single trip, rather than every employee driving to and from the dry cleaners.
- **Childcare co-ops.** Providing on-site child care is a workplace benefit employees really value. See Chapter 9 for more about creating child care co-ops at work.
- **Organize an optional sharing meeting.** Educate employees about sharing and encourage them to form sharing groups.

Sharing Things That Aren't Related to Work With Coworkers

The workplace provides a rich source of sharing possibilities because it brings people together, often in large numbers, on a daily basis. As a result, workplaces are a convenient forum for building sharing relationships of all types, even to meet needs that aren't work related. Most people who work see coworkers daily, so it's very easy to hand shared items off to coworkers. You can even keep many shared items at work. Here are some ideas for sharing in the workplace that aren't related to work.

Share all types of goods with a coworker. Just as you can own durable goods with a neighbor or friend, you might be able to share them with a coworker. A pair of binoculars, camping equipment, luggage, folding chairs and tables, kitchen appliances you don't use every day (such as a crock pot, dehydrator, ice-cream maker, or bread machine), cookbooks, supplies for do-it-yourself chores (like painting equipment, a tile saw, or outdoor tools), and much more can be handed off at work.

Make collective purchases with coworkers. The workplace provides a ready group of potential partners for making collective purchases and benefiting from bulk buying discounts. You and your coworkers could make bulk purchases of anything from dog food to toilet paper, and have it delivered to the office. Collective buying saves money, time, transport, and packaging.

Purchase services with other employees. Negotiate a group discount and have a monthly dry cleaning pick-up and drop-off. Have a hairdresser come in for appointments in the office.

Share season tickets. Purchase season tickets for a sports team, theater, symphony, lecture series, opera, or theme park. Keep them at work with a signup sheet so people can reserve them in advance.

Share subscriptions. Share a copy of the daily paper; perhaps you can read it at home, then bring it in for a coworker to read during lunch. You can also share magazines, journals, and trade publications.

Start a general workplace sharing group. Have a lunchtime meeting and brainstorm ways to share more, whether at work or off the job.

What things do you each want or need? What are ways you'd like to save money? Ways you could be more green? See Chapter 2 for more ideas and some helpful tools for brainstorming. After your meeting, create a workplace bulletin board or email list to make sharing connections.

Organize group projects or volunteer work. Schedule a blood drive at your workplace. Organize a group of coworkers to spend a few hours or a day volunteering at a local animal shelter, charity thrift store, or neighborhood clean-up project. Work together to decorate the office, paint a mural on your building, or care for a garden.

When the Work Runs Out: How Sharing Can Ease the Blow of Unemployment

Sharing can help us all ride out waves of economic recession and depression. Even when the economy is in good health, there are always people who are out of work or unable to work for reasons such as disability. Forming an off-work sharing group with friends and coworkers can provide support in a community-based way.

EXAMPLE: When his friends Jack and Andrew became unemployed, Austin was inspired to create an Unemployment Sharing Group. He formed an online discussion group and invited about 20 friends, who invited about 40 more friends. Of the 60, eight were unemployed and needed some support.

The group did many things: They helped each other find work. Those who could afford it hired those in need of work for child care, cooking, or housework. Some offered loans to others. They came up with ways that everyone—employed or not—could save money and cooperate more. When one group member was on the verge of eviction, many chipped in some cash to help him pay the rent.

The group's website contained two bulletin boards: One contained a list of needs and the other contained a list of offerings. Here's a sample of some of the list postings:

When the Work Runs Out: How Sharing Can Ease the Blow of Unemployment (cont'd)

Needs:

Anne: *I'd like to share my car, as a way to cut my auto expenses. Anyone want a car three days per week?*

Susan: *Looking for someone to rent a room in my house.*

Jay: *Need a loan to help pay my mortgage for a month or two.*

Fred: *Looking for work related to teaching, music, gardening, or childcare.*

Betsy: *I need occasional childcare.*

Offerings:

Paul: *Use my truck; I can help with heavy labor.*

Katie: *Can provide childcare on Tuesday nights.*

Robin: *Free leftover food from my restaurant; will box up at the end of each day.*

Aric: *I can do graphics for someone starting a new business.*

Blakelea: *I can make small loans.*

Bodhi: *I can help with plumbing needs.*

Solution 6: Sharing Ownership With Employees

There are ways that employees can either share ownership of a business or have some form of investment in the business beyond simply getting a paycheck. Workplace democracy can create a sense of accountability for the enterprise and its activities, which in turn can lead to improved job satisfaction and employee retention. Employees are motivated by more than just pay—and employees who feel their input and opinions are taken seriously are more committed to a company.

Worker-Owned Cooperative Businesses

A worker-owned cooperative business is one that is owned and democratically run by its employees, who have both jobs and ownership interests. The National Cooperative Business Association counts around 300 worker-owned businesses in the United States. Some of the types of businesses in which cooperatives are currently flourishing include:

- foodservice businesses, bakeries, restaurants, grocery stores, and other retail operations
- child care (see Chapter 9)
- home health care
- cleaning services, both commercial and residential, and
- manufacturing and distribution.

Democratic governance can mean different things in different businesses. A co-op has a board of directors, generally selected from the workers. Sometimes outside directors are brought in because they have valuable experience, advice, or skills to offer, but the board is always comprised primarily of workers. Some co-ops develop a traditional business structure with a hierarchical management tree, while others involve workers in decision making at all levels.

Profits from a cooperative business are distributed to the owner-workers. The distribution shares may be entirely equal in a management structure that eschews hierarchy or may depend on the employee's tenure, position, salary, or responsibilities.

In long-running cooperatives with a significant number of employees, new members usually undergo a probationary period during which they don't receive an ownership share. If accepted for membership, they buy in, either with a lump sum payment or by deductions from their paychecks.

Co-Op Profile: South Mountain Company

South Mountain Company is a cooperatively-owned architecture, building, and renewable energy business on Martha's Vineyard. South Mountain has 33 employees: 17 are owners and the others are on track to join them. Owners share in profits and decision making, as well as in the responsibility, risks, and rewards of owning a business.

South Mountain converted from a sole proprietorship to an employee-owned cooperative in 1987. John Abrams, owner of South Mountain, knew that some employees were interested in making their careers in the fast-growing company and having a greater stake. Abrams ultimately sold part of his ownership to two employees and together they formed a cooperative. Abrams first weighed the pros and cons of relinquishing part of his ownership and control. He writes, "It occurred to me that perhaps I had the most to gain: Aside from the lure of clearing this new path and seeing where it led, the possibility of shared responsibility and ownership promised new freedoms for me and new achievements for this company (and these people) that I loved."

On sharing ownership, Abrams writes: "I think those who are moved to distribute ownership ... embrace the view that organizational consultant Robert Leaver expresses: 'Power is infinite; if I take more and you take more, there's more of it.' That has been my experience: Bring more people to the table and you create new potency and ability that did not previously exist."

South Mountain Company has a website detailing the workings of the cooperative (www.somoco.com), and John Abrams wrote an excellent book about the company and its transformations: *The Company We Keep: Reinventing Small Business for People, Community, and Place*. In 2008, he released *Companies We Keep: Employee Ownership and the Business of Community and Place*, which has a broader focus on employee ownership of enterprise and offers tools to help businesses make these transitions. You can find more resources on cooperative businesses in Appendix A.

Employee Stock Ownership Plans

Employee stock ownership plans (ESOPs) are offered by some companies as a benefit of employment. They don't create the same kind of ownership as a cooperative, because they don't always allow employees to have a meaningful say in how decisions are made. But they do create an ownership interest by allowing employees to purchase stock in the company, generally at a favorable price, as part of a retirement benefit package and as a way for the company to reward and motivate employees.

> TIP
> **Creating an ESOP or co-op can benefit employers.** While often described as a benefit of employment, an ESOP is actually a stock sale by the company to the employees, as a result of which the employees become part owners of the company. The IRS rewards employers for creating ESOPs by allowing them to defer taxes on capital gains realized from the sale. The same tax benefits apply to a company that sells stock to a worker-owned cooperative made up of the company's employees. This is a fairly technical area of tax law. If you are part of an employee group that wants to create an ESOP or cooperative form of ownership, or an employer looking to do so, you'll need to consult with a tax professional—as well as a lawyer—to put a program in place.

Employee Profit Sharing and Gainsharing Plans

Profit sharing plans, in which employers share a portion of profits with employees according to a set formula, are usually established as part of a retirement plan. Contributions are made to the plan by the employer only, and then distributed to employees annually based on company profits and the employee's longevity. The distribution may be in the form of cash or stock, but sharing occurs only when the company is profitable. The idea is that by sharing in profits, employees will also share the motivation to make the company more successful.

Gainsharing is more of a direct reward system, in which employees share in profits created directly through productivity or cost-saving measures developed and implemented by the workers themselves.

The Bigger Picture: Sharing at Work

Here are some ways that businesses, nonprofits, employers, community leaders, and government can facilitate more work-related sharing:

- Employers: Create employee incentive programs for sharing, such as cash back on commuter vouchers for carpoolers, cash incentives for office sharing, and free parking for carpoolers and carsharers.
- Employers: Create resources and opportunities for employee sharing, such as office vanpools, a stocked kitchen for employee lunch sharing, common space for mealsharing, an employee-run child care center, and job sharing opportunities.
- Employers: Offer an employee stock ownership plan or a profit sharing program.
- Credit unions and banks: Provide specialized loan programs to finance and encourage worker-owned cooperatives.
- Nonprofits and community leaders: develop incubator programs for small businesses, which make available shareable offices, studio, workshop, and commercial kitchen spaces, and shareable work equipment, such as specialized tools, massage tables, and copiers.

Your Triple Bottom Line: The Benefits of Sharing at Work

Social and Personal Benefits

- Sharing with your work colleagues can make your work week much more pleasant and lead to new business and personal relationships.

- Sharing can save you money, which may allow you to work less and enjoy more free time.
- Job sharing gives employees more flexible work options, and can give them more time at home and with their families.

Environmental Benefits

- Sharing work space means the use of fewer natural resources for building, heating, and lighting work spaces.
- Engaging in collective purchasing with coworkers saves packaging, travel, and other resources.
- Carpooling or vanpooling to work or sharing a car or bike at work save a significant amount of energy and resources.

Financial Benefits

- Sharing work-related resources like equipment, space, and subscriptions can decrease your costs by half or more, depending on how many people you share with.
- Sharing can allow you to purchase, lease, or otherwise acquire things you wouldn't be able to afford on your own.
- Sharing employees can lessen the burden of employment-related taxes and other costs.

Resources

This appendix contains some of our favorite sources for more information on the ideas and topics covered in this book. The universe of resources is vast, so this list is by no means comprehensive. If we've missed anything you think is crucial, let us know; send us an email at sharing@janelleorsi.com.

Resources on Sustainable Communities and Living Green

Superbia: 31 Ways to Create Sustainable Neighborhoods, by Dan Chiras and Dave Wann (New Society Publishers)

The Green Collar Economy: How One Solution Can Fix Our Two Biggest Problems, by Van Jones (Harper One)

Hot, Flat, and Crowded: Why We Need a Green Revolution—and How It Can Renew America, by Thomas L. Friedman (Farrar, Straus, and Giroux)

Deep Economy: The Wealth of Communities and the Durable Future, by Bill McKibben (Holt)

Toward Sustainable Communities: Resources for Citizens and Their Governments, by Mark Roseland (New Society Publishers)

The Natural Step for Communities: How Cities and Towns can Change to Sustainable Practices, by Sarah James and Torbjörn Lahti, (New Society Publishers)

EcoCities: Rebuilding Cities in Balance with Nature, by Richard Register, (New Society Publishers)

Ecotopia, by Ernest Callenbach (Bantam Books)

Sustainable Living: For Home, Neighborhood and Community, by Mick Winter (Westsong Publishing)

Radical Simplicity: Small Footprints on a Finite Earth, by Jim Merkel (New Society Publishers)

Simple Prosperity: Finding Real Wealth in a Sustainable Lifestyle, by David Wann (St. Martin's Griffin)

One Makes a Difference: Inspiring Actions That Change Our World, by Julia Butterfly Hill (Harper San Francisco)

True Green: 100 Everyday Ways You Can Contribute to a Healthier Planet, by Kim Mckay and Jenny Bonnin (National Geographic)

True Green Kids: 100 Things You Can Do to Save the Planet, by Kim Mckay and Jenny Bonnin (National Geographic)

The Green Book: The Everyday Guide to Saving the Planet One Simple Step at a Time, by Elizabeth Rogers and Thomas M. Kostigen (Three Rivers Press)

Toolbox for Sustainable City Living: A Do-it-Ourselves Guide, by Scott Kellogg, et al (South End Press)

Yes! Magazine—www.yesmagazine.org

E, The Environmental Magazine—www.emagazine.com

Green America (formerly Co-op America)—www.greenamericatoday.org (Helps consumers, investors, and businesses to create a socially just and environmentally sustainable society.)

Eartheasy—www.eartheasy.com (Ideas for environmentally sustainable living.)

Worldchanging—www.worldchanging.com (An online magazine covering tools, models, and ideas for building a better future.)

Center for Neighborhood Technology—www.cnt.org (A "think-and-do tank" focused on transportation and community development, energy, natural resources, and climate change.)

New American Dream—www.newdream.org (An organization that helps people consume responsibly to protect the environment, enhance quality of life, and promote social justice.)

Solar Living Institute—www.solarliving.org (Promotes sustainable living through inspirational environmental education.)

Community Building Resources

Smart Communities: How Citizens and Local Leaders Can Use Strategic Thinking to Build a Brighter Future, by Suzanne W. Morse (Jossey-Bass)

Building Communities from the Inside Out: A Path Toward Finding and Mobilizing a Community's Assets, by John P. Kretzmann and John L. McKnight (ACTA Publications)

The Great Neighborhood Book: A Do-it-Yourself Guide to Placemaking, by Jay Walljasper and Project for Public Spaces (New Society Publishers)

Creative Community Builder's Handbook: How to Transform Communities Using Local Assets, Arts, and Culture, by Thomas C. Borrup (Fieldstone Alliance)

Legal Resources from Nolo

Negotiate the Best Lease for Your Business, by Janet Portman and Fred S. Steingold (Nolo)

How to Form a Nonprofit Corporation, by Anthony Mancuso (Nolo)

101 Law Forms for Personal Use, by Ralph Warner and Robin Leonard (Nolo)

How to Represent Yourself in Court, by Paul J. Bergman (Nolo)

Everybody's Guide to Small Claims Court, by Ralph Warner (Nolo)

Check out our full line of products at www.nolo.com.

Resources on Communication, Decision Making, and Conflict Resolution

Communication

Taking the War Out of Our Words: The Art of Non-Defensive Communication, by Sharon Ellison (Bay Tree Publishing)

Non-Violent Communication: A Language of Life, Marshall B. Rosenberg (Puddledancer Press)

Difficult Conversations: How to Discuss What Matters Most, by Douglas Stone, Bruce Patton, Sheila Heen, and Roger Fisher (Penguin)

Getting to Yes, by Fisher, Ury, & Patton (Penguin)

Communication Workshops

Powerful Non-Defensive Communication with Sharon Ellison—www.pndc.com

Nonviolent Communication with Marshall B. Rosenberg—www.cnvc.org

Consensus Decision Making and Facilitation

Facilitator's Guide to Participatory Decision-Making, by Sam Kaner, et al (Jossey-Bass)

The Zen of Groups, by Dale Hunter (Da Capo Press)

The Skilled Facilitator: A Comprehensive Resource for Consultants, Facilitators, Managers, Trainers, and Coaches, by Roger Schwarz (Jossey-Bass)

Consensus: A New Handbook for Grassroots Social, Political, and Environmental Groups, by Peter Gelderloos (See Sharp Press)

Breaking Robert's Rules: The New Way to Run Your Meeting, Build Consensus, and Get Results, by Lawrence E. Susskind and Jeffrey L. Cruikshank (Oxford University Press)

On Conflict and Consensus: A Handbook on Formal Consensus Decision-making, by C.T. Butler and Amy Rothstein (This whole guidebook is available online at www.ic.org/pnp/ocac.)

Seeds for Change—www.seedsforchange.org.uk (Resources on consensus decision making.)

Conflict and Mediation

The Mediator's Handbook, by Jennifer E. Beer and Eileen Stief (New Society Publishers)

The Mediation Process: Practical Strategies for Resolving Conflict, by Christopher W. Moore (Jossey-Bass)

Interpersonal Conflict, by William Wilmot and Joyce Hocker (McGraw-Hill)

Narrative Mediation, by John Winslade and Gerald Monk (Jossey-Bass)

Resources on Shared Housing

Home Buying, TICs, and Condos

Nolo's Essential Guide to Buying Your First Home, by Ilona Bray, Alayna Schroeder, and Marcia Stewart (Nolo)

Buying a Second Home, by Craig Venezia (Nolo)

How to Buy a House in California, by Ralph Warner, Ira Serkes, and George Devine (Nolo)

The Essential Guide for First-Time Homeowners, by Ilona Bray and Alayna Schroeder (Nolo)

The Home Equity Sharing Manual, by David Andrew Sirkin (John Wiley & Sons, Inc.)

Paul Sirkin Associates—www.andysirkin.com (A great resource on TICs, condos, and fractional ownership.)

Shared Housing and Group Houses

The Group House Handbook, by Nancy Brandwein, et al (Acropolis Books)

HIP Housing Home Sharing Program—www.hiphousing.org/programs/sharing.html

National Shared Housing Resource Center—www.nationalshared housing.org

Cohousing, Ecovillages, Cooperatives, and Intentional Communities

Cohousing: A Contemporary Approach to Housing Ourselves, by Kathryn McCamant, Charles R. Durrett, and Ellen Hertzman (Ten Speed Press)

The Cohousing Handbook: Building a Place for Community, by Chris ScottHansen and Kelly ScottHansen (New Society Publishers)

Senior Cohousing: A Community Approach to Independent Living, by Charles Durrett (Ten Speed Press)

Communities Directory: A Comprehensive Guide to Intentional Communities and Cooperative Living (Fellowship for Intentional Community)

Rebuilding Community in America: Housing for Ecological Living, Personal Empowerment, and the New Extended Family, by Ken Norwood and Kathleen Smith (Shared Living Resource Center)

Collaborative Communities: Cohousing, Central Living, and Other New Forms of Housing with Shared Facilities, by Dorit Fromm (Van Nostrand Reinhold)

Creating a Life Together: Practical Tools to Grow Ecovillages and Intentional Communities, by Diana Leafe Christian (New Society Publishers)

EcoVillage at Ithaca Pioneering a Sustainable Culture, by Liz Walker (New Society Publishers)

Ecovillages: A Practical Guide to Sustainable Communities, by Jan Martin Bang (New Society Publishers)

Finding Community: How to Join an Ecovillage or Intentional Community, by Diana Leafe Christian (New Society Publishers)

Ecovillage Living: Restoring the Earth and Her People, by Hildur Jackson and Karen Svensson, (Green Books)

Collaborative Communities: Cohousing, Central Living, and Other New Forms of Housing With Shared Facilities, by Dorit Fromm (Van Nostrand -Reinhold)

Ecovillages: New Frontiers for Sustainability, by Jonathan Dawson (Green Books)

Sustainable Community: Learning from the Cohousing Model, Graham Meltzer (Trafford)

Intentional Communities—www.ic.org (A directory of ecovillages, cohousing, and other intentional communities throughout the U.S. and the world.)

Cohousing Association—www.cohousing.org (A national directory of cohousing, with detailed information and statistics about each community, and lots of great articles and links.)

Cohousing Partners—www.cohousingpartners.com (Cohousing development and consulting.)

Cohousing Resources—www.cohousingresources.com (Cohousing development and consulting.)

North American Students of Cooperation—www.nasco.coop (A good resource on student housing cooperatives.)

Federation of Egalitarian Communities—www.thefec.org (Network of North American egalitarian communities ranging in size from small agricultural homesteads to village-like communities to urban group houses.)

Global Ecovillage Network—www.ecovillage.org (Includes a directory of ecovillages all over the world.)

Hospitality Exchange ("Couch Surfing") Websites

CouchSurfing—www.couchsurfing.org

The Hospitality Club—www.hospitalityclub.org

Global Freeloaders—www.globalfreeloaders.com

Home Swapping Websites

Digsville Home Exchange Club—www.digsville.com

HomeLink International—www.homelink.org

Intervac International Home Exchange—www.intervac.com

Resources on Sharing Household Goods, Purchases, Tasks, and Space

Sustainable Buying and Home Care

Green Guide: The Complete Reference for Consuming Wisely, by the Editors of The Green Guide Magazine (National Geographic)

Home Enlightenment: Practical, Earth-Friendly Advice for Creating a Nurturing, Healthy, and Toxin-Free Home and Lifestyle, by Annie Berthold Bond (Rodale Press).

Green Remodeling: Changing the World One Room at a Time, by David R. Johnston and Kim Master (New Society Publishers)

The Home Energy Diet: How to Save Money by Making Your House Energy-Smart, by Paul Scheckel (New Society Publishers)

Affluenza, by John Degraaf, et al (Berrett-Koehler Publishers)

The GoodGuide—www.goodguide.com (Provides information on the health, environmental, and social impacts of the products in your home.)

GreenPeople—www.greenpeople.org (Directory of eco-friendly products and services.)

Real Goods Catalog—www.realgoods.com (Provides products and information related to renewable energy and sustainable products.)

Oasis Design—www.oasisdesign.net (Great resource on grey water systems.)

Home Power Magazine—www.homepower.net (Information about reducing your home's carbon footprint.)

Tool Lending Libraries

List of Tool Lending Libraries: en.wikipedia.org/wiki/List_of_tool-lending_libraries

Other

Neighbor Law: Fences, Trees, Boundaries, & Noise, by Cora Jordan and Emily Doskow (Nolo)

Resources on Sharing Food

Food and Sustainability

The Omnivore's Dilemma: A Natural History of Four Meals, by Michael Pollan (Penguin)

In Defense of Food: An Eater's Manifesto, by Michael Pollan (Penguin)

Slow Food Nation: Why Our Food Should Be Good, Clean, and Fair, by Carlo Petrini (Rizzoli Ex Libris)

Animal, Vegetable, Miracle: A Year of Food Life, by Barbara Kingsolver (Harper Perennial)

Sharing the Harvest: A Citizen's Guide to Community Supported Agriculture, by Elizabeth Henderson and Robyn Van En (Chelsea Green Publishing)

Civic Agriculture: Reconnecting Farm, Food, and Community, by Thomas A. Lyson (Tufts)

Closing the Food Gap: Resetting the Table in the Land of Plenty, by Mark Winne (Beacon Press)

City Bountiful: A Century of Community Gardening in America, by Laura J. Lawson (University of California Press)

Growing Better Cities: Urban Agriculture for Sustainable Development, by Luc J. A. Mougeot (In Focus)

For Hunger-Proof Cities: Sustainable Urban Food Systems, by Mustafa Koc, et al (IDRC Books)

Everything I Want To Do Is Illegal: War Stories From the Local Food Front, by Joel Salatin

Holy Cows and Hog Heaven: The Food Buyer's Guide To Farm Friendly Food, by Joel Salatin

Chefs Collaborative—www.chefscollaborative.org (A community of chefs, farmers, fishers, educators, and food lovers is dedicated to promoting sustainable cuisine.)

Food Routes—www.foodroutes.org (Resource on buying local food.)

Mealsharing and Cooking for Large Groups

Here are a few books that could be useful if you will be cooking for a large group. There are also many books by caterers and food service professionals, which can be helpful in this endeavor.

The Tassajara Recipe Book, and other cookbooks by Edward Espe Brown (Shambhala) (Include practical recipes, use common ingredients, and were designed to serve large groups.)

The Zen Monastery Cookbook, by Zen Monks and Cheri Huber (Keep It Simple Press) (Contains simple vegetarian recipes from a monastery kitchen.)

Church Suppers, by Barbara Greenman (Black Dog & Leventhal)

The Church Supper Cookbook, by David Joachim (Rodale)

Large Quantity Recipes, by Margaret E. Terrell and Dorothea B. Headlund (Wiley)

Eartheasy: One Pot Cooking—www.eartheasy.com/eat_one_pot_meals.htm

Grocery Co-ops and Buying Clubs

Storefront Revolution: Food Co-Ops and the Counterculture, by Craig Cox (Rutgers University Press)

How to Form A Buying Club, by Ann Evans (NaSCO)

The Food Co-Op Handbook: How to Bypass Supermarkets to Control the Quality and Price of Your Food, by The Co-op Handbook Collective and Bob Marstall (Houghton Mifflin)

Food Co-ops for Small Groups, by Tony Vellela (Workman Publishing Company)

Co-op Directory Service—www.coopdirectory.org (Directory of grocery co-ops and buying clubs, plus other helpful info about starting a buying club.)

Local Harvest—www.localharvest.org (Directory of food cooperatives, CSAs, community farms, and much more.)

Cooperative Grocery Magazine—www.cooperativegrocer.coop

More resources on buying clubs: See www.morningsidefarm.com and www.unitedbuyingclubs.com

Community Supported Agriculture

Sharing the Harvest: A Guide to Community Supported Agriculture, by Elizabeth Henderson, with Robyn Van En (Chelsea Green Publishing)

Farms of Tomorrow Revisited: Community Supported Farms—Farm Supported Communities, by Trauger Groh and Steven McFadden (Biodynamic Farming and Gardening Association)

The Real Dirt on Farmer John (Movie featuring a community supported farm.)

Local Harvest—www.localharvest.org/csa/ (National Directory of CSA farms)

Community Gardens

Community Gardening, by Elizabeth Tehle Peters and Ellen Kirby, Eds. (Brooklyn Botanic Garden)

Food Not Lawns: How to Turn Your Yard into a Garden and Your Neighborhood Into a Community, by Heather Coburn Flores (Chelsea Green)

Garden Your City, by Barbara Hobens Feldt (Taylor Trade Publishing)

Edens Lost & Found: How Ordinary Citizens Are Restoring Our Great American Cities, by Harry Wiland and Dale Bell (Chelsea Green)

Backyard Market Gardening: The Entrepeneur's Guide to Selling What You Grow, by Andy Lee (New World Publishing)

Allotments, by Twigs Way (Shire)

The Power of Community—www.powerofcommunity.org (A wonderful documentary about urban gardening and cooperation in Cuba.)

American Community Gardening Association—www.community garden.org (National directory of community gardens and resources on starting community gardens.)

Green Thumb—www.greenthumbnyc.org (Large community garden organization based in New York City.)

Guerilla Gardening—www.guerillagardening.org

Revive the Victory Garden—www.revivevictorygarden.org

Resources on Sharing Care

Cooperative Child Care and Schools

Smart Mom's Baby-Sitting Co-Op Handbook: How We Solved the Baby-Sitter Puzzle, by Gary Myers (Tukwila)

Bringing Families Together: A Guide to Parent Cooperatives, by E. Kim Coontz (University of California, Center for Cooperatives)

Parent Cooperative Preschools International—www.preschools.coop

Transportation Resources

Carsharing

How to Live Well Without Owning a Car: Save Money, Breathe Easier, and Get More Mileage Out of Life, by Chris Balish (Ten Speed Press)

Bringing Car-Sharing to Your Community, by City CarShare (Entire handbook available at www.citycarshare.org/download/CCS_BCCtYC_ Long.pdf.)

Carsharing.net—www.carsharing.net (Contains a list of carsharing programs throughout North America and a library of information on carsharing.)

Carsharing.US blog—www.carsharing.us (Information, issues, and ideas for U.S. and North American carsharing services and partners.)

Some Ridesharing Matchmaking Websites

PickupPal—www.pickuppal.com (A huge network of ridesharers throughout the United States and the world.)

GoLoco—www.goloco.org (Helps you find a match for one-time rideshares and regular carpools.)

Zimride—www.zimride.com (A rideshare matchmaking site that can be used as a facebook application.)

Ridester—www.ridester.com

Rideshare 511—www.511.org (San Francisco Bay Area)

Craigslist—www.craigslist.org

Bikesharing and "Yellow Bikes"

The Bike-Sharing Blog—bike-sharing.blogspot.com

International Bicycle Fund—www.ibike.org/encouragement/freebike.htm

Austin Yellow Bike Project—www.austinyellowbike.org

Resources on Work and Sharing

Sustainable Businesses and Workplaces

True Green at Work: 100 Ways You Can Make the Environment Your Business, by Kim Mckay, Jenny Bonnin, and Tim Wallace (National Geographic)

The Triple Bottom Line: How Today's Best-Run Companies Are Achieving Economic, Social and Environmental Success—and How You Can Too, by Andrew W. Savitz (Jossey-Bass)

Raising the Bar: Integrity and Passion in Life and Business: The Story of Clif Bar & Co., by Gary Erickson (Jossey-Bass)

Going Local: Creating Self-Reliant Communities in a Global Age, by Michael H. Shuman (Routledge)

Small-Mart Revolution: How Local Businesses Are Beating the Global Competition, by Michael H. Shuman (Berrett-Koehler)

The Ecology of Commerce, by Paul Hawken (Collins Business)

Business Alliance for Local Living Economies (BALLE)—www.livingeconomies.org (A network of sustainable businesses committed to building local economies.)

Green America's Green Business Program—www.coopamerica.org/greenbusiness (Networks, resources, and technical assistance for socially and environmentally responsible businesses.)

Green Business—www.greenbusiness.net (Online Community for Eco Entrepreneurs.)

The Green Workplace—www.thegreenworkplace.com (A blog for those who design, manage, or occupy green workplaces.)

Workplace Democracy and Cooperatives

Putting Democracy to Work: A Practical Guide for Starting and Managing Worker-Owned Businesses, by Frank T. Adams and Gary B. Hansen (Prima Lifestyles)

We Own It: Starting & Managing Cooperatives & Employee-Owned Ventures, by Peter Jan Honigsberg, Bernard Kamoroff & Jim Beatty (Bell Springs)

A Legal Sourcebook For California Cooperatives: Start-up & Administration, by Van P. Baldwin (Complete book available online at www.cooperatives.ucdavis.edu.)

In Good Company: A Guide to Cooperative Employee Ownership, published by Northcountry Cooperative Foundation, available online at www.ncdf.org/documents/worker_coop_toolbox.pdf

Grassroots Economic Organizing—www.geonewsletter.org (Organization promoting an economy based on democratic participation, worker and community ownership, social and economic justice, and ecological sustainability.)

National Cooperative Business Association—www.ncba.coop (Develops and advances the interests of cooperative businesses.)

U.S. Federation of Worker Cooperatives—www.usworker.coop (Works to advance worker-owned, -managed, and -governed workplaces through cooperative education, advocacy and development.)

International Cooperative Alliance—www.ica.coop (Uniting, representing, and serving cooperatives worldwide.)

International Cooperative Alliance Group—www.ica-group.org (Providing employee ownership, business development, and job retention services.)

Arizmendi Association of Cooperatives—www.arizmendi.coop (Contains a helpful list of resources on cooperatives.)

Green Worker Cooperatives—www.greenworker.coop (Bronx-based organization serving as an incubator for green worker co-ops.)

University of Wisconsin Center for Cooperatives—www.uwcc.wisc.edu (Contains many helpful resources on cooperatives.)

Shared Workspaces and Coworking

National Business Incubation Association—www.nbia.org (Business incubators are often a good way for entrepreneurs to find shared workplace opportunities.)

Coworking—coworking.pbwiki.com (Contains information about coworking and links to coworking groups around the country.)

Forms

Money and Property Worksheet

Time and Efficiency Worksheet

Environmental Worksheet

Community Building Worksheet

Getting Help Worksheet

What Could I Share?

Neighbor Questionnaire

Checklist for Discussing the 20 Questions

Communication Checklist

Worksheet: Rate Your Housing Priorities

Goods to Lend and Borrow

Home Improvement Group: Tools and Skills Assessment

Diet Preferences for Mealsharing

Fruit Harvest Agreement

Information Sheet for Children's Carpool

Worksheet: Annual Car Expenses

Information Sheet for Carpool Members

Worksheet: Work Expenses to Consider Sharing

Money and Property Worksheet

How I Spend Money	How Much I Spend Per Month	Ways to Share and Possible Savings
Food		
Car/Transportation		
Housing		
Entertainment/ Vacations/Recreation		
Household goods		
Child care		
Pets		
Utilities/Phone/ Internet		
Clothes		
Healthcare		
Other		

Time and Efficiency Worksheet

How I Spend Time	Ways to Save Time by Sharing
Commuting	
Home repair/ Housework/Yard work	
Caring for others (children, adults, pets)	
Working	
Running errands	
Preparing meals	
Other	
I would like more time for:	

Environmental Worksheet

Green Goals	Ways to Live More Sustainably By Sharing
Drive less	
Buy fewer consumer goods	
Obtain food from more sustainable sources	
Reduce home energy use and use renewable energy sources	
Reduce waste	
Be greener at work	
Buy environmentally friendly products	
Other	
Other	

Community Building Worksheet

Community Building Goals	Ways to Build Community by Sharing
Get to know neighbors	
Help neighbors and get help in return	
Get to know coworkers better	
Other	
Other	
Other	

Getting Help Worksheet

What I Could Use Help With	Ways to Get Help by Sharing
House care	
Yard care	
Taking care of other possessions	
Meal preparation	
Chores and errands	
Child care	
Elder care or care for other adults	
Other	

What Could I Share?

Categories of Things to Share	What I Have to Share	What I Hope to Get Through Sharing
Tangible Items		
Household appliances		
Household goods		
Electronics		
Tools		
Vehicles		
Work equipment		
Recreation/ Hobbies		

What Could I Share? (continued)

Categories of Things to Share	What I Have to Share	What I Hope to Get Through Sharing
Fitness/ Outdoors		
Clothing/ Accessories		
Other		
Space		
Housing		
Yard		
Laundry room		
Storage space		

What Could I Share? (continued)

Categories of Things to Share	What I Have to Share	What I Hope to Get Through Sharing
Vacation home		
Work space		
Other		
Services, privileges, and subscriptions		
Services		
Privileges		
Subscriptions		
Other		

What Could I Share? (continued)

Categories of Things to Share	What I Have to Share	What I Hope to Get Through Sharing
Purchasing		
Food		
Goods/Supplies		
Utilities		
Other		
Other		
Other		

What Could I Share? (continued)

Cooperation	Ways to Cooperate with Others
Carpools and rides	
Child care	
Adult care	
Pet care	
Meals	
Gardening/ Yard work	
Home repair/ Improvement	
Chores/Errands	
Skills	
Other	

Neighbor Questionnaire

Name: _____

Address: _____

Phone number: _____

Email address: _____

Would you like to join a neighborhood email listserv? ☐ Yes ☐ No

Emergency contact (someone we can call if we think you need emergency help):

Home phone: _____ Work phone: _____

Cell phone: _____

How long have you lived in this neighborhood? _____

Where are you from originally? _____

What do you like to do for fun? _____

What kind of work do you do? _____

What city do you work in? _____

Do you drive to work? ☐ Yes ☐ No

Would you be interested in carpooling if a neighbor works near you? ☐ Yes ☐ No

Do you own a car? ☐ Yes ☐ No

Would you ever be interested in sharing a car with a neighbor? ☐ Yes ☐ No

If you work from home, are you interested in sharing office equipment? ☐ Yes ☐ No

Do you have children? ☐ Yes ☐ No
If yes, how many and how old? _____

Would you ever like to trade child care with other neighbors, whether through casual babysitting, sharing a child care provider, or otherwise? ☐ Yes ☐ No

Do you have pets? ☐ Yes ☐ No
If so, who are they? _____

Would you ever like to coordinate with neighbors to take turns walking dogs or caring for other animals? ☐ Yes ☐ No

Would you be interested in joining a neighborhood gardening group?   ☐ Yes   ☐ No

Would you be interested in joining a neighborhood home improvement group, which will meet to work on home repair and building projects at each member's house?   ☐ Yes   ☐ No

Would you like to be invited to neighborhood games nights?   ☐ Yes   ☐ No

Would you be interested in doing mealsharing with neighbors?   ☐ Yes   ☐ No

Do you have a fruit tree that you'd like help harvesting or fruit you'd like help eating?   ☐ Yes   ☐ No

Do you or does anyone in your household have any disabilities or health problems you would like your neighbors to know about, or you might need help with?
☐ Yes   ☐ No

If so, what are they? _____

_____

Would you be interested in sharing any of the following:

☐ Tools, ladders, etc.

☐ Washer and dryer

☐ Household appliances, like vacuum cleaners

☐ Household goods and electronics

☐ Toys and sports equipment

Checklist for Discussing the 20 Questions

When you sit down to discuss the details of your sharing arrangement, here's a checklist to guide your conversation:

☐ **1. Why Are We Sharing?**

- What are our personal, practical, financial, or environmental goals?

☐ **2. What Are We Sharing?**

- What are we not sharing?

☐ **3. Whom Are We Sharing With?**

- Do our cosharers need to meet any particular qualifications?

☐ **4. How Many People Are We Sharing With?**

- What are the pros and cons of having a large or small sharing group?

☐ **5. How Will the Timing of Our Arrangement Work?**

- When will it start and stop?
- Will it happen in phases?

☐ **6. Who Owns the Shared Item(s)?**

- Will one person own it and let others use it?
- Will we each own specific items or parts of the property?
- Will we each own a percentage share of the whole property? If so, in what proportions?

☐ **7. Should We Form a Separate Legal Entity?**

☐ **8. What Should We Call Ourselves?**

☐ **9. What Do We Get to Do?**

☐ **10. How Will We Make Decisions?**

- Will we all take part in decision making or delegate decisions to a small group?
- Do we all have equal decision-making power?
- Must all decisions be unanimous or made by majority vote?

☐ **11. What Responsibilities Will Each of Us Have?**

- Will we assign roles and tasks?

- Will we rotate responsibilities?

- Will anyone receive extra benefits in return for extra responsibilities?

☐ **12. What Are the Rules for Using Our Shared Property or Meeting Our Shared Responsibilities?**

☐ **13. How Will We Handle Administrative Matters Like Scheduling, Communication, and Record Keeping?**

☐ **14. How Will We Divide Expenses?**

- Will there be initial buy-in or start-up contributions? Will we need any loans?

- How will we divide overhead and variable costs?

- How will we collect money? Through regular dues or by reckoning expenses in some other way? Will we start a bank account?

- What kinds of unexpected costs could arise and how will we prepare for them?

- Who will keep track of our money?

- What happens if a member cannot pay?

☐ **15. How Will We Manage Risk and Liability?**

- What risks are involved in our sharing arrangement and how can we reduce them?

- How is the risk distributed (that is, who could suffer loss or be liable for damages)?

- Do we want to redistribute risk by making agreements with each other or purchasing insurance?

☐ **16. Are There Legal Requirements We Need to Follow?**

- Are there any required licenses or permits?

- Will this bring up any tax or employment law questions?

- Are there any legal roadblocks arising from zoning laws or private land covenants?

- What steps must we take to become a legal entity?

☐ **17. How Will We Resolve Conflicts or Disputes?**

☐ **18. How Will We Bring New People Into the Group?**

- What procedures will new members follow?
- How will new members be oriented?
- What is our policy on guests?

☐ **19. How Can a Member Leave the Group?**

- What steps must be taken when a member leaves voluntarily?
- Under what circumstances can a member be asked to leave the group?

☐ **20. How Do We End the Sharing Arrangement?**

Communication Checklist

Here's a handy checklist for you and your cosharers to review:

☐ Have we talked through the logistics of our arrangement (for example, the 20 questions in Chapter 3)?

☐ Have we discussed each of our concerns or worries regarding the sharing arrangement?

☐ Do we all feel comfortable voicing our needs?

☐ Do we each feel that our needs and values are understood by other sharers?

☐ Do we have a plan for checking in with each other periodically?

☐ Are any of us interested in taking a communication training class? (See Appendix A for training resources.)

☐ Have we chosen a decision-making process?

☐ Have we decided what conflict resolution methods we will use?

☐ Do we want to choose a mediator in advance?

☐ Do we all feel prepared to approach difficult conversation in a constructive, non-judgmental, and non-defensive manner?

Worksheet: Rate Your Housing Priorities

Rate each of the following priorities by circling a number (1 = least important; 5 = most important).

The Space:

1   2   3   4   5   I would like to have my own unit.

1   2   3   4   5   I would prefer my own bathroom.

1   2   3   4   5   I would like to have a large kitchen.

1   2   3   4   5   I would like access to a yard.

1   2   3   4   5   I would like to be able to garden.

1   2   3   4   5   I would like on-site laundry facilities.

1   2   3   4   5   I would like on-site parking.

1   2   3   4   5   I would like a large storage space.

1   2   3   4   5   I would like other amenities, such as _____

_____

Material Needs and Long Range Plans:

1   2   3   4   5   I would like to own my residence and build equity.

1   2   3   4   5   I prefer to rent my residence.

1   2   3   4   5   I hope to save money from this arrangement.

1   2   3   4   5   I am looking for a place that I can live in for a long time.

1   2   3   4   5   I am looking for a short-term arrangement.

1   2   3   4   5   I would like to share furnishings.

Furnishings I own and could share include: _____

_____

_____

_____

Furnishings I need or would like to have include:_____

_____

_____

_____

Home Environment, People, and Lifestyle:

1 2 3 4 5 I want to live in a way that is environmentally sustainable.

1 2 3 4 5 I want to feel free to have social events where I live.

1 2 3 4 5 I want to live in a nonsmoking home.

1 2 3 4 5 I would like to have some rules about drug and alcohol use.

1 2 3 4 5 I want to be able to have overnight guests.

1 2 3 4 5 I would like a quiet space (or quiet times).

1 2 3 4 5 I need space to practice trumpet (or other loud activity).

1 2 3 4 5 I want to share housing with someone who can help care for my child/pet.

1 2 3 4 5 I am open to caring for others and/or their children and pets.

1 2 3 4 5 I hope to feel a sense of community with people I live with.

1 2 3 4 5 I want to live with like-minded people. This means:

_____

_____

1 2 3 4 5 I would like to do activities with my cosharers, such as: _____

_____

1 2 3 4 5 I would like to do mealsharing and collective food buying.

Other wants and needs: _____

_____

_____

_____

_____

_____

_____

Goods to Lend and Borrow

Name: _____

Address: _____

Phone: _____

Email: _____

Please list all items you are willing to lend, as well as items you would be interested in obtaining by sharing or borrowing them from others. If an item cannot be moved, but you are willing to let people use it in your house or yard, please list this in the second column. For items that you would be willing to lend, please note any limitations. For example, if you will lend your vacuum cleaner only for an hour at a time, or if you will lend your ceramics wheel only to experienced users, please note this.

Categories of Goods	Items to Lend	Immobile Items Others May Use	Items I'd Like to Borrow or Buy With Others
Tools			
Cleaning			
Cooking			

Categories of Goods	Items to Lend	Immobile Items Others May Use	Items I'd Like to Borrow or Buy With Others
Yard			
Sports/Fitness/ Outdoor			
Fun/ Entertainment			
Clothing/ Accessories			
Hobbies/Arts/ Crafts			

Categories of Goods	Items to Lend	Immobile Items Others May Use	Items I'd Like to Borrow or Buy With Others
Travel			
Furniture			
Electronics			
Health			
Other			

Home Improvement Group: Tools and Skills Assessment

Name(s): _____

Address: _____

Phone: _____ Email: _____

Preferred Work Day (check one): ☐ Saturday   ☐ Sunday

Skills			
Skills	Seen It Done	Done Some	Done a Lot
Carpentry			
Plumbing			
Electrical			
Masonry			
Tile work			
Painting (exterior)			
Painting (interior)			
Gardening			
Demolition			
Basic wiring			
Other (list)			

Tools I Have for the Group to Use:

☐ Basic garden tools

☐ Basic hand tools

☐ Saw(s)

☐ Drill

☐ Ladder(s)

☐ _____

☐ _____

Comfort Level				
Tool or Activity	Expert	Fine	Willing	Rather Not
Power tools				
Lifting				
Heights/Ladders				
Attics/Basements				
Managing logistics				
Other (list)				

Possible Projects for Our Household

1. _____

2. _____

3. _____

4. _____

5. _____

6. _____

Diet Preferences for Mealsharing

Types of Food	Food I Don't Eat	Food I Prefer Not to Eat (but I Can Be Flexible)	Food That Is Fine If I Can Pick Out	Food That Is Fine in Small Amounts

Fruit Harvest Agreement

This agreement is between the _____("Harvesters") and
_____ ("Owner"). We enter into this
agreement to allow Harvesters to pick fruit from Owner's fruit tree(s) and bushes.

1. On the following dates and times, Harvesters will pick the following fruit:

   _____ : Harvesters will pick _____ .

   _____ : Harvesters will pick _____ .

   _____ : Harvesters will pick _____ .

2. Check one of the following:

   ☐ It is okay for Harvesters to enter the yard when Owner is not home. If
   owner is not home, Harvesters should _____
   _____

   ☐ Harvesters should enter the yard only when Owner is at home.

3. Harvesters will follow these rules when in Owner's yard: _____
   _____
   _____
   _____
   _____

4. Harvesters will pick all fruit that appears ready to be picked and leave less
   mature fruit on the tree.

5. Harvesters will take care to avoid damaging the tree or breaking branches.

6. Harvesters will give _____ of fruit to Owner.

7. Harvesters may do the following with the remainder of the fruit. (Check all
   that apply.)

   ☐ Give fruit to other neighbors

   ☐ Donate fruit to a food bank or other charity

   ☐ Consume the fruit

   ☐ Preserve or prepare the fruit, to eat or share

8. Harvesters will take reasonable steps to ensure that the fruit is not wasted.

9. Harvesters will use all proper care and safety precautions when climbing trees
   and ladders. (Or: Harvesters will not climb the trees or use ladders. Harvesters
   will use extension fruit pickers, which they will provide.)

10. Owner does not ask for any compensation.

11. Harvesters, as consideration for the right to harvest fruit from Owner's tree(s), agree not to make a claim against or sue Owner for injury, loss, or damage that occurs during fruit harvest and/or consumption of Owner's fruit, including injury, loss, or damage arising from the negligence of Owner. Harvesters agree to indemnify, hold harmless, and defend Owner from all claims, liability, or demands that Harvesters or any third party may have or in the future make against Owner for injury, loss, or damage arising from harvesting and/or consuming fruit from Owner's trees, including from food-borne illness.

HARVESTERS:

Name: _____

on behalf of _____

Signature: _____

Date: _____

OWNER(S):

Name: _____

Signature: _____

Date: _____

Name: _____

Signature: _____

Date: _____

Information Sheet for Children's Carpool

Child's Name: _____

Address for Pickup: _____

Parent/Guardian Names: _____

Parent 1: _____

Phone (please put a check mark by the best number to reach you)

☐ Home: _____ ☐ Work: _____

☐ Cell: _____ ☐ Other: _____

Email: _____

Parent 2: _____

Phone (please put a check mark by the best number to reach you)

☐ Home: _____ ☐ Work: _____

☐ Cell: _____ ☐ Other: _____

Email: _____

Name of Parent Who Will Drive Carpool: _____

Drivers' license no.: _____

Car make/model: _____ License plate: _____

Insurance co.: _____ Policy number: _____

Emergency Contact

Name: _____

Relationship to child: _____

Best number to reach: _____

Child's Physician

Name: _____

Best number to reach: _____

Worksheet: Annual Car Expenses

Type of Expense	Annual Costs	Costs to Share a Car	Costs to Carpool
Annual registration cost			
License fees			
Smog check (where applicable)			
Insurance (average is $850 per year)			
Depreciation			
Interest on car loan (finance charges)			
Roadside assistance program membership			
Fuel			
Parking			
Maintenance (regular replacements, tires, fluids, filters, tune-ups, windshield wipers, cleaning)			
Major repairs			
Tolls			
Title fee and transfer tax (usually applies only when car changes ownership)			
Total			

Information Sheet for Carpool Members

Name: _____

Address for Pickup: _____

Phone Numbers (please put a check mark by the best number to reach you)

☐ Home: _____

☐ Work: _____

☐ Cell: _____

☐ Other: _____

☐ Email: _____

Emergency contact

Name: _____

Relationship: _____

Best number to reach: _____

Driver information

Drivers' license number: _____

Car make and model: _____

License plate: _____

Insurance co. and policy number: _____

Worksheet: Work Expenses to Consider Sharing

Expense	Amount	Sharing Ideas

Index

Get the Latest in the Law

Nolo's Legal Updater
We'll send you an email whenever a new edition of your book is published! Sign up at **www.nolo.com/legalupdater**.

Updates at Nolo.com
Check **www.nolo.com/update** to find recent changes in the law that affect the current edition of your book.

Nolo Customer Service
To make sure that this edition of the book is the most recent one, call us at **800-728-3555** and ask one of our friendly customer service representatives (7:00 am to 6:00 pm PST, weekdays only). Or find out at **www.nolo.com**.

Complete the Registration & Comment Card...
...and we'll do the work for you! Just indicate your preferences below:

Registration & Comment Card

NAME _____ DATE _____

ADDRESS _____

CITY _____ STATE _____ ZIP _____

PHONE _____ EMAIL _____

COMMENTS _____

WAS THIS BOOK EASY TO USE?   (VERY EASY)   5   4   3   2   1   (VERY DIFFICULT)

☐ Yes, you can quote me in future Nolo promotional materials. *Please include phone number above.*

☐ Yes, send me **Nolo's Legal Updater** via email when a new edition of this book is available.

Yes, I want to sign up for the following email newsletters:

   ☐ **NoloBriefs** (monthly)
   ☐ **Nolo's Special Offer** (monthly)
   ☐ **Nolo's BizBriefs** (monthly)
   ☐ **Every Landlord's Quarterly** (four times a year)

☐ Yes, you can give my contact info to carefully selected partners whose products may be of interest to me.

SHAR1

NOLO

Send to: **Nolo** 950 Parker Street Berkeley, CA 94710-9867, Fax: (800) 645-0895, or include all of the above information in an email to regcard@nolo.com with the subject line "SHAR1."

NOLO and USA TODAY

Cutting-Edge Content, Unparalleled Expertise

The Busy Family's Guide to Money

by Sandra Block, Kathy Chu & John Waggoner • $19.99

The Busy Family's Guide to Money will help you make the most of your income, handle major one-time expenses, figure children into the budget—and much more.

The Work From Home Handbook

Flex Your Time, Improve Your Life

by Diana Fitzpatrick & Stephen Fishman • $19.99

If you're one of those people who need to (or simply want to) work from home, let this book help you come up with a plan that both you and your boss can embrace!

Retire Happy

What You Can Do NOW to Guarantee a Great Retirement

by Richard Stim & Ralph Warner • $19.99

You don't need a million dollars to retire well, but you do need friends, hobbies and an active lifestyle. This book shows how to make retirement the best time of your life.

The Essential Guide for First-Time Homeowners

Maximize Your Investment & Enjoy Your New Home

by Ilona Bray & Alayna Schroeder • $19.99

This reassuring resource is filled with crucial financial advice, real solutions and easy-to-implement ideas that can save you thousands of dollars.

Easy Ways to Lower Your Taxes

Simple Strategies Every Taxpayer Should Know

by Sandra Block & Stephen Fishman • $19.99

Provides useful insights and tactics to help lower your taxes. Learn how to boost tax-free income, get a lower tax rate, defer paying taxes, make the most of deductions—and more!

First-Time Landlord

Your Guide to Renting Out a Single-Family Home

by Attorney Janet Portman, Marcia Stewart & Michael Molinski • $19.99

From choosing tenants to handling repairs to avoiding legal trouble, this book provides the information new landlords need to make a profit and follow the law.

Stopping Identity Theft

10 Easy Steps to Security

by Scott Mitic, CEO, TrustedID, Inc. • $19.99

Don't let an emptied bank account be your first warning sign. This book offers ten strategies to help prevent the theft of personal information.

ORDER ANYTIME AT WWW.NOLO.COM OR CALL 800-728-3555

Prices subject to change.

NOLO *Online Legal Forms*

Nolo offers a large library of legal solutions and forms, created by Nolo's in-house legal staff. These reliable documents can be prepared in minutes.

Online Legal Solutions

- **Incorporation.** Incorporate your business in any state.
- **LLC Formations.** Gain asset protection and pass-through tax status in any state.
- **Wills.** Nolo has helped people make over 2 million wills. Is it time to make or revise yours?
- **Living Trust (avoid probate).** Plan now to save your family the cost, delays, and hassle of probate.
- **Trademark.** Protect the name of your business or product.
- **Provisional Patent.** Preserve your rights under patent law and claim "patent pending" status.

Online Legal Forms

Nolo.com has hundreds of top quality legal forms available for download—bills of sale, promissory notes, nondisclosure agreements, LLC operating agreements, corporate minutes, commercial lease and sublease, motor vehicle bill of sale, consignment agreements and many, many more.

Review Your Documents

Many lawyers in Nolo's consumer-friendly lawyer directory will review Nolo documents for a very reasonable fee. Check their detailed profiles at **lawyers.nolo.com**.

Nolo's Bestselling Books

Nolo's Essential Guide to Buying Your First Home
$24.99

Buying a Second Home
Income, Getaway or Retirement
$24.99

Neighbor Law
Fences, Trees, Boundaries & Noise
$29.99

101 Law Forms for Personal Use
$29.99

Every Nolo title is available in print and for download at Nolo.com.

NOLO *Law for All*

Find a Quality Attorney

- *Qualified lawyers*
- *In-depth profiles*
- *Respectful service*

When you want help with a co-ownership contract, real estate transaction, agreement to retrofit a home, or purchase shared personal property, you don't want just any lawyer—you want an expert in the field, who can provide up-to-the-minute advice to help you protect your loved ones. You need a lawyer who has the experience and knowledge to answer your questions and help you draft the necessary paperwork.

Nolo's Lawyer Directory is unique because it provides an extensive profile of every lawyer. You'll learn about not only each lawyer's education, professional history, legal specialties, credentials and fees, but also about their philosophy of practicing law and how they like to work with clients. It's all crucial information when you're looking for someone to trust with an important personal or business matter.

All lawyers listed in Nolo's directory are in good standing with their state bar association. They all pledge to work diligently and respectfully with clients—communicating regularly, providing a written agreement about how legal matters will be handled, sending clear and detailed bills and more. And many directory lawyers will review Nolo documents, such as a will or living trust, for a fixed fee, to help you get the advice you need.

www.lawyers.nolo.com

The attorneys shown above are fictitious. Any resemblance to an actual attorney is purely coincidental.